THE FARAWAY HILLS

THE FARAWAY HILLS ARE GREEN

Voices of Irish Women in Canada

To Ann,

beannaiz Brid ort

Síle

Sheelagh Conway
(Síle Ní Chonmhacháin)

women's
P R E S S

Half of the royalties for this book are donated to a special fund of the Mary Quayle Innis Foundation to benefit economically disadvantaged single-parent Irish women in Canada who wish to further their education. Written enquiries can be sent to the Irish Women's Committee, c/o Women's Press.

CANADIAN CATALOGUING IN PUBLICATION DATA

Conway, Sheelagh
    The faraway hills are green : voices of Irish women in Canada
Includes bibliographical references.
ISBN 0-88961-176-9

1. Irish-Canadian women — History.* 2. Irish-Canadian women — Social conditions.* 3. Women immigrants — Canada. 4. Canada — Emigration and immigration — History. 5. Ireland — Emigration and immigration — History.
I. Title.

FC106.I6C65   1992   305.48'89162071   C92-095052-3
F1035.I6C65   1992

Editing: P. K. Murphy
Copy editing: Kate Forster
Cover design: Linda Gustafson/Counterpunch
Front cover photograph: Adam Cherechowicz
Harp illustration: Siobhán Conway-Hicks

Women depicted in photographs on back cover from top to bottom: Nora O'Grady, Connie Sullivan, Maggie Thompson, Ena McClearn-O'Brien, Norita Fleming, Anna Copeland

Back cover photographs: Sheelagh Conway (Connie Sullivan), Micah Gampel (Maggie Thompson), Anne Weniger (Ena McClearn-O'Brien), Arlene Fleming (Norita Fleming), Maria Bowman (Anna Copeland)

This book was produced by the collective effort of Women's Press. Women's Press gratefully acknowledges the financial support of the Canada Council and the Ontario Arts Council.

Printed and bound in Canada
1 2 3 4 5   1996 1995 1994 1993 1992

*For Nellie O'Donnell, whose stories on our
walks down by the river inspired this book.
Her spirit speaks.*

Contents

IT IS NEW STRUNG AND SHALL BE HEARD

Acknowledgments

My deepest appreciation goes to Nellie O'Donnell, to whom this book is dedicated. Her story matters. I thank the women who made this book possible. Their stories make an important contribution in affirming Irish women's presence in Canada. These women gave their time and hospitality. Most of all, they gave me inspiration and strength. Mary Broderick, Norita Fleming, Maria O'Kane and Connie O'Sullivan became close friends and I appreciate their support and encouragement.

Twice in the last three years, just as this book was about to be published, the publishers went under. I would like to thank Dennis Deneau, the first publisher, who gave me tremendous support. Once, when I was halfway across Canada and had run out of money, he generously gave me a cheque for $1,000. I would also like to remember the second publisher, Gordon Montador of Summerhill Press, who died of AIDS in June 1991, six months after Summerhill Press went down.

I would like to thank the women at Women's Press for making way for writing by women on the margin. Their work is critical in making Canada's writing scene more equal. I appreciate very much their confidence in me. Special thanks to Angela Robertson, the co–managing editor at Women's Press, for her skill and patience in navigating the manuscript through to completion, and to Deborah Barretto for her promotional work.

This book has benefited from the skilled hand of my editor, Pat Murphy, whose eagle eye has earned her the title "Reverend Mother." I've come across many women like her who get things done. I owe her my thanks. Thanks also to Marlene Nourbese Philip for reading the manuscript and offering valuable suggestions; our friendship which developed over cappuccino during conversations about sexism, racism and classism have kept my oft-lagging spirit going. Ann Clarke did the transcribing of the tapes. For her energy and patience, which often saw us into the night, I thank her. Thanks also to Kate Forster for her sensitive copy editing, to Linda Gustafson for designing a cover that connotes the faraway hills, and to Heather Guylar for her design and production work.

I would like to thank all those people across Canada who offered me a place to stay: Kristine Hansen in Winnipeg, Nancy Mulligan-McCaldin and Heather Copeland in Montreal, and Anne Hart in St. John's, Newfoundland.

Many people helped in the making of this book. Their efforts and interest were immensely encouraging: author Marianna O'Gallagher for her help on the Irish in Quebec, Janet Fontaine for leads in Montreal, Dennis Leyne of Action Grosse Île, the Irish Freedom Association, and Simon Kwok and Garry Lawrence for help with the computer. The section on Irish women in Canadian religious orders was possible thanks to Sr. Esther Hanley, the archivist for the Loretto Sisters, Sr. Mary Jane Trimble, the archivist for the Sisters of St. Joseph, and Sr. Theresa Ryan of the Sisters of Mercy in Newfoundland. Thanks also to Anne Weniger, Maria Bowman, Ulrike Karzai, Marian Lydbrooke, Maggie Thompson, Ann Thomson, Marc Montebello, Mary Broderick and Brian Boyer for taking photographs. Mary Holland of *The Irish Times*, Olive Braiden of the Rape Crisis Centre in Dublin, Nuala Kelly of the Toronto Metro Action Committee on Violence Against Women and Children, and Tom Kelly provided helpful information. Thanks also to the Vancouver *Sun*, the *Winnipeg Free Press*, *The Gazette* in Montreal, *The Toronto Star* and the *Telegram* in St. John's for their help in soliciting Irish women's responses for this project.

Funding for this book came from the Canada Council, the Ontario Arts Council, the City of Toronto, the Jackman Foundation, and a small donation from the hat, organized by Doug Tottle of Winnipeg. Without these funds this book would not have been possible.

Thanks to my friends who have navigated me emotionally, spiritually and politically through a difficult passage: Sue Leather, Denise Zakoor, Marie Lord, Beth Perrott-Lightening and Anne Innis Dagg.

Thanks to my daughters, Siobhán and Ann, who have been patient and understanding when this book claimed long hours. Siobhán's help in transcribing Dorothy Taylor's tape ensured the inclusion of another important voice. Thanks to my faithful collie Toby, who has sustained me through this book. Thanks to my mother for her intrepidness; she is one of the feistiest Irish women I know. This is a woman who single-handedly raised six children. Well do I remember how she used to lift a twelve-gallon milk churn out of a drain and onto a platform by the roadside twice a week ready for the creamery in Nenagh; how she used to go to the fairs to sell and buy sheep and cattle; how she struggled against the odds. She has no time, she says, for all that highfalutin' talk of big-shot eejits. Thanks to my father for his class analysis; to educated people he was a peasant, but he had a better reading of Marx than I found in any university. Thanks to my old schoolmaster, Dermot Nolan of Loughrea, who taught me never to use the word "nice." Thanks to old Jack Melia, who taught me Irish history, culture and location around the hearth. What a peasant indeed. May he rest in peace. Most of all, thanks to the mothers and the grandmothers of Ireland, Mná na hÉireann.

"The Stone" beside Victoria Bridge, Montreal, commemorating Irish Famine victims of 1847. Photo: Brian Boyer

Nellie O'Donnell near Timmins, Ontario, circa 1940.

Vi Moore and her pupil, in Irish dancing costume.

Maura Keohane. Photo: Sheelagh Conway

Maggie Thompson. Photo: Micah Gampel

Back from the war: Brigid Ryan and her husband Patrick with their daughter Theresa at Bonavista Bay, Newfoundland, in 1945.

Dorothy Taylor, founder of the Toronto Irish Players.
Photo: Kevin Kennedy

Connie O'Sullivan, day-care worker. Photo: Sheelagh Conway

The Ice Cream Seller: Nora O'Grady at Brock House Senior's Club
Garden Party in Vancouver, 1988.

Marie O'Kane: "Sometimes I find myself looking out the window of a Sunday morning thinking: My God, what's it all for?"
Photo: Ulrike Karzai

Patricia Willoughby. Photo: Sheelagh Conway

"The Bag of Spuds": And their spirit will come through in the music. Ena McClearn-O'Brien. Photo: Anne Weniger

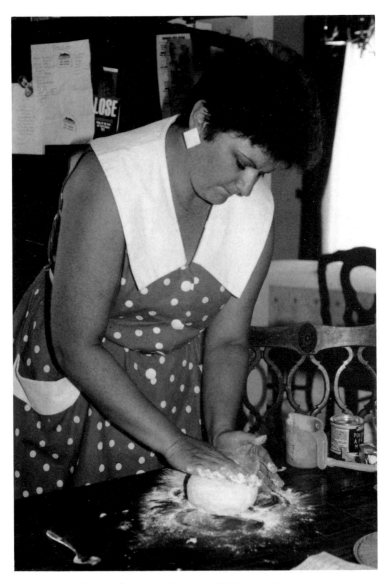

Making the brown bread. Margaret O'Connor-Lefas.
Photo: Sheelagh Conway

Belfast wall mural. Photo: Maggie Thompson

Derry wall mural. Photo: Ann Thomson

Introduction

The heart is a bird who should sing the song of truth.

Jagjit Chuhan

It was during evening strolls with my dog over the course of the summer of 1984 that I got to know Nellie O'Donnell. When I first came to Canada I lived in Windsor, which has a lovely pathway on the banks of the Detroit River where many people stroll on summer evenings. I couldn't help but notice this woman in her eighties who, despite her frailness, walked with such a sprightly step and had an unmistakable alertness. It wasn't long before we introduced ourselves, surprised to find we were both Irish immigrants. And soon Nellie began telling me stories about growing up in Co. Tipperary and coming to Canada as a domestic worker in the 1920s.

On those evenings by the river, Nellie's stories took me back to the hearth of my home in a small village near Loughrea, Co. Galway. The hearth was the focus of our culture when I was growing up in the 1950s. Indeed, down through the centuries it was always that way. Around the hearth the neighbours came for *cuairt* (to visit). Yarns would be told, songs would be sung, and poems would be recited. Some of the finest music and dancing took place at wakes, mummer dances[1] and times when one of our own returned from the United States for a holiday. Those were happy occasions where we celebrated our culture with laughter and tales and brown bread with freshly churned butter, with fresh buttermilk and tea, and sweetcake, and bottles of porter, and, on the odd occasion, poteen — an illegal brew distilled from potatoes. Old Jack Melia, our neighbour, said that Raftery, the poet himself, used to visit our old house on his travels around Co. Galway in the first half of the nineteenth century.

But amidst the laughter there was always a sadness. It was around the hearth that we also learned of our history and the songs of grief and heartbreak, passed on to prepare us, to warn us, to teach us. These songs always placed the facts of Irish lives, such as emigration, in their historical and political context. Our history is a blood-red tapestry of oppression and resistance. For hundreds of years we have been dominated by the English and that, with its attendant poverty and exploitation, made our leaving unavoidable. The Famine of 1847, when some two million people died by the roadsides, on coffin ships[2] and on foreign shores, is etched deep in our collective memory. The Famine is in our blood. Who we are today cannot be separated from our history.

Those of us who had to leave remember the songs and the stories. In the morning sunlight of our leavings, last goodbyes with our loved ones are heightened by vivid images of our native land: green fields, the wild cry of the curlew, the silent oak trees, ancient stones, the purple heather. The very landscape seems to join with our songs and our poems to mourn our leaving, as we go across the water, beyond, abroad, in search of places where we can live our lives, where we can find fulfilment for our hopes and dreams. My Aunt Frances used to say that the thing to do was never look back as you were going up the boreen[3] towards the gate. Whatever you do, never look back.

Every evening I'd wait for Nellie, eager to hear the next part of her tale. As she spoke, I would remember it all. What is it about emigration that etches such a deep scar? And every evening my listening gave Nellie a voice. She told me stories about that day she left on the ship, the journey from Tipperary to Belfast, her father telling her to make sure not to bless herself in case any Protestants might see, how she got a job as a servant girl, as she put it, in a big house in Toronto, how she got married to an English eejit, how he took her child, how she divorced him, kidnapped the child back and dashed off to Union Station in Toronto where she caught the train leaving for Kapuskasing. I could hardly wait for the next evening. "An' what happened then in Kapuskasing, Nellie?"

Many times I urged Nellie to record her stories — for history, you know. But she'd laugh and tell me to be quiet. These were, she said, the ramblings of an old woman living in the past. "Who'd be bothered with them anyway? An' the other day didn't what's-her-name tell me that it was time I got out of it, this living in the past business. It's not good for you, Nellie, she said." But the more Nellie told me the more convinced I was that her story must be heard. Then it occurred to me that there must be many more stories to be told by Irish women across Canada, many voices to be heard. In short, this was history that had to be retrieved. So it was that this book claimed me.

This book is a sort of fireside coming together of Irish women to tell their immigration stories: stories of hopes, dreams, disappointments, achievements and insights. Before we come to the fireside, however, we must ask what it was about Nellie's stories that compelled me to travel across Canada in search of more Irish women to tell stories. Why Irish women in Canada? To answer these questions we must locate what it means to be women, what it means to be Irish and what it means to be Irish women in Canada. From our location we experience and view the world in a particular way. I will begin from the location of being women.

Being female in a male-dominated world means living under patriarchy. Feminist historian Gerda Lerner defines patriarchy more narrowly, as a system based on Greek and Roman law which gives the male head of household economic and legal power over the female, who is made dependent, as are other family members. According to Lerner, patriarchal dominance dates back to the third millennium B.C. and was well rooted by the time of the writing of the Hebrew Bible. More broadly, patriarchy in today's world is the institutionalization of male dominance not only in the family but in every aspect of society. "It implies that men hold power in all the important institutions of society and that women are deprived of access to such power."[4] Men dominate every institution: law, the Churches, business, the professions, education, the media, the arts and government.

Men don't dominate institutions in just the physical sense.

They also dominate ideas, beliefs and images — the symbols by which the institutions forming our whole social structure are thought out and put together. Men's ideas dominate *history*, philosophy and theology. Our culture is manufactured by men for men. Men's ideas and experiences are presented as the norm, women's ideas and experiences as an aberration, a deviation from the norm. Women are thus excluded from the making of culture.[5] Sexism and patriarchy are mutually supportive. According to Lerner, "sexism defines the ideology of male supremacy, of male superiority and of beliefs that support and sustain it."[6] When a woman is told that she ought to be subservient to her husband, that is sexism.

Patriarchy has had and continues to have a profound impact on Irish women. The patriarchal Christian Church, which came to Ireland in the fifth century, brought with it negative ideas about women, ideas that have shaped women's role in Irish society. Irish women have been written out of Irish history in Ireland and out of the records of the Irish in Canada. It is mostly men who have presented the accounts of what happened, producing a history that is one-sided and flawed.

Over the last 150 years, women have begun publicly to question this system of patriarchy and have identified the distorted and hateful views it presents of women, beliefs which restrict women's ability to achieve their full potential. Patriarchal ideas — Freud's notion of women suffering from penis envy; English common law, which rendered women the chattels of their husbands; the denial of the vote to women; the belief that women's sole role is that of wife/mother/homemaker — permeate our everyday lives as women. Women who question the assumptions of patriarchy, women who present a vision of equality for women and a new way of ordering the world, a vision that respects the earth and its people, are feminists. Feminists uphold and advance the interests and perspectives of women. Feminists show that women have a particular location, a different standpoint,[7] precisely because patriarchy has tried to erase our footprints and blot out our perspectives.

As the author of this book, I also begin from the location of being a feminist. I join with other feminists in recovering and validating the experiences and perspectives of women.[8] My task in this book is to *begin to make known the presence of* Irish women in Canada by claiming the space for the women I interviewed to voice their own experiences and perspectives. The women here are not representative of all Irish women, but at least the task has begun.

I hope that this book will stimulate Irish women in Canada to do justice to our history, and that these stories will encourage women of Irish descent to comb the archives and registry books and study family letters and diaries to recover the details of the lives of the three centuries of Irish women who came to this land where they thought the faraway hills were green.

The women in the book who identify themselves as feminists, like Patricia Willoughby and Vi Moore, look beyond the confines of women's role as prescribed by the Catholic Church to another era of Irish history when God was female. The Celtic Goddesses Brigid and Maeve of Connaught provide inspiration and encouragement to Irish women disillusioned with the patriarchy of the Catholic Church.

The journey of recovering the heritage buried by patriarchy leads to inspiring work, work in which Irish women create and reinterpret our culture. Vi Moore talks of using Irish dancing to reinterpret Irish legends from a woman's perspective. Ireland's President, Mary Robinson, also provides us with encouragement. Her election in 1990 unsettled Ireland's patriarchal foundation and her words resounded when she declared, "The women of Ireland, instead of rocking the cradle, rocked the system." The work of Irish feminists such as historian Margaret MacCurtain helps Irish women to rediscover our past and power in Ireland.[9] I have drawn extensively on her work and that of other Irish feminists in the chapter "Women of Ireland/Mná na hÉireann."

Many women in this book talk about their religion and its impact on their lives. Whether Catholic or Protestant, they speak about patriarchy. Others, like Anna Copeland, a Protestant woman from Belfast, find in their church a means of expressing their faith: "My faith is a great comfort to me, so I suppose I'm lucky in that respect." For Brigid Ryan, a Catholic, "The Church is the most important thing in my life and in our family. Everything else fades." While many women abandon the church, others stay within it, believing that women ought to have full participation. Síle Ní Bhreanach advocates women's ordination in the Catholic Church. "It would have a softening effect and it would mellow a lot of this harshness," she says.

Many Irish women have strong connections with the Catholic Church. Despite its sexism, to which many do not subscribe, they find in it a means for expressing their spirituality. The Church, in Ireland and Canada, faces opposition from many feminists because of its exclusion of women and its moves to limit women's rights. On questions of abortion and birth control, Irish women in the Catholic Church are divided, some adhering to Church authority, some questioning it.

The experiences of Irish women in Canada must be seen within the context of patriarchy as a global problem. Awareness of this is revealed in the comments of Connie O'Sullivan, a daycare worker in Toronto: "A lot of young Irish women like myself come out here thinking that because things aren't so good in Ireland they will be better off in Canada....If you work in daycare, after a while you realize that if you spend your life working in low-paying jobs here in Canada you are no better off than you are in Ireland." Joan Bridget says, "Jobwise, I mean any old guy could come over here from Ireland, from anywhere, and work in an unskilled job and make twice the money I make." Maria O'Kane puts it this way: "If I'm not going to be educated...if I'm going to work in an office or something then I might as well stay home and be poor with my family."

Male violence against women is common to all cultures, so Irish women do not necessarily escape sexual harassment, rape, pornography or battering by emigrating.

The women in this book are particular women, which provides another location: They are Catholic and Protestant. Ireland has been colonized since 1169, a fact pivotal in understanding what it means to be Irish. I am no longer a member of the Catholic Church because of its patriarchy,[10] but I am nevertheless Catholic, as opposed to Protestant, which is an important political distinction. What is reported in the press as "sectarian strife" masks a centuries-long struggle between colonizer and colonized.[11] England occupied the whole of Ireland until 1921 when Southern Ireland won independence; it later became a republic. Britain still occupies the North, also known as Ulster. Irish Protestants, the descendants of English colonizers from 1609, were and are loyal to England and had come to dominate Ulster.

As Irish people we cannot be separated from our history. The brief history of Irish women and of Ireland locates the voices of the women in this book. The section on the Troubles in Ulster provides gripping accounts of how the lives of two Irish women were shaped by this struggle. The two speak of what it means to be Catholic and Protestant.

The many themes in this book are threads in our historical and cultural tapestry. The heartbreak of emigration forms the weft of the fabric. "That I had to give up my homeland was maybe the saddest thing in my lifetime. It's a struggle and it'll be a struggle when I'm ninety" is how Bridget Grealis-Guglich puts it. For Joan Bridget, "It just broke my heart. Some essential tie to the country broke." It was this that struck me most as I listened and let the tapes roll. Many of the women were composed until they came to the part about leaving. It was here they broke down as they recalled vividly images of family and friends bidding farewell. Often they recounted the small events of the day of leaving and the particular things they did before that bitter, wrenching moment of parting and separation. Many times, as women told me their stories, I had to stop the tape at this point so that both of us could regain our composure.

I too have memories. My mother standing at the door, waving goodbye. Aunt Frances's advice never to look back could not lessen the pain. Standing on the platform of the little railway station in Loughrea in 1970, with a one-way ticket for London,

England, I was just eighteen. All I knew was my village and the stories and our slow meandering way of life. And the history. And the inevitability of leaving.

The certainty of leaving surfaces in the stories; this certainty too is tied very closely to our history. Poverty and lack of opportunity have made leaving inevitable. And though the 26 counties of Ireland are now a republic, hundreds of years of colonialism still leave their mark. Foreign capital still controls Ireland. Máire gan Ainm speaks of the British army in Armagh; it made leaving a certainty.

Many a summer's evening my mother would sit by the hearth of our old cottage around twilight, cleaning the glass globe of the paraffin oil lamp, our only source of light even in the 1950s and 1960s, with a crumpled page of *The Connaught Tribune*. Polishing the glass till it would squeak, and occasionally puffing her moist breath to remove a stubborn piece of grit, she would gaze at the turf burning red. In a sweet melancholic voice she'd sing "Noreen Ban," the story of a young Irish emigrant woman: "Then one day there came a letter with her passage paid to go/ To a land of Mississippi where Missouri waters flow. Very soon she'd all things ready, then one morning at the dawn/ A brokenhearted mother parted with her Noreen Ban...."

The women in the book also speak about the racism they experienced in England. Joan Bridget talks about the signs warning "No Blacks, No Irish, No Dogs," which were common in London, England, even up to the 1970s. Such signs, together with the insults hurled at Irish people on London streets, led me to leave Britain in the late 1970s. The Irish in Canada faced similar attacks, as we will see in historical accounts, during and after the Famine in the latter half of the 1800s. Into the 1930s, as Nellie O'Donnell recounts, "Oftentimes Irish Catholics were called 'Dogan.' Sometimes they'd call you 'a bloody Irish Dogan' when they'd get mad.... In Toronto, the 12th of July was a big day for them Orangemen. It was terrible. If you were Catholic you had to keep the hell out of there when the Protestants were marching on the 12th." Toronto too featured signs stating "No Irish. No Dogs."

Another important theme which emerges in this book is Irish women as keepers of the culture. Traditionally, women have done the work behind the scenes in Irish associations across Canada while the men have defined and expressed our culture at centre stage. These are the women who have organized the events, baked the bread and done the washing up. So much talent wasted in washing dishes. But times are changing. Ena McClearn-O'Brien takes her place on the stage as a fine accordion player; Dorothy Taylor takes hers as an inspiring actor. Vi Moore goes further with her feminist interpretation of Irish dancing. Norita Fleming has a small catering business, specializing in Irish foods, and her work is no longer volunteer work only. In addition to continuing the tradition of the soda bread which marks every Irish event, she makes an important contribution by recovering traditional Irish recipes. Her story connects us with the part food plays in our culture. Her story also connects us with history and the memory that almost two million of us died from *lack* of food. "I don't hold it against the potato that it failed us during the Famine," she says, referring to the blight which destroyed the potato crop. "When I think of the Famine I feel an anger against the invaders, at the abuse of the food in our land, and the way they denied it to our starving people." The bread is a reminder of home. When I come back to Canada, my mother always packs two cakes into plastic bags, the ancient packaged in the modern.

Many women in the book recall the story-telling, music and songs around the hearth. Mary Broderick opens a window into what that was like, and her close connection with the landscape gives insight into our love of the land. In this respect, Nancy Mulligan-McCaldin, from war-torn Ulster, gives another picture of the North: "I can still smell the heather; I hear the reapers in the fields; I hear the corncrakes and the cuckoos and the magpies.... I see all the beautiful sheep running free over the mountains. I can still smell the ocean."

In putting together this book, I have another location. I am a peasant Irish woman from a part of Ireland untouched by the industrial revolution even up to the 1950s. We drew water from the well. We churned our own butter and baked our own bread. We drank fresh buttermilk. We had oil lamps and candles. We went to Finnerty's watermill to have our corn ground into flour. We walked to school through the fields. The pony and trap were tied up outside the church for Mass on Sunday. We cut turf with a slane in the bog. We cut hay in the meadows with a sickle and a scythe. Life went according to the seasons. Pollution was unknown to us. Recycling and care for the environment were what we did naturally.

Like me, many women in this book *know* what it means to have someone from the town who has more money, privilege and education look down on us, exclude us, deride us, and use our labour because they consider us less than, inferior to and even subordinate to them because we came from the bog or the mountain or even the countryside. We also know that class is linked to unequal relations of power and privilege, relations that favour those who rule and dominate. In Ireland we call it "class distinction." Here some call it "classism." It took years for many of us to overcome this internalized oppression such that we could look on our humble roots with pride and see the richness of our rural culture and the wisdom of our people, and rejoice in our love of the bog and the mountain. On a global level, classism comes out of the capitalist mode of production that emerged from colonization, a mode that uses patriarchy and racism to segregate women, people of colour and peoples of the Third World so that their labour can be appropriated for profit.[12]

Many Irish women will see themselves in Bridget Grealis-Guglich's reflection on growing up in Co. Mayo, where she faced "class distinction" because she was poor. "Going off with the little bag" shows the power of the link between poverty and emigration. She says: "Not having any proper degree or education...I saw the winds of change. I decided I wasn't going to stay. The nuns were not down in the poor places like Mayo and Galway. They were in the rich places. You think we weren't conscious of that?" Dorothy Taylor looks at the classism among Irish emigrants to Canada:

You have the top level people in the Irish community who have absolutely no knowledge of what the lower level of the Irish community is all about, the working class. They don't mix…. Then you have what I call the intellectual Irish…they figure that they're too high up in the scale to sort of get down to the nitty gritty of the ordinary guy who's not afraid to say, "Listen, I was a street-sweeper when I was in Dublin."

As these women and others in the book speak about "class distinction," we come to see how those who hold the power shape the lives of those who do not, and what this means for women in Ireland and in Irish communities abroad. More particularly, class distinction is about how those with power and privilege discriminate against those who are poor and/or uneducated or who work at little-valued jobs.

The story of Irish women in Canada also speaks about Canadian history. Edith Pringle gives a detailed account of the Depression of the 1930s as she lived it homesteading in Alberta. Nellie O'Donnell's story also yields insight into the Depression and its impact on women in domestic service and factory work. She reflects on that time: "Nobody knows what it was like, only them that lived it like myself. They were putting us in awful jobs. Bringing boatloads of us out — farm help and domestic help — from Ireland or wherever they could pick them up." Brigid Ryan's experience as a war bride provides yet another perspective into Canada's history.[13] Irish women were there too during the Winnipeg polio crisis of 1950. Nora O'Grady, a nurse, speaks: "It was just a terrible situation. Neighbour helping neighbour, but nobody wanted to have anything to do with polio. The nurses weren't allowed to go to a movie. They didn't want us getting on the buses going downtown. They said we were covered with bugs."

We must examine one further location, that of Irish women's immigration to Canada as part of the global pattern of immigration, structured within a First World–Third World division. With respect to women of colour, Canadian immigration patterns today reflect both racism and sexism rooted in a history of colonialism

and imperialism. In this context, while Irish women today encounter sexism they do not meet with the pervasive discrimination embedded in racist ideologies and practices that women of
colour experience.

The First World–Third World division itself is rooted in racism
and racism's colonial past. Racism, the system of belief and power-
holding that deems people of colour inferior, excludes them from
any real say in social, political and cultural life and segregates
them as a group into low-paying, ghettoized jobs. It intersects with
patriarchy and classism. Under capitalism, it is used to make
profits and maintain power and rule.[14] This issue will be further
explored in the section "Irish Women in Canada."

I began this project by placing announcements in newspapers
across Canada. I got letters from women telling me I *must* talk to
an Irish grandmother or a mother, letters full of pride and admiration. I got letters from the women themselves, saying they had
stories to tell, they'd love to meet me and wasn't it about time
something was done too. With a Canada Council grant and little
money, I spent the summer of 1989 travelling across Canada with
my tape recorder and camera, talking to some of the many women
who responded to the announcements. Often I stayed in their
homes. The interviews usually took place at the kitchen table,
where the women said they were most comfortable. I'd get a great
welcome with the tea and brown bread, and after a long meandering chat, the interview would begin. Very soon, it became clear to
me that recording a life story was very much like sitting around
the hearth at home. And I could no more interrupt the teller than
I could the story-teller around the hearth. Each story had to *emerge*
with its own rhythm and resonance. Rather than circumscribe a
story with a list of set questions, I let the tape roll. And, sure
enough, each story came into its own. I did ask questions occasionally to explore a point, but always, I hope, with the respect
I learned around the hearth, where there is an understanding that
the story-teller has the power to speak, to tell events as she or he
chooses. What we learned around the fire, giving the story-teller

an uninterrupted forum, listening, is now being advocated by feminist oral historians.[15] *The listener must listen.*

The women whose voices we hear in this book are young, middle-aged and old. They are working-class and middle-class. They come from different parts of Ireland and they have settled in different parts of Canada. Their marital status, sexual orientation and religion differ. Because time and finances were always limited, I have only included Irish-born women. It is my hope that this book will generate interest in the history and experiences of second-generation women too.

What fascinated me most was finding the "vein" in each story, the coursing through a life, with its knowledge, time, circumstance, will and fate. Although all the stories have common themes, each story has its own vein. I never knew what it would be. Sometimes the woman herself didn't know until she got talking. But soon she would be talking passionately about a particular event or point or issue.

The edited versions of the transcripts came out of collaboration with the women. I was careful to retain Irish idioms, remnants of our Gaelic-speaking past, in the transcripts. Some women had kept these idioms, others had lost them in conforming to a more "polished" tongue. That the Gaelic has never fully left us is a mark of resistance to English colonialism's attempts to crush our language and culture.

A transcript can be surprisingly revealing, even to the person whose words are converted to written form. Something happens in that place where the spoken word is transformed into the written word. The spirit of presence and being somehow gets lost. My intervention in transcribing and editing these stories into text cast me in the role of arbitrator on many occasions. I had to decide which words, sentences and paragraphs to keep and which to drop. That's a judgment call. Some women were happy with the edit. Some wanted changes. Some wanted many changes. One woman was annoyed because she thought she came across only as a housewife, when she also worked outside the home. It was important to her that she be recognized as a working mother. Two women withdrew after they saw the transcript. One woman's estrangement from her mother dominated the transcript to such an extent that it overshadowed her remarkable achievements. She withdrew with little comment. When issues were particularly sensitive and women still wanted to talk about them, rather than forfeit their voices, they chose anonymity or changed their names.

I learned a valuable lesson: A life story is not as fixed as it appears to be in text. It is fluid and moving and can only be captured in the to-and-fro between people. "Yes, I said that, but that's not quite what I meant" is an example of this.[16] What was said was captured by a machine, put into words in a text, where it now lies fixed in a book, stopped in time. But what was said and meant *carries on*. Things change. Life goes on. Perceptions change. Views change. But some things also stay the same.

It is important to acknowledge our differences as well as our commonalities. While there are many common themes in the lives of the women in this book, there are also differences. Some women are staunch feminists; some are not. Some women want to forget what happened in history; some do not. Some women in the book may well be at odds with my location as a feminist, as a nationalist, as an activist, which is reflected in how I have constructed the histories. Each woman's story must stand on its own, and the women's stories and voices must remain primary in this book. My interpretations are secondary to those stories. Some will agree with my interpretations; others will not. These diversities must be celebrated.

The commonalities of women's lives nevertheless bond these women who discuss motherhood, their mothers, their grandmothers, old age, sexuality, relationships, abortion, spirituality and more.

For me, as an Irish woman in Canada, this book became a double journey. The journey across Canada from Vancouver to Winnipeg to Montreal to St. John's put into perspective for me the vastness and the beauty of my adopted land. It also brought into focus the diversity of its peoples and the tensions between regions focus the diversity of its peoples and the tensions between regions and cultures. As Irish people we are used to tension and conflict. I will never forget that clear blue dome of a sky over the flat lands of the Manitoba prairies. I had been invited to visit a farm there and I went out to a field, so vast I couldn't say how big, and I lay on my back looking up, staring at its perfect symmetry and beauty. I thought of two of the women from war-torn Ulster, women who described their sense of freedom when they first saw this sky. As Maggie Thompson put it, "The blue sky made it all seem possible."

Growing up in Ireland, I envisioned Canada as a vast country with acres of forests and high mountains. Visiting Vancouver, I remembered the time my father took a notion to write to the Canadian Embassy in Dublin for information on Canada. He said he wanted to emigrate. The brochures showed pictures of the forests and the mountains, which became associated for me with Canada and emigration. My father never did emigrate. He was too old and besides, he said, he could never get used to the timing of a clock. The sun was his time. Finally seeing these beautiful mountains of the brochures was almost like coming full circle.

The stone at Victoria Bridge in Montreal commemorating the Famine victims brought me back to the hearth and old Jack's stories. And I felt again his anger at the English whose brutality left us dying on these foreign shores. But somehow that anger also seemed strange to me. Unlike London or Boston, where the Irish have their own neighbourhoods, there is no neighbourhood in any of Canada's major cities with a distinct Irish population. The discrimination the Irish once faced has found new targets: today's immigrants from the Caribbean and Asia.

On St. Patrick's Day in Canadian cities, much green is worn — even the horses in the parade are painted green. And the pubs are filled with dancing and singing and green beer. But it lacks the *feeling* that goes with our culture, the feeling for the history and the land and the stories. We weave tales of modern-day life, using faxes and vcrs. And when St. Patrick's Day is over, we go our separate ways and life goes on. Occasional flashes of memory bring the wild cry of the curlew, or the wind in the heather in the bog. Maybe that's why the haunting call of the Canadian loon has such an intimation for us. And yet this dormancy can spring to life, as in the recent case of Grosse Île, burial place of thousands of Irish Famine victims. The Irish have mobilized across Canada to protest the Canadian government's plans to turn Grosse Île into a theme park. As this book goes to press, Action Grosse Île has sprung up, demanding that Grosse Île be preserved as sacred ground to the memory of perhaps as many as 20,000 Irish Catholics buried there in mass graves. Action Grosse Île is also demanding a recognition of the Famine as the outcome of English colonialism, a fact dismissed by the Canadian government, which is representing the Famine as simply the result of overpopulation.

In Newfoundland I travelled around the Avalon Peninsula, thinking how like home it must have felt to the Irish immigrants who first landed there some 200 years ago. The little fishing villages could have been my own village, with all its characters, its gossip and its stories. There was that same sense of humour, and the accent was incredibly like that of my native Galway.

As I travelled across Canada collecting these stories and hearing these voices, the other journey for me was an inner one, back to my mother and to her mother before her. The mothers and the grandmothers — the strength of a nation. One memory lingered, of my paternal Grandmother Conway when I was about five years old. My mother and I were about to leave after a visit, and she told me to kiss my grandmother. I couldn't bring myself to kiss her wrinkled old face. Instead I kissed her hands. I remembered those hands and the thin purple veins barely discernible beneath the translucent skin, the blood slowing through them. This blood that is in our veins. How would it carry on in me? How would it change course? At the top of the stairs I gave one last look back. My grandmother lay sleeping quietly on her bed, her old face pale. I caught a glimpse of the view from the little window of her room in Ballinagrieve, outside Loughrea. It was the sleek outline of the

Aughty Mountains in the distance, sweeping pale shades of purple into the evening sky.

> *Sheelagh Conway (Síle Ní Chonmhacháin)*
> *Toronto, Canada*
> *1 May (Bealtaine) 1992*

Notes

1. On St. Stephen's Day (December 26), neighbours would dress in disguise and travel from one house to another with great music and dancing on the kitchen floors. A donation would be taken and put towards a dance for the parish.
2. During the Famine, thousands of emigrating Irish died of cholera, typhus and other diseases while crossing the Atlantic in filthy, overcrowded ships. The vessels became known as coffin ships.
3. Laneway.
4. See Gerda Lerner, *The Creation of Patriarchy* (New York: Oxford University Press, 1986), pp. 238–39. The first extensive writings on patriarchy include Kate Millett, *Sexual Politics* (New York: Doubleday, 1970); Mary Daly, *Beyond God the Father: Toward a Philosophy of Women's Liberation* (Boston: Beacon Press, 1973); Betty Friedan, *The Feminine Mystique* (New York: Dell, 1963).
5. See Dorothy Smith, *The Everyday World as Problematic: A Feminist Sociology* (Boston: Northeastern University Press, 1987), pp. 19–20.
6. Lerner, *The Creation of Patriarchy*, p. 240. Ideology is not defined here, but very broadly it means the body of ideas reflecting the beliefs and interests of a culture, a nation, a political system and so on. For an individual, it is also shaped by gender, race and class. In turn, this body of ideas is carried by the culture and shapes everyday life. Patriarchy is an ideology shaped by male supremacy. The ideas of patriarchy permeate Christian doctrine, for example, where women are the "helpmates" of men. These

ideas exclude women from full participation in religion and also shape women's lives in the family, where the male is supposed to be superior to women and therefore is head of the family.

7. Smith, *The Everyday World as Problematic*. Smith, along with other feminist theorists such as Sandra Harding, developed the notion of standpoint. Referring to the development of a sociology for women, Smith says, "The knower who is construed in the sociological texts of a sociology for women is she whose grasp of the world *from where she stands* [her emphasis] is enlarged thereby" (pp. 105–6). Smith's theory is complex; simplified, it contends that all knowledge and truth is socially constructed; that the notion of "objectivity" or "neutrality," such as that claimed by science, is false because it is one-sided. Smith refers to the structure of society as "the ruling apparatus" of manufactured male-defined power relations — that "complex of management, government administration, professions, and intelligentsia" which rule women in the "organization of particular places, persons, and events" which are formulated in rules and laws (pp. 107–8). According to Smith, women cannot begin to know truth from a patriarchal standpoint which excludes women's reality and presents a male-defined distortion. Instead, women must create a new knowledge and a new truth from the standpoint of women, where women know what is true about our everyday experiences. Thus, when women articulate their experiences and put forward their ideas in any forum — the law, the arts, education — this must be done from a women's understanding of what truth is.

8. Feminists define the task of women's equality from different locations, including radical, liberal, conservative, marxist and socialist, and Black feminism. In recent years, women of colour and women of the First Nations have rightly criticized the first and second waves of the women's movement for excluding them. For an overview of different feminisms, their analyses and strategies for change, see Alison M. Jaggar and Paula M. Rothberg, eds., *Feminist Frameworks: Alternative Theoretical Accounts of the Relations Between Women and Men*, 2nd ed. (New York: McGraw-

Hill, 1984). For a discussion of Black feminism, see bell hooks, *Feminist Theory: From Margin to Centre* (Boston: South End Press, 1984); hooks says, "A central tenet of modern feminist thought has been the assertion that 'all women are oppressed.' This assertion implies that women share a common lot, that factors like class, race, religion, sexual preference, etc. do not create a diversity of experience" (p. 5).

9. See Margaret MacCurtain and Donncha ó Corráin, *Women in Irish Society: The Historical Dimension* (Dublin: Arlen House, 1978).

10. In 1984, I left the Catholic Church after a struggle of many years against its sexism. The Catholic Church is not alone in this. Virtually all religions are founded on patriarchy. See Sheelagh Conway, *A Woman and Catholicism: My Break with the Roman Catholic Church* (Toronto: PaperJacks, 1987).

11. For a brief discussion of this, see Sheelagh Conway, "History Weaves a Blood-Red Tapestry," *The Globe and Mail*, November 1, 1991. Today, the Republic of Ireland has a Roman Catholic majority (95 percent); Ulster has a Protestant majority (65 percent). See Ursula Barry, *Lifting the Lid: Handbook of Facts and Information on Ireland* (Dublin: Attic Press, 1986), p. 6.

12. For a discussion on class, see *Fireweed* no. 26 (Winter/Spring 1988), "This Is Class Too," and *Fireweed* no. 25 (Fall 1987), "Class Is the Issue" (special issues on class); Anne Cameron, "Classism, Racism, and Academic Elitism Run Head-long into Low-Rent Criticism," in Angela Miles and Geraldine Finn, *Feminism: From Pressure to Politics* (Montreal: Black Rose, 1989), pp. 313–26. For sources on the capitalist mode of production and its use of class, patriarchy and racism in making profits, see Maria Meis, *Patriarchy and Accumulation on a World Scale: Women in the International Division of Labour* (London: Zed, 1986). For information on multinational corporations and Third World women, see Swasti Mitter, *Common Fate, Common Bond: Women in the Global Economy* (London: Pluto Press, 1986).

13. For more information on this topic, see Joyce Hibbert, ed., *The War Brides* (Toronto: PMA Books, 1978).

14. See Audre Lorde, *Sister Outsider* (New York: Crossing Press, 1984);

Barbara Smith, ed., *Home Girls: A Black Feminist Anthology* (New York: Kitchen Table/Women of Colour Press, 1983); Jesse Vorst *et al.*, *Race, Class, Gender: Bonds and Barriers* (Toronto: Between the Lines, 1989). In Vorst *et al.*, see especially Tania Das Gupta, "Introduction."

At a demonstration against racism in the 1990 PEN World Congress, held in Toronto, demonstrators were told to "fuck off" by the incoming president of Canadian PEN. For Joyce Nelson, Marlene Nourbese Philip and Ayanna Black's responses to this attack and their analyses of racism in the arts in Canada, see "Disturbing the Peace: Commentary on 54th International PEN World Congress" in *Fuse* 13, no. 3 (Winter 1989–90), pp. 17–22. See also Marlene Nourbese Philip, *Frontiers: Essays on Racism and Culture* (Stratford, Ontario: Mercury, 1992).

15. Kathryn Anderson and Dana C. Jack, "Learning to Listen: Interview Techniques and Analyses" in Sherna Berger Gluck and Daphne Patai, eds., *Women's Words: The Feminist Practice of Oral History* (New York: Routledge, 1991), pp. 11–26. The role of the listener is also explored by Beverley Grace, a Toronto story-teller, in her Ph.D. thesis at the University of Toronto.

    Remember too the old Armenian proverb: Three apples fell from heaven: one for the story-teller, one for the listener and one for the one who heard.

16. This point is explored by Katherine Borland, "'That's Not What I Said': Interpretive Conflict in Oral Narrative Research" in Berger Gluck and Patai, eds., *Women's Words*, pp. 63–75.

History

Women of Ireland/
Mná na hÉireann

For many schoolchildren, history is a dry and lifeless subject. It was quite the contrary for me. That was because of Jack Melia, John O'Malley in English, an old man and neighbour when I was growing up in the fifties in the small village of Limehill near Loughrea, Co. Galway. Whenever my mother and father would cycle off to the pictures in Loughrea, Jack would be left to look after us kids. In his sixties, Jack lived alone, the last of ten children, seven of whom had emigrated to the United States at the turn of the century.

Around the hearth he would tell us of Irish history, of the Norman Invasion in 1169, the Battle of Aughrim in 1691 and the Easter Rebellion of 1916. Jack would first build a big turf fire in the hearth. When it would be in full blaze he would take out his old pipe and a block of tobacco, carefully pare it, then place the soft brown chips in his pipe. With the pipe lit, he would weave the tales, his old grey sweat-rimmed felt hat flopped down over his ruddy face.

A few years ago, beyond in de bog road comin' down from de village of Ranamacken one moonlit night, dere was meself an' Pateen Joe. An' outta nowhere sure wasn't dere an almighty fierce big woolpack[1] dat took up de whole a de road an' id rollin' down de hill from de village of Ranamacken. Rollin' up towards de bog 'twas. An' sure 'twas all we could do but ta lep inta de ditch before we got knocked down. An' sure de nexht ting didn't we hear de marchin' a de soldiers. De Lord save us, dere musht a been about 200 of dem, marchin' dere in de moonlight, an' deir rapiers glistenin', an' de finesht music yer ears ever heard. An' no sooner did de woolpack reach de road goin' up ta Clonlee, de crossroads at de foot of Limehill bog, den didn't id disappear, an' de soldiers after id. An' dere wasn't a sound nor a footshtep left. Dey all disappeared. De whole lot of dem, woolpack an' all, just up by Ranamacken crossroads. 'Twas from Aughrim dey were. 1691. 'Twas an awful ting dey losht de battle. Sure if id wasn't for St. Ruth gettin' killed dey'd a won, an' Ireland would a been saved. Sarsfield an' de Wild Geese would never a had to leave poor Ireland.[2]

Always at the end of that story Jack would tip the old hat a little sideways with his hand, flat, worn and rough from working in the fields and the bog, and shuffling his heels in the ashes he would start into the only verse he'd sing of his favourite song. He'd sing it with renewed vigour, even anger, the old pipe held in his right hand, and his gaze burrowed deep into the glowing red core of the turf fire: "Ah sure don't you fret/ Dere'll be good times yet/ When Ould Ireland will be free/ An' grá mo croí I long ta see/ Ould Ireland free once more."

Then he'd tell us about the Famine of Black '47:

Ara sure didn't tousands of us die. De spud failed us. But 'twasn't de spud altogether d'ya see. Sure wasn't dere enough corn[3] altogether if 'twasn't for de Sassenachs[4] takin' id outta de country an' we dyin' before deir very eyes. Sure around here dey were dyin' all along de boreens. Whole village wiped out above dere on top of Limehill, behind de house. Ah Jasus, sure dey put de bodies all inta big graves dey dug up after dey had landed dem off de side of de boreens. Horses an' carts dey used ta load dem up on. Chrisht Jasus, sure id mushta been a fierce job altogether. An' de graves, dey put dem above in de callas up dere by de big river.

Where above by de river, Jack?

Ara what would ya be wantin' ta know a ting like dat for!

But justa see id, Jack.

What would ya be wantin' ta see a ting like dat for an' dem graves all covered up anyways. Go 'way now!

More than anything else I wanted Jack to give me the location of these mass graves. I could never understand his exasperation: Was he collaborating with the earth in keeping secret what would confirm his tale, or would the truth of it be horrifying for the ears of a small child? Still and all, above on top of Limehill, behind our house, were the markings of foundations of small cabins that had been razed to the ground. Jack said that was one of the villages wiped out. The little mounds were barely discernible beneath the mossy grass. There was something about these ruins that brought an overwhelming sense of the past into my child's awareness. Somehow the very sight of them triggered a deep collective memory.

Long after old Jack had returned to the earth and its secrets I discovered his legacy. He had given me the realization that time, place and person have a location by which the world is known. Before he died he gave me one more gift, an Irish history book published in 1902. Its pages are disintegrating with age and its cloth cover torn and ragged now. It has that musty smell of long ago. Its heroes, Jack's heroes, are all men — the likes of Patrick Sarsfield, and Michael Davitt, and Padraic Pearse. They stare out of the yellowed, fraying pages with frowns and scowls and silent indignation.

Etched in gold on the faded magenta cover is the figure of a woman in front of a tall tower playing a large harp. The years have made her shadowy, her young face barely visible as she looks off sideways. By her side sits a large hound, looking off in the same direction. In the background are the waves of the ocean, lapping gently. At the base of her harp is an unfurled scroll, the gold so faded the inscription can hardly be made out:

IT IS NEW STRUNG AND SHALL BE HEARD.

Men have strung this harp to play only their tunes of Irish history, inventing a silent harpist, the young and beautiful Róisín Dubh, the Dark Rosaleen. Posing with the harp but not playing it, she is, for the men who created her, the romantic symbol of

Ireland. Men would die to rescue her from the Sassenachs who stole her. She is Mangan's "saint of saints" and MacNeice's "bore and a bitch" who "gives her children neither sense nor money."[5] And then there is Yeats's romantic Cathleen Ní Houlihan, the female symbol of free Ireland.

Myth and stereotype have created an image of Irish women which has been woven into the poetry, literature and songs of Irish men down through the centuries. Always fixed in the political, this romantic image characterizes women as receptive vessels of virginity, whoredom and motherhood, replete with passivity, tragedy, and abandonment. Irish feminist historian Margaret Mac-Curtain locates native Irish poetry and songs in the political circumstances out of which they arose, where women were portrayed in the *Aisling*, or vision poetry, as "the ideal of the 'passive' beautiful young woman" and "the captive *spéirbhean* who was a figure of unliberated Ireland needing to be rescued by her 'prince' across the waters of Europe. Occasionally she was pictured in bondage to the powerful John Bull," the symbol of England.[6] Nowhere is there a woman's definition of this woman. Nowhere is the space.

Celtic Ireland and the Coming of St. Patrick

Long before Róisín Dubh, however, there was a period in the history of Celtic Ireland when the feminine was revered and goddesses were worshipped. These deities, with many characteristics and names, included a spiritual Great Mother, concerned with fertility and agriculture.[7] There was a triad of war goddesses, Morrígan, Badb and Macha, and great sagas were built around their fierceness and victories. The most famous war goddess, who also took human form, was Queen Maeve of Connaught.[8] Historians disagree about women's status in Celtic times. Nevertheless, the fact that goddesses were worshipped indicated value was placed on the feminine and also suggested women's possibilities and aspirations.

St. Patrick introduced Christianity to Ireland in 432, and with the new religion provided the impetus for a "Golden Age" of learning which was to place Ireland, "the island of saints and scholars," at the forefront of Europe until the Viking invasion of 795. The Vikings continued their raids — often sacking monasteries for their gold — until they were finally defeated at the battle of Clontarf in 1014. During this Golden Age, Christian monasteries flourished in Ireland and spread out to the continent. Great works of art such as the *Book of Kells* were created. Unfortunately, the new Christianity spelled the end of any power women had held under Paganism.

The new Christianity in Ireland did not occur in a vacuum. Feminist historian Gerda Lerner argues that the creation of patriarchy in Western "civilization" occurred when men invented new meanings for the major symbol of female power, the Mother-Goddess, rendering the masculine superior and the feminine inferior. She also argues that the invention of writing, about 3100 B.C. in Mesopotamia, helped men accomplish this by manipulating symbols. Patriarchal ideology is the linchpin of Greek philosophy, Judeo-Christian theology, and legal systems which transmit male-defined views of the world.[9]

In the centuries after St. Patrick's arrival in Ireland, the Christian Church launched a massive campaign to stamp out[10] the old Celtic religion. The Church assigned the attributes and functions of Pagan deities to Christian saints to make the new religion more acceptable. St. Brigid is one example. A Pagan goddess in Celtic society, she became St. Brigid of Kildare who founded a monastery around the end of the fifth century and assumed spiritual responsibility for Christians in her vast jurisdiction.[11] Not all goddesses were easily transformed into Christian saints. The powerful Badb appears in folk tradition as the *bean sí* (banshee or fairy woman), whose keening still foretells death to certain Gael (old Irish) families. Old Jack always said that the *bean sí* cried for the O's and the M's.

The new Christian religion, buttressed by early Greek philosophy,[12] would introduce ideas about women alien to Pagan Ireland. St. Augustine, a fifth-century Catholic theologian, declared that women were an "inferior mix," prone to sin, and did not reflect the image of God; Augustine was adamant that only men were created in God's image. Such views, the foundation of much Christian doctrine, contributed to the establishment of patriarchal religion.[13] Christian misogyny would have a profound impact on every aspect of women's lives up to and including the present day. It would lead to the Christian witch hunts and the holocaust of hundreds of thousands of women, often eccentric or nonconformist, in sixteenth- and seventeenth-century Europe. The male inquisitors used the *Malleus Maleficarum* (*The Hammer of Witches*), a 1486 handbook designed by two Dominican priests for the persecution of witches. The *Malleus* linked witchcraft to women's inferior nature:

> And it should be noted that there was a defect in the forma-
> tion of the first woman, since she was formed from a bent rib,
> that is, a rib of the breast which is bent as it were in a contrary
> direction to a man. And since through this defect she is an
> imperfect animal [*sic*], she always deceives.[14]

Margaret Murray advances the view that these witch hunts were an attempt by the new male-dominated Christianity to suppress the ancient female-oriented Pagan goddess religions.[15]

Under the Brehon laws, the traditional laws of early Irish society, women had rights in marriage, divorce and property.[16] According to Irish historian Donncha Ó Corráin, however, early Irish society was patriarchal, and records from the sixth and early seventh centuries, the earliest period for which they are available, show legal and political life governed by men. Nevertheless, under the Brehon laws women had more rights than under the later English common law. At the end of the seventh century, if the couple came from the same social class, the typical marriage (*lánamnas comthincuir*) ensured that both parties retained owner-ship of land, stock and household equipment. Under the law, the wife was "a woman of joint dominion" and "a woman of equal lordship." For a contract or business dealing to be legally binding, both partners had to consent. There were also generous grounds for women seeking divorce, including sexual dissatisfaction and vagrancy. The Brehon laws also covered male violence against women; a woman could divorce her husband if he beat her and could claim the equivalent of her total bride-price, or dowry, and compensation for the injury. The husband could also be fined for the assault.[17]

Women were also expected to become warriors, and were not exempted from martial duty until 697 A.D. by the Synod of Tara. They had the right to pursue a case at law and to recover debts equally with men. They could inherit property, but primacy in inheritance went to men. If a man had no sons, then his daughter inherited, and daughters were always entitled to a dowry from the general estate.[18]

However, as Christianity began to gain a foothold and Celtic influence declined, the power, prestige, and authority of Irish women also waned. A Christian text, *Cáin Adomháin*, would contend that the Church's ban on women warriors had improved Ireland.[19] By the twelfth century, a woman might hold the clothing and linens she brought into marriage, but officially she would come under her husband's control.[20]

Colonization

The Normans, under William the Conqueror, invaded Ireland in 1169.[21] Unlike the Brehon laws, where land was vested in the clan, Norman-British property rights rested on the personal ownership of land. Under English common law, women became the chattels of marriage. In addition, male violence against women was promoted according to the "rule of thumb" — a man was encouraged to beat a recalcitrant wife so long as the stick he used was no wider than his thumb. It would take four centuries for common law to root out the Brehon laws.[22] Irish women of the Middle Ages lost more ground as Christian Europe moved to consolidate itself.

Central to any examination of Irish women, then, is the impact

of Christian and English colonizations on their role. Both colonizations conspired to the same end: the subjugation of women. The
Christian Church, from the fifth century onwards, would
obliterate ancient goddess Paganism. Its patriarchal religious and
political colonization of Ireland would radically change women's
role, defining them according to the doctrine of Augustine and
others. The English were the second to colonize. As Christian
colonization merged with English colonization, women would be
more effectively subjugated under English common law.

The merging of colonizations was not simple, however. The
relationship of Irish women to the Catholic Church is distinct and
particular. The Christian Church had erased women's power from
Pagan times and rendered women inferior to men. Later, the
Catholic Church — as opposed to the English-identified Protestant
Church — would provide women with a native Irish identity and
a refuge from English colonialism. Thus, in a most unusual twist,
while Catholicism and English colonialism would each oppress
Irish women, Catholicism would provide an Irish identity, the
means for Irish women (and men) to fight English colonialism.
This conflict for Irish women lasts to the present day. Today, as we
will see, what may appear as a Catholic–Protestant conflict in
Ulster is more precisely an Irish–English one.

The English colonizations of the seventeenth century ensured
the overthrow of the political, social and economic structures of
Irish society. Irish women's rights were further eroded. English
common law rendered women the chattels of their husbands and
compromised Irish women's property and inheritance rights inside and outside marriage. Women might, however, continue to
hold some control over land: "Into the twentieth century in County Clare ... mothers held the land until the heir came of age."[23]
Women were to be wives and mothers, performing within the
private sphere of the home and subject to the husband. English
colonialism now buttressed Christianity, which had subordinated
women within the social structure as well as within the patriarchal
nuclear family.[24]

The seventeenth and eighteenth centuries brought the Plantation of Ulster, the Cromwellian Invasion and the Penal Laws, all designed to complete the English colonization of Ireland.[25] All had a profound impact on Irish women's lives.

MacCurtain cites Gearóid Ó Tuathaigh's summation of Irish women's lot in the aftermath of the plantations and conquests in sixteenth- and seventeenth-century Ireland:

> Firstly, they [women] were totally without formal political rights; secondly, their property and inheritance rights, both within and outside of marriage, were now governed by English common law; and thirdly, theirs was a subject and subsidiary role to the male, and it was performed, for the most part, within a domestic context.[26]

Implicit in Ó Tuathaigh's investigation of women's role in Ireland under "the new English order" is colonization. According to MacCurtain, this new order established the pattern for further British colonization throughout the world: a stratified state achieved by military conquest. MacCurtain outlines its characteristics: a growth in state bureaucracy making it possible for English settlers and planters to control the country's resources; the transformation of an older pastoral economy; wealth now consolidated in the hands of an English landed aristocracy backed up by force and law. By the beginning of the eighteenth century, vast numbers of producers would be at the bottom of a class pyramid, living in poverty, the fruits of their labour appropriated by the administrators, nobility, churchmen, army officers and great merchants resting at the top.[27] What happened in Ireland, England's first colony, would serve as a model for its colonial adventures elsewhere. It would culminate in the English Crown's vow that the sun would never set on the British Empire.

The Plantation of Ulster

The Plantation of Ulster in 1609 would echo through the centuries. This Plantation lies at the root of "the Troubles" in Ulster today.

Elizabeth's successor, James I of England, seized some 500,000 acres of Irish land in the North and gave it to English and Scottish Protestants. Catholics, the native Irish, were driven off their own lands in mass evictions to make way for the colonizers. Some of the evicted took to the hills and bogs. Some emigrated.[28] By 1641, Protestants had taken three million of the three and a half million acres that made up the six counties of the North — Armagh, Cavan, Coleraine,[29] Donegal, Fermanagh and Tyrone. Catholics owned the rest.

The native Irish have always resisted. In 1641, the Irish rose, demanding the restoration of all seized land and recognition for Catholicism, in a rebellion that would last eight years. Thousands strong, the English parliamentary army under Oliver Cromwell landed in Ireland in 1649. Bent on bringing the rebels to heel, Cromwell's army slaughtered the defenders and townspeople of Drogheda and Wexford. His war cry to the native Irish was "To Hell or Connaught," which drove them to the poorer land in the west. Between 1652 and 1660, more than eleven million acres of Irish land was taken over by English soldiers and settlers. Under what became known as the Settlement, "Irish landowners found east of the river Shannon after 1 May 1654 faced the death penalty" or forced labour in the West Indies and Barbados.[30]

With the collapse of Cromwell's Commonwealth and the restoration of the English monarchy under Charles II, many Irish hoped to get their lands back. But Charles, reluctant to risk confronting the parliamentary army, would change little. However, after James II, a Catholic, took the throne as King of England and Ireland in 1685, the Catholic-dominated Irish Parliament repealed the Settlement imposed by Cromwell. In response, the English Parliament called in the Netherlands' William of Orange, a Protestant.

James raised an army in Ireland, but his troops fell before William's at the Battle of the Boyne on July 12, 1690. James fled Ireland. The Irish harried William's army in the South for more than a year after William defeated James, holding out until they lost the Battle of Aughrim in 1691. The conquest was not complete, however, until the Treaty of Limerick was signed in 1691.

The Penal Laws

Power now lay in the hands of the Protestant Ascendancy, the English colonial governing class, who became the wealthiest land-owners in Ireland. Between 1695 and 1727 they brought in the Penal Laws, designed to destroy the spirit of the native Irish by eradicating their culture. The Laws consolidated the colonizers' power and wealth and remained in force for more than a century.

The Penal Laws banned Catholicism, the political stronghold of the native Irish. They also forbade the native Irish Catholic majority to vote or hold public office, educate their children or take up a profession, purchase or lease land, keep more than one-third of the profits from rented land, or own a horse worth more than £5 — the last to prevent Catholics from raising a cavalry. The Laws also banned the speaking of the Irish language and traditional expressions of culture. In desperate attempts to preserve reading and writing and the old traditions, the native Catholic Irish set up hedge-schools (schools hidden under hedges) taught by itinerant schoolteachers. Catholics worshipped illicitly, under pain of death. Irish poets wrote secretly in Gaelic throughout the 1700s, their audience the native Irish. Roísín Dubh became the secret symbol for Ireland.

Emigration Begins

Although many eighteenth-century Protestant colonizers in Ulster amassed sizeable landholdings and others moved as industrialists into the textile industry, thousands chose to emigrate, at a rate of some 4,000 a year throughout the century.[31] Native Irish subsisted on small plots of land, once theirs, now the property of English Protestant landlords, who exacted extortionate rents plus a portion of the often meagre crop. The potato had come to Ireland from the Americas in the late 1600s. Producing strong yields on small plots and requiring less labour than other crops, within two centuries it would become the staple diet of small tenant farmers. In the meantime, the emerging Irish wool and glass industries, hit by English protectionist measures, gave way to the needs of English trade and commerce. Linen weaving continued; there was no linen industry in England. By 1700, the native Irish — four-fifths of the population — lived on one-seventh of the poorest land.

The results of English colonialism left Irish people dispirited and broken. Irish emigration began in earnest. Between 1700 and 1776, 250,000 to 400,000 Irish emigrated to the North American colonies.[32]

The Protestant Orange Order was founded in 1795. Its chief celebration, held annually on July 12, commemorates the Orange victory at the Battle of the Boyne in 1690, when the Protestant King William III defeated the Catholic King James II. For the Orange Order, the Battle of the Boyne meant the final defeat of the Catholics, the final defeat of Ireland. In Ulster, political and economic power would remain in Protestant hands. The native Catholic Irish were shut out, a situation that prevails in Ulster to the present day.[33]

The French Revolution of 1789 brought a new era, the Enlightenment, and inspired the native Irish to rise again in 1798. But the English quashed the rebellion, and once again the Irish were left dispirited.

The Famine

In the nineteenth century, the Famine was the most conspicuous consequence of the English colonization of Ireland. The Famine came about because of English colonial oppression. In 1841, Ireland's population numbered slightly more than eight million. That year's census classed seven in ten Irish as labourers and smallholders with fewer than five acres. These people would bear the brunt of the Great Famine. Ireland had known famine before, but crop failure had been localized. By 1845, the year the potato blight — a fungus that rotted the crop to pulp — first showed up, the potato was the basic food of nearly one in three native Irish. In 1846, 1847 and 1848, the blight led to mass starvation — but only in Ireland, even though the potato crop had failed throughout Europe.[34] At the time of the Famine, Ireland was intensely cultivated, with three-quarters of the soil growing wheat and other grains and vegetables untouched by the blight — enough to feed the starving. But as thousands of Irish lay dying on the roadsides, English landlords shipped Ireland's abundant harvest to England.[35]

Malthusians and their successors, anxious to absolve England of responsibility, have argued that the Famine was the inevitable outcome of overpopulation.[36] The English politicians of the time insisted that the native Irish use the good crops to pay land rents, or be evicted. Some writers have pointed to England's 1846 repeal of the Corn Laws — a protective tariff on wheat, known at the time as corn — as meant to relieve the Famine in Ireland.[37] But so long as wheat prices in England remained high under the tariff, English manufacturers faced demands for higher wages from English workers who could not afford the price of wheat. English manufacturers wanted and got the Laws repealed.[38] By then the Famine had devastated the native Irish.

> So many people died in so short a period of time, that mass graves were provided, often in ground specially consecrated for the purpose. Emigration soared from 75,000 in 1845 to 250,000 in 1851. Thousands of emigrants died during the Atlantic crossing (in 1847 there were 17,465 documented deaths) in "coffin ships".... Thousands more died of sickness at disembarkation centres.[39]

By the time the Famine had abated, the population was cut in half. The population of Ireland today is smaller than it was before the Famine. Many smallholders and labourers who lived through the early part of the Famine later fell victim to scurvy, fever, dysentery and cholera.[40]

Emigration to North America reached enormous proportions; estimates put the number of Irish emigrating at close to a million and a half between 1841 and 1845. In 1852 alone about 220,000 people emigrated. For the next sixty years emigration to America was steady. Emigrants usually paid their own expenses and when settled abroad sent back money for relatives to follow.[41]

Irish women had begun in the 1790s to emigrate in search of a better life in the Americas, and their numbers increased in the nineteenth century. Nineteenth-century Famine Ireland was largely a pre-industrial class society, its economy rooted in land ownership and great estates held by English landlords.[42] Irish people farmed as tenants on these estates, lands rightfully theirs, making a precarious living, stymied by lack of tenure, rents far in excess of what anyone could pay and fear of eviction by the 800 English landlords who owned the country.[43]

In 1879 Michael Davitt founded the Land League and Charles Stewart Parnell became its president. The League, financed largely by Irish exiles in the United States, formed to combat the massive evictions of peasant farmers. It also fought rack-renting, the jacking up of the rent at the end of the lease. This practice forced hundreds of thousands of families off the land and out of their homes. Between 1874 and 1881 alone, there were 10,000 evictions. The poor harvest of 1879 led to nearly 2,600 evictions in 1880.[44] The League used the boycott in the fight for secure tenure and fair rents.[45] On a tenant's eviction, the League prevented anyone else from taking the land, leaving the landlord without rent.

Tenant farmers facing eviction also fought back. Women often proved formidable opponents for the landlords. When the first battle against eviction took place at Carraroe, Connemara, on January 5, 1880, the "fierce daring" women who led the "bloody conflict" forced the bailiffs and police, with their bayonets, to withdraw.[46]

In the post-Famine years, harsh economic times saw an increase in male dominance. Women did not benefit from the early industrial revolution, and their diminished status was reflected in their poor representation in the work force: The 1861 census recorded 29 percent of women employed outside the home, but by 1911 that figure had fallen to 19.5 percent.[47]

Miriam Daly's examination of women in Ulster points out that it was only in the North that large numbers of women could find waged labour. Beginning in the late seventeenth century, economic prospects for women in Ulster were largely shaped by Protestant-dominated industrial development. Linen cloth produced from home-grown flax became central to Ulster's industrial prosperity. The domestic manufacture of linen had begun after 1660 and increased in importance until the outbreak of the Revolutionary and Napoleonic Wars in the late 1700s. Ulster women spun flax and wove linen at home and away from home. They also worked the fields. Their oppression was exacerbated or ameliorated by their class and religious/political allegiances. With the Industrial Revolution came the mechanization of weaving, and in the 1860s women's work as home weavers came to a halt. Women — and children — went into factories where they worked in poor conditions for less than subsistence wages.[48] About 75 percent of the work force in the Belfast linen industry were female.[49]

While working-class Ulster women faced increased oppression in the factories, women from middle-class families had one other option: Fired by the spirit of Evangelicalism which arose in the mid-1800s, they found new opportunities in the churches. Protestant women went into the missions, sailing for China as early as the 1840s. Catholic women joined convents, which opened schools, orphanages, hospitals and homes for the physically and mentally disabled throughout Ireland.[50]

According to MacCurtain, although distinctions can be made between working-class women and middle- and upper-middle-class women, as well as between rural and urban women, Irish women's choices were limited overall. They could choose between marriage and becoming the property of men, or remaining single with its corresponding economic and social vulnerability. The only prospects for employment were domestic service, the family farm or the factory. Single women, 43.3 percent of the female population in 1861 and increasing to 48.6 percent in 1911, emerged as a substantial group at the turn of the century, but their opportunities and rights remained limited.[51]

After the Famine, the subdividing of land gave way to inheritance by one family member, usually a son. Dowries became more common, but for smallholder and labouring families the land or cattle or cash for a favourable match could equal a decade's rent. Nor would single women easily find work in the towns and cities, where colonial policy had long undercut the development of trade and commerce.[52] For the many Irish women who boarded ships bound for New York and Montreal, leaving Ireland was the only option.

Irish emigrants favoured the United States over England, and women made up more than one-third of Irish immigrants to the States in the mid-1800s. They were usually single, and on average younger than the male emigrants. For the rest of the nineteenth century and at times in the twentieth, Irish women emigrants outnumbered the men; "sisters, aunts, cousins and friends abroad became an encouragement to those at home to follow."[53]

The women who left did more than encourage others. Part of the money they earned as domestic or factory workers they sent home, providing an important source of foreign exchange. Their earnings also helped pay the passage for other family members. They continued this trend even to the 1950s, when the net amount of monies Irish emigrants, including women, sent home accounted for £12 million of Ireland's gross national product.[54]

Irish Women's Resistance and Revolution

In Irish women's struggle over the last hundred years, the "woman question" and the "national question" have been at odds, or at best ill at ease with each other. All too often, Irish women in the male-dominated resistance movements have found the space for nationalist struggle but not equality for women. Irish women in the broader feminist movement have found the space for feminist struggle but little understanding of or support for their demand for their right to self-determination as Irish. This conflict makes Irish women's full emancipation more difficult.

Despite this conflict, Irish women do resist, whether that resistance is to patriarchy, political oppression, or both. One form of resistance emerged in the many important women's organizations founded around the turn of the century. These organizations include The Ladies' Land League (1881–1882), Inghinidhe na hÉireann (Daughters of Erin; 1900–1914), Cumann na mBan (the Irishwomen's Council; 1914–present), the Textile Operatives' Society (1890s) and the Irish Women's Franchise League (1908).

Margaret Ward explores the work of the Ladies' Land League, Inghinidhe na hÉireann and Cumann na mBan, each devoted in different ways to Irish independence, each a means of Irish women's engagement, and each a record of Irish women's participation in the "national question."[55]

The Ladies' Land League

The Ladies' Land League began in the late 1800s, after the outlawing of the Land League and jailing of its male leaders for conspiracy in blocking rent payments and resisting evictions. To hold what had been won, the Land Leaguers had to set up an alternative leadership of women. The male leadership accepted Michael Davitt's proposal to engage women — a proposal deemed a "most dangerous experiment" by his colleagues — and the leadership passed to Anna Parnell, Charles Stewart Parnell's sister. On their release from prison, however, Parnell and Davitt dissolved the Ladies' Land League, much to the disillusionment of Anna Parnell, who never spoke to her brother again and died a recluse in an artists' colony in Cornwall.[56]

Despite being betrayed by the men, the Ladies' Land League accomplished a remarkable amount of work that has been written out of history. They helped evicted families, built huts for those left homeless and took care of prisoners and their dependants. Simultaneously, they spread the resistance throughout the country. Some of their leaders were arrested and imprisoned.[57]

Having dared to step beyond women's prescribed role, they also pointed out the complicity of the two colonizers — the Christian Church and England — in the subjugation of women. Their definition of these issues in the public sphere, the domain of men only, drew the wrath of both the press and the churches, a show of brotherhood across English Protestant–Irish Catholic lines that had never been seen before. Catholic Archbishop McCabe of Dublin was appalled by these women who were prepared to "forget the modesty of their sex and the high dignity of their womanhood" "before the public gaze in a character unworthy of a child of Mary."[58] The Protestant *Belfast News-Letter* condemned the "distasteful spectacle of women making a harangue from a public platform."[59] The *Times* sneered, "when treason is reduced to fighting behind petticoats and pinafores it is not likely to do much mischief."[60]

Cumann na mBan

Cumann na mBan formed to assist male Irish Volunteers in their fight against England. The Volunteers joined with the Citizen Army in the Easter Rebellion of 1916. Led by Padraic Pearse and James Connolly, about 1,800 rebels occupied a number of public buildings in Dublin, including the General Post Office, which became their headquarters. From the steps of the GPO, Pearse proclaimed Ireland a republic. The British declared martial law and executed sixteen of the leaders, including many signatories to the Proclamation.[61]

Cumann na mBan's role in the Rebellion was significant. Its members had trained with rifles and knew first aid. They also washed, cooked and cleaned for the men. The Irish Women's Franchise League, while agreeing with Cumann na mBan on the importance of Home Rule,[62] nevertheless contended that Cumann was a setback to women's emancipation because it lacked equal standing with the Volunteers, who relegated the women to traditional women's work.

During the Rebellion, sixty Cumann na mBan members acted

as messengers, organized the cooking, administered first aid and transported ammunition, hidden in their clothing and in prams, between garrison posts. In an extraordinary portent of things to come, one commandant, Eamon de Valera, refused to admit women to his post at Boland's Mills. In 1937, when the Dáil (the Irish parliament) debated the Irish constitution, a constitution which would sharply curtail women's rights, de Valera, then president of Ireland's Free State, bluntly justified his exclusion of the women during the Easter Rebellion. "I said we have the anxieties of a certain kind here and I do not want to add to them at the moment by getting untrained women, women who were clearly untrained for soldiering — I did not want them in any case."[63]

Ward sums up Cumann na mBan's assisting-the-men role in the Easter Rising as "an account of the tensions generated by this

"PRES." PEARSE AND 3 OTHERS HAVE BEEN SHOT

Canadian Press Despatch.

London — Four signatories to the Republican Proclamation in Ireland have been tried by court martial and found guilty, and were shot this morning.

Padraic (Peter) H. Pearse, the "provisional president of Ireland," was among them.

Another of the rebels found guilty and shot this morning was James Connolly, who was styled "Commandant General of the Irish Republican Army." The other two shot were Thomas J. Clark and Thomas MacDonagh.

Three other signers of the proclamation were sentenced to three years' imprisonment.

Premier Asquith made an announcement to this effect in the House of Commons this afternoon.

Pearse, the "provisional president of Ireland," who was shot this morning, was one of the best-educated of the rebel leaders, and headmaster of a boys' school in Dublin at the outbreak of the rebellion. He had been connected with Sinn Hein activities for some time, and at a secret gathering of rebels immediately before the outbreak, was chosen provisional president of the new Irish republic.

Pearse led the assault on the general post office, resulting in its capture by the rebels on the first day of the rebellion. He was wounded in the leg in last Thursday's fighting, and surrendered to the Government forces unconditionally. Later he signed a proclamation calling upon his followers to lay down their arms.

Connolly, the "commandant general of the Irish republican army," also shot this morning after trial by court-martial, had been wounded in the street fighting.

The Easter Rebellion in Ireland was quashed and four of its leaders shot, *The Toronto Daily Star* reported May 3, 1916. Reprinted with permission —*The Canadian Press.*

CASEMENT HANGED TO-DAY, SOME CHEERS, SOME GROANS

Small Early-Morning Gathering Grew to a Crowd That Extended Two Blocks.

London — Roger Casement, former Knight and consul, was hanged at 9 o'clock this morning in Pentonville jail for high treason. He was convicted of conspiring to cause an armed revolt in Ireland, and with having sought German aid to that end.

Two hours before the execution a crowd of men, women and children gathered before the prison gates. Twenty minutes before Casement mounted the scaffold the great prison bell commenced to toll.

The sound was greeted with cheers from the crowd, mingled with some groans.

At 9 o'clock the crowd had swollen to such proportions that it extended for two blocks from the prison front. At one minute after nine a single stroke on the big bell announced that the trap had been sprung. It was the signal for another yell from the crowd which suddenly died away into dead silence.

Casement met his death with calm courage, according to eye witnesses. Early in the morning two priests of the Roman Catholic Church administered the last rites in the cell of the condemned man, and shortly afterward a little procession, headed by the clergymen, with Casement following, a warder on either side, proceeded toward the execution shed, only five yards away.

The priests recited the Litany of the dying, Casement responding in low tones: "Lord have mercy on my soul."

As the party reached the shed where the gallows was erected, the special executioner, a hair dresser named Ellis, approached Casement and quickly pinioned him. The two chaplains, the under sheriff of London, and the under sheriff of Middlesex, then took up their positions in front of the scaffold. Casement mounted the gallows steps firmly and commended his spirit to God as he stepped on the trap. A moment later the lever was pulled.

Immediately after the trap was sprung the prison engineer and physician descended into the pit, where after the application of the usual tests, Casement was pronounced dead at nine minutes after nine.

According to the custom in the case of prisoners hanged for crimes similar to that of Casement, his body will be buried in quicklime in the prison yard.

An affecting incident took place outside the prison wall as the execution was in progress. At the back of the prison a little distance from the crowd about the gates was a group of about thirty Irish men and women. When the dull clang of the prison bell announced that the doomed man had paid the last penalty this little group fell on their knees, and with bowed heads remained for some moments silently praying for the repose of the soul of their dead fellow-countryman.

All the members of Casement's family were Protestants, and he was brought up in that faith, but became a convert to Roman Catholicism within the last few weeks.

On June 29 he was registered as a member of the Roman Catholic Church, and since that time Fathers McCarroll and Carey of Eden Grove Church, near the prison, have been ministering to him.

He received his first and only communion at seven o'clock this morning, when he assisted at mass in his cell. According to one of his attendants, the last words of the condemned man, apart from his prayers, were: "I die for my country."

Roger Casement's execution was reported on August 3, 1916. Reprinted with permission — *The Toronto Star Syndicate.*

subordination and of the repeated attempts by some women to establish a greater degree of autonomy for themselves."[64] Cumann na mBan members had risked their lives just as the men had, and some were arrested following the Rising. Countess Markiewicz, a member of Cumann na mBan, was court-martialled but her death sentence was commuted to life imprisonment because of her sex.

Inghinidhe na hÉireann

Inghinidhe na hÉireann[65] made a very important contribution to the rekindling of native Irish culture through its revival of Gaelic language, literature, music, history, art and theatre. Staunchly nationalist, it aimed in part "to discourage the reading and circulation of low English literature, the singing of English songs, the attending of vulgar English entertainments at theatres and music halls, and to combat in every way English influence, which is doing so much injury to the artistic taste and refinement of the Irish people."[66]

For years, the poet W. B. Yeats had envisioned an Irish theatre, a theatre he believed would establish a new identity for Irish people and propel a new generation of Irish writers. It was Irish women who fulfilled this dream. Inghinidhe and the Celtic Literary Society put together a series of plays illustrating such figures from Irish legend as Queen Maeve, the Children of Lir and Red Hugh. Pressed by activist Maude Gonne to be more nationalist, Yeats wrote the poetic and nationalist *Cathleen ni Houlihan*, launched with Maude Gonne in the role of Cathleen, the symbol of Ireland.[67] The work of Maude Gonne and Inghinidhe na hÉireann led to the founding of the Abbey Theatre in Dublin,[68] a fact often missing from male accounts.

Inghinidhe eventually dissolved, having joined Cumann na mBan and Cumann na nGaedhael, out of which formed Sinn Féin, a republican organization. From Sinn Féin's beginnings, in 1908, women held executive positions. Many of its women members had belonged to Inghinidhe.

Irish Women and Suffrage

In the mid-1800s, women's suffrage became an important issue for women in Europe and North America. Ireland was no exception. In 1876, Anna Haslam, a Quaker, founded the Irish Suffrage Society. On behalf of Irish women, Haslam signed the first women's suffrage petition, brought by John Stuart Mill to England's House of Commons.[69] Mill, in collaboration with Harriet Hardy Taylor Mill, had published *The Subjection of Women* in 1869, providing encouragement for the women's suffrage movement in Europe and the United States.

The militant Irish Women's Franchise League, co-founded in 1908 by Hanna Sheehy-Skeffington, fought from its inception to include women's suffrage in the Home Rule Bill. Reflecting the woman-or-nation conflict, the IWFL frequently found itself at odds with the leaders of the nationalist movement, who were often quick to dismiss suffrage. While Sheehy-Skeffington acknowledged that women could find prominence in republican movements such as Sinn Féin, she also pointed out that the work allotted to them reinforced their domestic role, running counter to women's full emancipation. The Republican movement dismissed her criticisms as nothing more than "English agitation," a sally implying that suffrage, an issue at the forefront of the day, was but an English phenomenon and therefore anathema to the Republican cause. Even Inghinidhe na hÉireann did not support this "English agitation."[70]

In 1911, the militant Irish Women's Suffrage Federation, an umbrella suffrage organization, was formed. The Irish Parliamentary Party said it was sympathetic to suffrage, but its leader, John Redmond, told a deputation of women that he opposed the vote for women. Sinn Féin hesitated. English suffragist Christabel Pankhurst spoke in Dublin in 1910 to huge crowds, and one suffragist was arrested for chalking notices for the event on pavements. Soon after, four members of IWFL were jailed for breaking government windows. The suffragists would meet with growing hostility from the nationalist movement. When they held a Poster

Parade advocating the vote for women, they were attacked by a mob mustered by the Ancient Order of Hibernians. The suffragists retaliated in 1912 on Home Rule Day by daubing a public platform where Redmond was due to speak with the slogan "Votes for Women." Redmond condemned the women and women's suffrage.

Between 1912 and the outbreak of the 1916 Rising, thirty-six women suffragists were convicted. In 1911, the suffragists took up the right to citizenship for women under Home Rule, a position supported by Cumann na mBan. In 1912 the Woman's Suffrage Bill, including women's suffrage amendments to the Home Rule Bill, was overwhelmingly defeated by the Irish Parliamentary Party.[71]

In a report dated January 18, 1913, *The Toronto Daily Star* carried the headline "WINDOWS OF DUBLIN CASTLE BROKEN BY THE SUFFRAGETTES." The *Star* reported that three of the women had been arrested, tried and sentenced to a month's hard labour each.[72] In 1918, two years after the Proclamation of the Easter Rising, a proclamation to Irish men *and* women, women older than thirty years finally won the right to vote. With Ireland still occupied, Irish women's suffrage came from England. Countess Markiewicz became the first Irish woman to be elected to public office.

The Textile Operatives' Society

Irish women also joined labour unions in the early nineteenth century. Miriam Daly points out that among the first labour conflicts in which women played a major role were the Belfast linen strikes of 1872 and 1874. Women and girls made up 70 percent of the work force in the linen mills. In 1897, Mary Galway, secretary of the Textile Operatives' Society, the first labour union for women textile workers in Ireland, led 8,000 workers in a strike against the strict discipline and penalties enforced on the shop floor.[73] Daly credits three women activists with providing the impetus for the ground-breaking vote on a resolution in favour of equal pay for equal work by the largest of the Irish trade unions, the Irish

WINDOWS OF DUBLIN CASTLE BROKEN BY THE SUFFRAGETTES

Special Cable to The Star
Dublin — Irish suffragettes at noon made an onslaught on Dublin Castle, the official building of the Lord Lieutenant of Ireland, and smashed several windows. Three of the women, Mrs. Cousins, Mrs. Conroy and Mrs. Hopkins, were promptly arrested, tried, and given a month's hard labor each.

Three Irish feminists each got a month's hard labour in prison after a window-breaking spree. This report appeared January 28, 1913.

Transport and General Workers' Union, in 1948. She argues that this vote paved the way for the Republic's historic 1974 Anti-Discrimination Act which established the right to equal pay.[74]

Irish Women and Class Distinction

That Irish women participated in and struggled for women's emancipation as well as for Irish emancipation is known largely because of Irish feminists who have sifted the records to unearth what has been covered over. The history of this dual struggle, however, reveals an unsettling trend. The women who participated in and defined the struggle were middle-class women with access to the education advocated by the English feminist theorist Mary Wollstonecraft (1759–1797) in her now famous political treatise, *A Vindication of the Rights of Woman* (1792).[75] This pattern was repeated in other parts of the West during the 1800s.

MacCurtain credits the education of middle-class Irish women from the 1830s on to the Catholic Church. Various religious orders, including the Ursuline, Loretto, Dominican and Sacré Coeur Sisters, set up convent boarding schools in Ireland to educate middle-class girls. This, together with the 1878 Intermediate Act on education, had an enormous impact on middle-class Irish women's educational and economic aspirations. Their families' economic status also afforded them university education and its corresponding relative economic freedom.

Thus access to education enabled middle-class Irish women to articulate the issues that would lead to the founding of the Free State in the South in 1922.[76] Although it was hardly the intention of Catholic educators, in yet another stroke of irony, the Catholic Church, having collaborated with the English over the centuries in colonizing Irish women, would now provide at least some Irish women with the skills to analyze and articulate the feminist and/or nationalist issues of the day.

It was largely this education, open only to middle-class Irish women, which inspired the first women's newspaper produced in Ireland. From the beginnings of *Bean na hÉireann* (Woman of Ireland) in 1908 until its collapse in 1911, Irish middle-class women voiced their positions on feminism and nationalism.[77] The editor, Helena Moloney, an active member of Inghinidhe na hÉireann who was disillusioned with the sexism of Sinn Féin, sounded the battle cry of the women's paper in an editorial: "Freedom for Our Nation and the complete removal of all disabilities to our sex."[78]

But Irish working-class women did not have the privilege of an education which would give them the opportunity for some economic freedom. Nor did they live in circumstances that would let them analyze, define and mobilize for feminist and/or nationalist goals. James Connolly summarized the conditions of the working-class Irish woman in the early 1900s:

> Driven out to work at the earliest possible age, she remains fettered to her wage-earning, a slave all her life. Marriage does not mean for her a rest from outside labour...she has the added duty of a double domestic toil — completing each day's work, she becomes the slave of domestic needs of family.[79]

Class divisions gave rise to yet another issue for Irish women, as conflicted today as it was nearly a century ago and reflected in feminism in the West. When a movement's aims are defined, voiced and mobilized by the few for the many, voices are suppressed, even erased, so that the dominant group can maintain power and privilege. Within the women's movement, that dominant group is middle-class white women.

The middle-class white suffrage movement, the first wave in the West at the turn of the century, and the second wave of feminism in the 1960s, dominated and defined the feminist agenda and ultimately left many women on the margin because of their race and class.[80] Ireland's story of the first and second wave is no exception. While working-class women did participate in union activity, only middle-class women could get an education. Only middle-class women could participate in nationalist and feminist causes. Only middle-class women could record what happened. Working-class women were shut out. That trend continued in the second wave.

Irish Women into Modern Times

In 1920 Partition created the Ulster State, which remains under English rule. The other 26 counties of Ireland became the Irish Free State, finally winning independence in 1922 after close to 800 years of foreign rule. The treaty establishing Partition split Irish politics, with some accepting Partition and others violently opposed. This split erupted into the Irish Civil War, which finally ended in 1923.

MacCurtain presses the question, "What then was the reality for the Irish woman in the decade following Yeats's romantic projection of her female presence in Irish nationalism?"[81] Alas, poor Cathleen Ní Houlihan was once again overruled by the menfolk of the revolution. She remained condemned to the poetry of men's dreams, still relegated to a secondary role. MacCurtain answers her own question:

> Around Irish women, as in a cage, were set the structures of family life and women were assigned a home-based, full-time role as housewives, whose talents and energies were devoted to looking after husband and children.[82]

Ward describes the ground Irish women lost under subsequent administrations which curtailed women's rights. Among other measures under de Valera, the draconian Employment Bill of 1935 prohibited women's work in industry and banned employers from employing more women than men where a ministerial decision on discrimination against women in a particular industry was in order.

The politicians hoped to ameliorate the economic depression of the time by excluding women from the work force and giving their ᴊᴏʙꜱ to men. In 1926, 60 percent of women in the labour force were employed in domestic service or farming. Between 1926 and 1936 women's participation in the industrial work force rose from 20 to almost 23 percent. In a time of political conservatism and economic recession, women's presence in the work force was construed as an affront to male ego; unemployed men used working women as a convenient scapegoat.[83]

In 1937, de Valera's Irish Constitution, much of which remains unchanged to this day, defined women as mothers and wives and worked to exclude them from paid work. The constitution reflected the special position the Catholic Church enjoyed within the state and gave state backing to the Church's opposition to abortion, contraception and other rights.[84] It also banned divorce, making it illegal for the first time since the fifth century,[85] and this ban continues today. In a 1986 referendum, after a massive campaign by the Catholic Church, two-thirds of the voters rejected divorce. Before the referendum, one male member of the Dáil urged a "no" vote, arguing: "A divorced woman is like a used car"![86]

Contraception has been outlawed since 1935, but recently became available to "married couples." Long illegal, abortion can bring a penalty of life imprisonment. The Constitution no longer grants special recognition to the Church. Nonetheless, Church policies still carry great weight. A 1983 referendum made abortion unconstitutional, and it is illegal even to provide Irish women with information on how to get an abortion elsewhere. More than 10,000 Irish women a year go to England for abortions.[87] The recent spectacle of a High Court judge banning a 14-year-old pregnant rape victim from doing so made headlines around the world. After an uproar by Irish women, the Court rescinded its decision and allowed the girl to make the trip.[88]

Like many post-colonial states throughout the world, the Republic of Ireland has been plagued by a poor economy since independence. Irish women emigrate today because of an economy that is still shaped by foreign capital, a situation that results in high unemployment and few job prospects. Ursula Barry notes: "The economy of the twenty-six counties is in a severe state of crisis: over 240,000 people are unemployed; over one-third of the population is dependent on welfare; penal taxation levels cut people's earned income in half; government expenditure on critical services like health and education is being cut back."[89]

Barry attributes much of the crisis to multinational companies' siphoning off and repatriating billions of pounds in profits a year from Irish-based subsidiaries. She notes that employment in manufacturing increased during the 1960s and 1970s as multinationals set up shop in Ireland. These companies were encouraged by an Irish government policy that opened the country to foreign investment after the severe depression and mass emigration of the 1950s. Barry points out that U.S. companies record their highest rates of profit in Ireland. Between 1980 and 1985 multinational corporations, taking advantage of tax concessions, took some £4,034 million in profits out of the country. Within ten years of opening shop in Ireland, about one-third of the multinationals leave. Barry reports around 20,000 jobs lost between 1973 and 1981 alone.

Barry also cites the part Ireland's national debt plays in the economic crisis. This debt, at £20,000 million, half of which is owed to foreign bankers, is of such magnitude that interest payments alone consumed the total value of all income tax collected by the government.

Barry notes that women make up just over 30 percent of the recorded work force in Ireland and are concentrated mainly in clerical work, making them especially vulnerable to job loss as capital investment moves away from labour-intensive industries. In manufacturing, women make up 27 percent of the labour force. The electronics industry did not bring women good jobs at high pay: In 1987, when women held 78 percent of jobs in the industry's general operations, they held only 15 percent of the specialized jobs and 3 percent of management jobs.[91] Irish women face particular hardships in employment, despite the Employment Equality Act of 1977 which prohibits discrimination on the basis of sex and marital status.[92] In an economy where unemployment shot to 17 percent in 1989, women were particularly hard hit.

Today, Irish women remain concentrated in the lower-paid, less-skilled jobs.[93] In the early 1980s, Irish married women showed the lowest rate of labour-force participation in the European Common Market — 17 percent.[94] According to the Employment Equality Agency in Dublin, in 1990 women were 32 percent of the work force in the Republic. Today married women are also staying longer in the work force.[95] But the bulk of women's jobs are in the service sector, rendering women more vulnerable as capital flees labour-intensive modes for the new electronic technologies that replace women workers.[96]

The Republic of Ireland does not gather statistics on male violence against women. According to Olive Braiden, the executive director of the Dublin Rape Crisis Centre, Ireland has no official statistics on the number of rapes reported to police. Ireland's six Rape Crisis Centres are dotted throughout the North and South and each gather data separately. In 1990, the Dublin Rape Crisis Centre handled 1,479 complaints of rape from women. Braiden notes that the Criminal Law Rape Act of 1990 prohibits the introduction of the victim's previous sexual history, except her relationship with the accused. Marital rape is also outlawed. The Republic does not compile official statistics on battered women. Braiden uses Canadian statistics, which show that one in ten women is battered by a male partner.[97]

The Equal Pay Act of 1974 implicitly covers sexual harassment. According to a spokesperson for the Employment Equality Agency in Dublin, the first successful sexual harassment case launched before the Irish courts in 1985 placed the onus for preventing sexual harassment on the employer. It became a landmark case for Europe.[98]

Irish women emigrate today because social and economic conditions still force them to leave. Faced with unemployment, travelling across the water is the only option. The patterns from the past repeat themselves in the present. Government statistics report that in 1989, 46,000 people emigrated, the highest number in the decade, and in sharp contrast to 1970 when only 5,000 left.[99] Some analysts compare recent rates of emigration to those of the Famine years,[100] with a dramatic rise beginning in the 1970s. In 1970, the number of people leaving Ireland balanced against those entering was 5,000. This increased to 20,000 in 1985 and reached a peak of 46,000 in 1989. But the preliminary figures for 1991 show a dramatic decrease to 1,000.[101]

The Troubles

Following Partition in 1920, the six counties of Ulster remained under British rule. The North's first Prime Minister, Sir James

Craig, assured the Protestant majority that he had brought in a "Protestant Government for a Protestant People."[102]

As a group, Catholics in the North face systemic discrimination in employment, voting rights, and housing. The Civil Rights Association, founded in Belfast in 1967, organized under the banner "One Man, One Vote." The Association also sought equality in jobs and council housing and an end to electoral boundaries drawn to favour Protestants. A 1968 march in Derry was outlawed, but marchers turned out anyway and were met by the Royal Ulster Constabulary. Dozens were wounded, including several police officers.

The more militant and avowedly leftist People's Democracy formed in 1968.[103] March and counter-march followed each other, often resulting in pitched battles. In early January 1969, a march organized by People's Democracy walked from Belfast to Derry, where it was attacked at a bridge outside town by

> a Protestant mob wielding cudgels with nails hammered through. The [Royal Ulster Constabulary] gave the marchers no protection. Later that day, RUC and "B" Specials [Loyalist paramilitary forces] ran amok in Londonderry's Catholic Bogside district. In retaliation, the residents there sealed off the Bogside and declared it "Free Derry."[104]

Several thousand Loyalists marched that August 12, celebrating the end of the siege of Derry in the seventeenth century. When Catholic and Protestant young people battled each other, the RUC attacked the Bogside, using tear gas, but were driven back. Two days later, on August 14, 1969, British troops entered Derry to bring about "peace." Any hopes of peace were short-lived; that night Belfast police fired machine guns at the homes of Catholics, and Protestant Loyalist mobs set houses aflame.

The British government of the time is reported to have considered dropping part of the Special Powers Act of 1922, laws which allow Britain's Minister of Home Affairs to arrest and imprison people without trial, search homes without warrants, seize property, suspend habeas corpus, and not hold inquests.[105] In 1971, however, the North's prime minister, Brian Faulkner, ordered internment. Between August 9, 1971, and December 5, 1975, more than 2,100 Northerners were jailed without trial.

In 1976, the European Commission on Human Rights found the British Government had used torture in Ulster. In 1978, however, the European Court of Human Rights would rule that Britain had treated suspected members of the IRA inhumanely and degradingly in 1971 but had not tortured them. Amnesty International registered "surprise" at the ruling and urged the British Government to set up a public inquiry to investigate allegations of maltreatment. The murders continued. Between 1969 and 1979, almost 2,000 people were killed in Ulster.[106] The Civil Rights Association responded with more demonstrations.

On Bloody Sunday, January 30, 1972, troops of the parachute brigade opened fire on demonstrators in Derry, killing thirteen Catholics. Derry's coroner would later write, "It seems that the Army ran amok that day and they shot without thinking what they were doing...it was sheer unadulterated murder."[107] Within a few weeks, the IRA would bomb the officers' mess of the parachute brigade, killing seven people, including a cleaning woman. For its part, the Ulster Defence Association, a merger of smaller Loyalist paramilitary groups in 1971, had vowed "It's lead bullets from now on. We are British to the core but we won't hesitate to take on even the British if they attempt to sell our country down the river."[108] In March 1972, Britain's Heath government suspended the North's parliament. Direct rule from Westminster began.

Today, as in yesteryear, prospects for a job in Ulster are drawn on political-religious lines, with Catholics often ruled out. In some Catholic neighbourhoods in West Belfast, unemployment runs as high as 80 percent. The rate of Catholic unemployment, having remained constant since 1968, has recently begun increasing. In 1991 the Fair Employment Commission found that Catholic men were two and a half times as likely to be unemployed as Protestant men. In Belfast's industrial giant, the Harland and Wolff shipyards, only 5.7 percent of the 2,691 workers in 1991 were Catholic.[109]

Ulster women have been politically active in what has come to be known as "the Troubles." The Civil Rights Association included both Catholic and Protestant women. However, Ulster women face exclusion and marginalization by men within the resistance movements. Margaret Ward outlines the marginalization of women in Sinn Féin and the IRA and argues that the Republican movement "has never included within its programme a strategy for the liberation of women."[110] Women continue the struggle to make their presence felt and take women's concerns to the forefront of the movement.[111] One woman volunteer in the IRA put it this way: "It still shocks me that I have two battles to fight — one against the Brits and secondly with the men of my own organization. If a guy makes a mistake, it's different. But if a woman does, it just reinforces their prejudices that you aren't competent in the first place."[112]

Catholic Ulster women, subject to strip-searches, internment and imprisonment by the security forces in Ulster and in Britain, often have but one alternative: political resistance. In recent years, two Irish women political prisoners held in England's Brixton Prison endured almost 500 strip-searches between them in a ten-month period. The purpose? To break their morale.[113]

Under the Emergency Provisions Act of 1973, the British Army and police in Northern Ireland can detain anyone "suspected" of an offence. The police and army can also search any premises without a warrant and seize and use any property accordingly. The Prevention of Terrorism Act of 1976 permits arrest and detention "upon reasonable suspicion of a terrorist offence." These provisions are used widely to harass and intimidate Irish Catholics in Ulster and Irish people travelling to Britain. Some 70 percent of arrests under this Act occur at airports or other ports of entry to Britain. That the goal of these arrests is harassment and intimidation is confirmed when we look at the disposition: On average, only 7 percent of those detained under this Act are ultimately charged with a criminal offence.[114]

The British military presence is always a hazard for native Irish Catholics, particularly for women. The British Army routinely raids and wrecks Catholic homes in the early hours of the morning, on the pretext of looking for arms. Residents are often taken away, interned and tortured. To many Catholics, unemployed, living in poor housing, subject to British Army raids and attacks, the real terrorists are not the IRA; they are the British Army. To the dispossessed, the IRA is a resistance movement fighting British colonial occupation. One woman living in a Catholic ghetto describes her views of the IRA, the British Army, and violence:

> People get upset and angry about the violence of the IRA, but forget to ask themselves why this violence exists. I remember the first person to die as a result of the Troubles. He was called Sammy Devenney and was batoned to death by the RUC in his own living room in April 1969.... It suits the Brits to portray us as mad murdering bastards and themselves as the neutral go-between. The truth of the matter is that the Brits are here to back up the Loyalists and their interests.... It was the Brits who made the country what it is....[115]

For Irish women, both the Christian and the British colonial pasts dictate an unforgiving legacy. Irish women cannot be separated from this past. The sexism of the broader society and the sexism of male-dominated Irish resistance movements also pose a major stumbling block to Irish women's self-determination. Additionally, Irish women face classism both in the dominant society and in the feminist movement. Irish women are not a homogenous group. Divided by class, physical ability, sexual orientation and age, they experience discrimination accordingly.

Moreover, within the broader women's movement, Irish women often find little understanding of the British occupation of Ulster. British feminists, in particular, are often unwilling to acknowledge that their country is occupying part of Ireland. Bernadette Devlin-McAliskey criticizes feminists who cling to relative political power and privilege:

There are differences between all of us as it were, up here and some of you down there. And I think the first difference that has to be understood is that while we are all women together with a common struggle, some of us are women in countries which are exploited by Imperialism and some of you are women in countries which are the Imperialist exploiters.... Like all the women here I don't know peace; I've never seen it. My mother never saw it, my grandmother never saw it. It is a commodity that has never been available in Ireland.[116]

For Irish feminists today, strip-searching, prisoners' rights, political rights for Catholics, and the "national question" rank as highly as women's employment, the need for daycare and an end to male violence against women. Women in the Republic also are fighting for reproductive rights and divorce.

Back to the Fireside

To come full circle in this story of Mná na hÉireann, we must now go back to Jack's stories by the fireside and the old history book full of men: how men came to shape the future of Ireland, how brave men were, how poetic, how passionate and fiery, how handsome. Jack told no stories of women, except for the Banshee and occasional verses of Mangan's "Róisín Dubh": "O my Dark Rosaleen, do not sigh, do not weep...."

Jack told no stories of the Goddess Brigid. He could have told us that St. Brigid's holy well up in the nearby village of Abbey came from another time, one when the symbols for women were more heartening, or how the ancient Brigid was honoured in the little Pagan circles that people made around that well, or how the eggshells we saw on the hawthorn bushes on the paths through the fields to school on May Morning (Beltane) were remnants of ancient Pagan goddess rituals. But there is more to it than that. Spinning yarns with Jack left me with one last legacy, a legacy for Irish women — for all women. A legacy that connects us to our past.

What are dem eggshells on de bushes, Jack?

Ara sure dey're good luck d'you see.

An' how would dey be good luck, Jack?

Good luck ta make de corn an' de spuds grow.

An' how do de good luck be workin' dat all de corn would be growin' so great, Jack?

Good luck now. Dat's all.

An' how do good luck work, Jack?

Ara how would I be knowin' how 'twould work! 'Twould work, dat's all!

But *how*, Jack?

Ara will ya shtop now from askin' all dem questions. Dat's enough now. Makin' yerself quare[117] in de head you'll be doin' now.

But how'd I be makin' meself quare in de head, Jack?

From askin' dem questions!

How do questions make ya quare in de head, Jack?

Ara g'way wid ya now!

Sure didn't Sarsfield an Padraig Pearse an all a dem lads get quare in de head den, Jack? Otherwise dey wouldn't a been able ta fight de Sassenachs? Would dey, Jack? Ishn't dat de truth now, Jack? If ya ask me now, Jack, I'd be tinkin' dat quare in de head ishn't a bad ting at all at all. 'Tis a mighty ting, Jack. A mighty ting altogether.

Hrumph. 'Tis mighty impertinent ye are now. Hrumph.

Now to the woman etched in gold on the faded magenta cover of my old history book. Playing the harp, she sits before the waves on the ocean, young and daring, her music strong and bold, her voice filling the air with possibilities. But lest we fall into the trap of male romanticizing, the trap of Róisín Dubh, let us remember that this woman is the woman whose hands are flat and worn from backbreaking work. This is Connie O'Sullivan, living in Canada, a daycare worker who earns a pittance and who asks in this book, "Am I really working for this?" This is the woman facing an abortion. This is the woman in an abusive relationship.

This is Maria O'Kane, lost and alone in Canada, torn between two cultures and reconciled with neither. This is Nellie O'Donnell, who came to Canada in the 1920s and whose life is an account of hardship and pain. This is the woman without education and class privilege who has laboured unknown at home and abroad. This is Ena McLearn-O'Brien, Margaret O'Connor-Lefas, Norita Fleming, and Vi Moore, strong women whose labour keeps Irish culture alive in Canada. Ireland's women *do not sigh or weep* so passively as Róisín Dubh. We never did.

And now to that unfurled scroll at the base of her harp. The faded inscription boldly proclaims:

IT IS NEW STRUNG AND SHALL BE HEARD.

Notes

1. A woolpack is a very large burlap bag for packing the wool from sheep at shearing time. It can hold the wool from as many as 25 sheep and usually is the size of a medium-sized room in a house.
2. Jack's story recalls the Battle of Aughrim. Patrick Sarsfield, a French-trained Irish soldier, helped lead the troops that hounded William's army in the South for more than a year after William defeated James, finally surrendering under the Treaty of Limerick in 1691. After defeat, Sarsfield and thousands of others, known as the Wild Geese, went into exile in France, where 5,000 Irish soldiers served in the French army's Irish Brigade. See John O'Beirne Ranelagh, *A Short History of Ireland* (Cambridge: Cambridge University Press, 1983) pp. 66–68.

    For years I had been confounded by the woolpack's unexplained appearance in Jack's story. I knew about St. Ruth, the French soldier who fought with Sarsfield and died, beheaded by a cannonball at the Battle of Aughrim. With victory almost secured, he is said to have risen in his stirrups to order the final charge that would defeat the enemy, but at that moment he was killed by the cannonball, whereupon the Irish army fell into confusion and was defeated. I could not imagine how Jack's woolpack came into the story. It was not until 1991, at the Galway Association in Toronto, that I met Tom Kelly from Killimor, which is about ten miles from Aughrim (Aughrim is about 20 miles from my village), who told me that, according to local stories, St. Ruth and his men are said to have commandeered thirteen sheep off a local farmer's land. The farmer demanded payment from St. Ruth, and when refused put a *mí-ádh* (curse) on St. Ruth which caused his demise. That piece of history — not folklore — is still told around the hearth some three hundred years later. Sadly, television, introduced in the 1960s, has undercut the telling of news around the hearth.

3. Wheat, known as corn, had to be exported to England.

4. A derogatory term for the English.

5. See David H. Greene, *An Anthology of Irish Literature* (New York: Modern Library, 1954).

6. Margaret MacCurtain, "The Historical Image," in *Irish Women: Image and Achievement*, edited by Eiléan Ní Chuilleanáin (Dublin: Arlen House, 1985), p. 44.

7. Mary Condren's *The Serpent and the Goddess: Women, Religion, and Power in Celtic Ireland* (New York: Harper & Row, 1989) is an excellent source for information on female deities in Celtic Ireland.

8. Helen Lanigan Wood, "Women in Myths and Early Depictions," in Ní Chuilleanáin, *Irish Women*, pp. 13–14.

9. Gerda Lerner, *The Creation of Patriarchy* (New York: Oxford University Press, 1986). See Chapter 10, "Symbols," pp. 199–229.

10. St. Patrick is said to have rid Ireland of snakes and is often portrayed stamping on snakes. This symbolism is important in Irish women's history. The snake was the symbol of the goddess in ancient times; because it shed its skin it represented life and death and regeneration. It also represented wisdom and divination. In pre-Christian Ireland, Celts revered trees, wells and stones. The overlay of Christianity on these key symbols of Celtic

worship can be seen in the restructuring of the legends around wells, which often feature contests between the early Christian saints and a serpent, "Oll Phiast," the saint coming out the winner and claiming the well. The contest is repeated in the lives of many early Irish saints. The wells then became Christian "holy wells," where people went to worship and to appeal to the saint rather than the goddess for favours. For more on the legends of the saints and these wells, see Patrick Logan, *The Holy Wells of Ireland* (Gerrards Cross, England: Colin Smythe, 1980). Christianity did not succeed entirely in stamping out Paganism. Now called "piseogs" or superstitions, Pagan rituals can still be found today in much of rural Ireland. Putting eggshells, the female symbol of fertility, on hawthorn bushes on May Morning, the Pagan feast of Beltane, is one. The Christian St. John's night is the Pagan Bonfire night, in celebration of the summer solstice.

11. See Condren, *The Serpent and the Goddess*, Chapters 3, 4 and 5, for more on this point.

12. For a discussion on Plato's and Aristotle's views of women and those of the early Christian theologians Paul, Augustine and Aquinas, see Rosemary Agonito, *History of Ideas on Women* (New York: Perigee, 1977).

13. See Rosemary Radford Reuther, *Sexism and God-Talk: Towards a Feminist Theology* (Boston: Beacon Press, 1983), pp. 94–95, for a discussion of Augustine's influence. For a general discussion on the goddess past and the foundations of and implications for patriarchal religion, see Mary Daly, *Beyond God the Father: Toward a Philosophy of Women's Liberation* (Boston: Beacon, 1973). See also Charlene Spretnak, ed., *The Politics of Women's Spirituality: Essays on the Rise of Spiritual Power Within the Feminist Movement* (New York: Anchor, 1982) and Merlin Stone, *When God Was a Woman* (New York: Dial, 1976).

14. Radford Reuther, *Sexism and God-Talk*, p. 170.

15. See Margaret Murray, *The Witch Cult in Western Europe* (London: Oxford University Press, 1921), and Margaret Murray, *The God of the Witches* (London: Oxford University Press, 1931).

16. See Donncha Ó Corráin, "Women in Early Irish Society," in

Women in Irish Society: The Historical Dimension, edited by Margaret MacCurtain and Donncha Ó Corráin (Dublin: Arlen House, 1978), pp. 1–13.

17. *Ibid.*, pp. 1–5.
18. Ranelagh, *A Short History of Ireland*, p. 17.
19. Bonnie S. Anderson and Judith P. Zinsser, eds., *A History of Their Own* (New York: Harper & Row, 1988), p. 453 n. 43.
20. Anderson and Zinsser, *A History of Their Own*, pp. 338–39.
21. Battle-hardened Norman mercenaries had already conquered England and half of Europe. When the Norman, Strongbow, was invited by the Irish King of Leinster, Diarmaid MacMurchadha, to help him in an internal land dispute, the course of Irish history was irrevocably altered as help quickly changed to outright invasion by Henry II of England. In 1154 Henry had announced his intention of invading Ireland. Chronicles of the period reveal the Normans' hatred for the Irish. Gerald de Barry, a Norman chronicler, describes the Irish as a "hostile race...always plotting some kind of treachery under cover of peace" who should be "fully submitted to the yoke of obedience." But within two centuries the Normans in Ireland would become "more Irish than the Irish themselves." See Ranelagh, *A Short History of Ireland*, pp. 35–41.

    Under a Papal Privilege, England's Henry II would invade Ireland at Waterford in 1171. Two hundred years later, in 1367, the Statute of Kilkenny tried to halt the Gaelicization of the Normans and the weakening of English power by forbidding intermarriage between the Norman Irish and the native Irish. It also banned the use of Irish speech, names, dress and customs, provided fines for "harbouring or encouraging Irish minstrels, rhymers or taletellers," and banned the Irish from grazing their cattle on lands granted by the English Crown.
22. "The Irish State Papers of the sixteenth century were peppered with laws and complaints against the continuing widespread use of Brehons and their law." See Ranelagh, *A Short History of Ireland*, p. 17.
23. Anderson and Zinsser, *A History of Their Own*, p. 141.

24. For a comprehensive account of Western Christianity's impact on women, see Karen Armstrong, *The Gospel According to Woman: Christianity's Creation of the Sex War in the West* (London: Pan, 1986).

25. England's Elizabeth I, determined to entrench Tudor government across Ireland but facing unexpected rebellion, waged the Irish Wars. Crown troops defeated the rebellious earls and the Crown seized their lands. The Flight of the Earls, who took up residence on the Continent, left the whole of Ireland under English control for the first time.

26. MacCurtain, "The Historical Image," p. 43, citing Gearóid Ó Tuathaigh's "The Role of Women in Ireland under the New English Order," in MacCurtain and Ó Corráin, *Women in Irish Society*.

27. *Ibid.*, pp. 42–43.

28. See Edmund Curtis, *A History of Ireland* (New York: Methuen, 1936), pp. 226–34. This is a useful source on Irish history.

29. The English later renamed Coleraine Londonderry.

30. Ranelagh, *A Short History of Ireland*, p. 65.

31. *Ibid.*, p. 71.

32. Kirby Miller, *Emigrants and Exiles: Ireland and the Irish Exodus to North America* (New York: Oxford University Press, 1985) p. 137.

33. Curtis, *A History of Ireland*, p. 394.

34. Ranelagh, *A Short History of Ireland*, pp. 110–13.

35. For a discussion of the Famine, see Cecil Woodham-Smith, *The Great Hunger, Ireland 1845 to 1849* (New York: Harper & Row, 1962), and Donald MacKay, *Flight from Famine: The Coming of the Irish to Canada* (Toronto: McClelland & Stewart, 1990).

36. The English social theorist Thomas R. Malthus's *Essay on the Principle of Populations as It Affects the Future Improvement of Society*, first published in 1798, promulgated the misleading notion that the more people there are, the fewer resources for each. The assumption is that, when individuals have more than the minimum for survival, populations increase to the point that "overpopulation" and fewer resources force everyone back to subsistence. A convenient theory for the ruling classes in unequal

societies, it allows the haves to argue that improving the lot of have-nots is futile because it will result in more people being poor. See Amiya Kumar Bagchi, *The Political Economy of Underdevelopment* (London: Cambridge University Press, 1982), Chapter 8, for a discussion of population growth in the Third World and how Malthusian theory is used to justify the rich/poor division of the world into First World and Third World.

37. Ranelagh, *A Short History of Ireland*. See also Magnus Magnusson, *Landlord or Tenant: A View of Irish History* (London: Bodley Head, 1978, p. 85).

38. For the economists' debate on the Corn Laws, land rent and the positions taken by English landowners and industrialists, see Leo Huberman, *Man's Worldly Goods: The Story of the Wealth of Nations* (New York: Monthly Review Press, 1968) pp. 204–20.

39. Ranelagh, *A Short History of Ireland*, p. 112.

40. "Cholera, caused by drinking water contaminated with sewage, infested European cities until the third quarter of the nineteenth century. With no adequate water supply, keeping minimally clean became an immense labour." Anderson and Zinsser, *A History of Their Own*, p. 235.

41. Curtis, *A History of Ireland*, p. 370.

42. MacCurtain, "The Historical Image," p. 43.

43. Margaret Ward, *Unmanageable Revolutionaries: Women and Irish Nationalism* (London: Pluto, 1983) p. 8.

44. Curtis, *A History of Ireland*, p. 379.

45. Parnell and Davitt recommended the boycott as part of "The Plan of Campaign." It was first used in 1880 against a Captain Boycott, a land agent in County Mayo. After people refused to work for him or to associate with him in any way, he left Ireland.

   One detailed example of rents, evictions and how "The Plan of Campaign" worked in the Clanricarde estate, a vast English landlord's holdings between Woodford and Portumna, Co. Galway, is examined in Thomas Gorman *et al.*, eds., *Clanricarde Country and the Land Campaign* (Galway: Woodford Heritage Group, 1987). See also Michael Shiel and Desmond Roche, eds., *A Forgotten Campaign* (Galway: Woodford Heritage Group, 1986).

46. Ward, *Unmanageable Revolutionaries*, p. 10.
47. MacCurtain, "The Historical Image," p. 48.
48. Miriam Daly, "Women in Ulster" in Ní Chuilleanáin, *Irish Women*, pp. 51–55.
49. Ward, *Unmanageable Revolutionaries*, p. 6.
50. Daly, "Women in Ulster," p. 55.
51. MacCurtain, "The Historical Image," pp. 47–48.
52. Mary Lennon, Marie McAdam and Joanne O'Brien, *Across The Water: Irish Women's Lives in Britain* (London: Virago, 1988), pp. 21–22.) See also Anderson and Zinsser, *A History of Their Own*, p. 122. For more on domestic service, see Anderson and Zinsser, *A History of Their Own*. In Europe "from the second half of the eighteenth century on, domestic jobs for women expanded tremendously, and between one third and one half of all women who earned income outside the home did so as domestic servants. These positions increased for two reasons: as wealth grew, more families could afford to hire a servant, and as new urban and industrial jobs opened up for men, they left domestic service to women" (p. 253).
53. Lennon *et al.*, *Across the Water*, p. 23.
54. *Ibid.*, p. 25.
55. Ward, *Unmanageable Revolutionaries*. The title of Ward's book comes from a comment by Eamon de Valera, a member of the Irish Revolution of 1916 and later Ireland's first President: "Women are at once the boldest and most unmanageable revolutionaries" (p. x). His comment reflected at the very least his discomfort with women. Information on these three groups comes from Ward.
56. *Ibid.*, pp. 15–39.
57. That women were arrested under statutes on the curbing of prostitution, not as political prisoners like the men, was additionally humiliating. *Ibid.*, pp. 27–28.
58. *Ibid.*, p. 23.
59. *Ibid.*
60. *Ibid.*, p. 22.
61. Eamon de Valera was the only commandant not to be executed; because of his U.S.-born mother he was able to claim U.S. citizen-

ship. The British feared that executing him would cause a diplomatic incident with the United States.

62. The Home Rule League formed in 1873. One of its passionate leaders was Charles Stewart Parnell, who advocated that Ireland manage internal affairs with a parliament in Dublin. Westminster would maintain control over the army and navy, trade, foreign policy and imperial matters. Generally, Home Rule was supported by the Protestant landlords but was anathema to the Irish Catholic majority — the poorer they were, the more nationalist they were. The Fenians, the Irish Republican Brotherhood, were firmly opposed to Home Rule, on the grounds that Ireland must become an independent Republic. See Curtis, *A History of Ireland*, p. 376.

63. Ward, *Unmanageable Revolutionaries*, p. 110.

64. *Ibid.*, p. 88.

65. Maude Gonne became its first president. Gonne, nationalist and suffragist, was the lost love for whom Yeats pined in his romantic poetry.

66. Ward, *Unmanageable Revolutionaries*, p. 51.

67. *Ibid.*, p. 56.

68. *Ibid.*, p. 57.

69. MacCurtain, "Women, the Vote and Revolution," in MacCurtain and ó Corráin, *Women in Irish Society*, pp. 46–47. Harriet Hardy Taylor Mill had published an essay in 1851 advocating women's suffrage. John Stuart Mill credited her with "the development of his new ideas concerning women." See Anderson and Zinsser, *A History of Their Own*, pp. 358–59.

70. Ward, *Unmanageable Revolutionaries*, pp. 71–72.

71. MacCurtain, "Women, the Vote and Revolution," pp. 46–50.

72. *The Toronto Star*, April 6, 1992, p. A2. The story was part of the *Star*'s centenary celebration.

73. Daly, "Women In Ulster," pp. 56–57.

74. *Ibid.*, p. 58.

75. For a reading of Wollstonecraft's treatise, as well as other middle-class, white "essential works of feminism," see Alice Rossi, ed.,

The Feminist Papers: From Adams to de Beauvoir (New York: Bantam, 1973).

76. MacCurtain, "Women, the Vote and Revolution," p. 47.
77. See Lerner, *The Creation of Patriarchy*, pp. 217–19. According to Lerner, key elements of patriarchy in maintaining male dominance include educational deprivation, gender indoctrination, denial of women's history, economic and political discrimination, and the awarding of class privileges to women who conform. These elements allowed men to maintain control over the symbol system.

   Once again we see the conflict facing middle-class Irish women in the Catholic Church. The Church enshrined in its doctrine each element, except education, listed by Lerner. But education, though not intended to be used as women did, would give women the means to challenge other elements of patriarchy and to benefit, at least partially, from class privilege and its corresponding economic resources and political power. In contrast, working-class women had no privilege, and they still have none. This difference is often either ignored or played down by middle-class white women who have the privilege of symbol making, albeit limited privilege in relation to men.
78. Ward, *Unmanageable Revolutionaries*, p. 69.
79. MacCurtain, "The Historical Image," p. 47.
80. Race and class have come more to the fore in society at large and in the women's movement over the past decade. There are many works that discuss classism (that is, discrimination against those who are poor and/or working-class) and racism. See, for example, Angela Davis, *Women, Race & Class* (New York: Vintage, 1983), and bell hooks, *Feminist Theory: From Margin to Centre* (Boston: South End Press, 1984).
81. MacCurtain, "The Historical Image," p. 49.
82. *Ibid.*
83. Ward, *Unmanageable Revolutionaries*, p. 234. For an excellent discussion on the Irish Constitution and its impact on women, and on the effect of subsequent legislation in the South, see Yvonne Scannell, "Changing Times for Women's Rights," in Ní

Chuilleanáin, *Irish Women*, pp. 61–72). Scannell cites numerous legislative gains for women from the 1970s on and attributes these gains to "the emergence of a strong and articulate women's movement in the early 1970s" and to Ireland's entry into the European Common Market in 1973 (p. 65). See also Mary Robinson, "Women and the New Irish State," in MacCurtain and Ó Corráin, *Women in Irish Society*, pp. 58–70.

84. See Lennon *et al.*, *Across the Water*, p. 24. See also Anderson and Zinsser, *A History of Their Own*, p. 507 n. 38, which cites Jack Goody's argument in *The Development of the Family and Marriage in Europe* (New York: Cambridge University Press, 1983) that the early European Church's position on divorce, marriage and adultery "had been intended to create more heirless families and thus more opportunities for the Church to acquire property, on which all power ultimately rested."

85. Ursula Barry, *Lifting the Lid: Handbook of Facts and Information on Ireland* (Dublin: Attic Press, 1986), p. 58.

86. From a short article in one of the Irish dailies during the debate on the divorce referendum.

87. Barry, *Lifting the Lid*, pp. 95–98.

88. In the spring of 1992, news came of another referendum, this one on the right of Irish women to travel freely abroad for abortion and for the right to access to information about abortion (*The Globe and Mail*, April 8, 1992).

89. Barry, *Lifting the Lid*, p. 14.

90. For an in-depth discussion on the role of multinational corporations in the global economy and how women's labour is exploited by the sexual division of labour, see Swasti Mitter, *Common Fate, Common Bond: Women in the Global Economy* (London: Pluto, 1986). Mitter notes that Shannon, in Ireland, became the first freeport for multinationals, and the idea soon spread to Third World countries as an innovative method of enticing foreign investment. Also see Maria Mies, *Patriarchy and Accumulation on a World Scale: Women in the International Division of Labour* (London: Zed, 1986). A good resource on neo-colonial economies in the Third World is Amiya Kumar Bagchi's *The Political Economy of Underdevelopment* (Lon-

don: Cambridge University Press, 1982). Unfortunately, Bagchi fails to provide any gender analysis.

91. These statistics were provided over the phone by the Employment Equality Agency in Dublin in April 1992. One of the largest electronics operations in Ireland is Digital, which has operated there since the 1970s. I placed several calls to the Digital head office in Maynard, Massachusetts, trying to find out the total number of people employed by Digital in Ireland, how many are women, how many women work in unskilled jobs, and how many women are in management. Having said that he would look into the matter, Digital's public relations spokesperson then stated, "I cannot find anyone who keeps these records." Later in the conversation he said, "We're encouraged not to provide these numbers over the phone. We just don't do that."

92. The Employment Equality Agency in Dublin.

93. Barry, *Lifting the Lid*, p. 34.

94. See Charles Jones, Lorna Marsden and Lorne Tepperman, *Lives Of Their Own: The Individualization of Women's Lives* (Toronto: Oxford University Press, 1990), p. 92.

95. This information was provided by a spokesperson for the Employment Equality Agency in a telephone call in April 1992.

96. Barry, *Lifting the Lid*, pp. 34–36.

97. Telephone conversation, April 1992.

98. According to the spokesperson, the Employment Equality Agency now receives about ten serious complaints a month.

99. These figures came from the Central Statistics Office of the Irish Government, St. Stephen's Green, Dublin.

100. Lennon *et al.*, *Across the Water*, p. 27.

101. These figures came from the Central Statistics Office in Dublin. The Office does not issue statistics on the number of people leaving, only "the number of people leaving balanced against the number of people coming in." Nor does the Office keep a breakdown by gender. A spokesperson told me on the phone that the dramatic decline for 1991 was due to fewer people leaving because of the recession in the U.S. and Britain.

102. See John Colleary, *Ireland's Case* (Grimsby, Ontario: Innisfree,

1985), p. 49. This book by an Irish-Canadian author provides a good synopsis of Ulster politics.

103. The best-known spokespersons of the time were the Rev. Ian Paisley, who had already pledged to "keep Protestant and Loyal workers in employment in times of depression, in preference to their Catholic fellow workers" (cited in Ranelagh, *A Short History of Ireland*, p. 264) and Bernadette Devlin of People's Democracy.

104. Ranelagh, *A Short History of Ireland*, p. 256.

105. Phil Evans and Eileen Pollock, *Ireland for Beginners* (London: Writers and Readers, 1983), p. 132.

106. Colleary, *Ireland's Case*, p. 216.

107. Evans and Pollock, *Ireland for Beginners*, p. 144.

108. *Ibid.*, p. 147.

109. This news item appeared in *The Globe and Mail*, March 1992; it did not report figures for women.

110. Ward, *Unmanageable Revolutionaries*, p. 254–55. In the 1980s, Sinn Féin also defeated a motion backing Irish women's access to abortion in Ireland. This motion was later overturned.

111. *Ibid.*, p. 256.

112. See Eileen Fairweather, Roisin McDonagh and Melanie McFayden, *Only the Rivers Run Free: Northern Ireland: The Women's War* (London: Pluto, 1984), p. 241. The authors interviewed several women, Catholic and Protestant, about their experiences of and views on "the Troubles." This book also recounts the terror imposed on Catholics by the British Army.

113. Barry, *Lifting the Lid*, p. 76.

114. *Ibid.*, pp. 87–89.

115. See Fairweather *et al.*, *Only the Rivers Run Free*, p. 232–233.

116. Bernadette Devlin-McAliskey, "Building a United Women's Movement," *Spare Rib*, December 1991–January 1992, London, pp. 69–72. (Published in London, England.)

117. "Quare" in Irish country language means queer, strange, odd, different. More generally, it means not conforming to things as they are. Thus, it can mean outrageous, incorrigible, impertinent, intemperate, impudent, an aberration, an infraction.... From a location on the margins, the list is endless!

Irish Women in Canada

Feminist scholars remind us that, beginning with the third millennium B.C., men have occupied the territory of the recording, defining, and interpreting of events, with women denied this ground until the nineteenth century. Rosalind Miles decries the phallocentric focus of history and its denial of women's contributions: "All this is lost when our history concentrates on men only, claiming a universal validity of the actions of less than half the human race." The result is "a one-eyed sham — fractured, partial and censored." The task for women's world history, according to Miles, is "[filling] the gaps left by conventional history's preoccupation with male doings, and [giving] attention and dignity to women's lives in their own right."[1]

For the past twenty years we have seen an outpouring of male academic literature on Irish immigration to Canada. We find page after page reflecting men's deeds and men's work but no acknowledgment of the three centuries of Irish women in Canada or of their work. A recent two-volume "comprehensive" account of the Irish in Canada gives no record of women's history.[2] Some Protestant historians also reflect a pronounced anti-Irish bias in their accounts of Irish immigration to Canada. One example is the Famine: Conveniently denying England's role, they attribute the mass starvation to the old standby, the Malthusian notion of "overpopulation."[3]

The Irish began coming to Canada in the seventeenth century, but it was only at the beginning of the nineteenth century that large-scale Irish immigration to Canada began. Nineteenth-century Irish immigration to North America falls into two stages: The first half of the century constituted the Canadian stage; the second half, the U.S. stage. Between 1825 and 1845, 450,000 Irish immigrated to Canada and another 400,000 to the United States.[4] The principal stage for Irish immigration to Canada was 1815 to 1855.[5]

Protestant Irish immigrants predominated in the earlier stage but did not represent the Irish population overall. Because of the high cost of passage, only those with some capital could afford to leave Ireland.[6] Thus, during the nineteenth century, Irish Protestant immigrants made up 55 percent of all Irish immigration to Canada. Most had come from the North of Ireland, but some came from the Protestant cores of Leinster and Munster. One-third of the Irish Catholics came from Ulster and two-thirds from elsewhere in Ireland. In the three decades before 1836, about 35,000 Irish, most of them Catholic, arrived in Newfoundland. They came from the southeast of Ireland, drawn by trade links between Newfoundland and the ports of Waterford, New Ross and Youghal.[7] The Irish settled throughout Canada, making homes in Newfoundland,[8] Quebec,[9] Nova Scotia,[10] New Brunswick,[11] and Ontario.[12]

Grosse Île

O windswept isle — your gnarled trees bend with the gales
that sweep
Above the hallowed ground wherein they lie
Those exiles who sought freedom but to die;
In foreign soil they take their last long sleep.

O silent isle — could you but tell the tale
That tragic story so few know too well
The dire results of laws conceived in hell
Which told today make valiant men [sic] turn pale.

O poor Grosse Ile — what awful scars you bore
When spades dug deep into your breast
Where speedily the dead were laid to rest
By brave Canadians who did this ghastly chore.

— from "Grosse Ile" (1910) by
Mary Eileen O'Gallagher Conway (1894–1987)

Irish immigration to Canada during the Famine years over-shadows all other Irish immigration in suffering and loss of life. The predominance of Irish Catholics signalled the political origin of the Famine. In an extensive discussion on the Famine Irish at Grosse Île, an island in the St. Lawrence, thirty miles below Quebec City, Marianna O'Gallagher notes: "The sadness of 1847 belongs to the Irish....The accumulation of hundreds of years of institutionalized injustice in Ireland came to an ugly head in 1847."[13]

In 1847, at the height of the Famine, Irish immigration to Canada peaked, with some 74,000 arrivals in Quebec City alone.[14] In contrast to the predominantly Protestant immigration from Ireland for most of the century, an estimated 90 percent of the Famine Irish arriving at Grosse Île were Catholic.[15] Overcrowded and filthy "fever ships" docked at the quarantine station set up on Grosse Île. On board lay hundreds of destitute women, men and children, many of them dead or dying of cholera. During the summer of 1847, the recorded death rate hit forty to fifty a day. Often, corpses lay everywhere on board ship. The living could not move, much less tend to the dead. Official statistics for Grosse Île show that between May 10 and July 24, 1847, some 4,572 people died on the voyage, on the ships at Grosse Île and in tents on the island. Another 1,458 people, including infants and children, died in the makeshift hospital on the island.[16] The *Ancient Order of Hibernians Magazine*, circa 1910, estimated the number dead at Grosse Île and Montreal at 18,000 for 1847. Estimates vary; some claim the real figure was as high as 25,000 but was lowered to avoid embarrassing the British government.[17]

Quebec authorities were overwhelmed as hospital staff and clergy tried to cope. Landings and inspections of food and housing came under military command, and soldiers policed the island to make sure the healthy stayed apart from the sick to prevent the spread of disease. Boatmen, soldiers and clergy carried bodies from the ships. One account tells of uncoffined bodies being hauled out of the hold of a ship on a winch, "the golden hair of a young girl moving in the slight breeze." One big field became a mass grave. Because of the thin layer of earth, soil had to be brought onto the island to fill the trenches. The clergy then began adopting out the desolate orphans to French-Canadian families.[18]

Once they got clearance at Grosse Île, the Famine refugees moved on. Weakened and emaciated, many were already ill with cholera and typhus as they travelled on to Montreal, Ottawa, Kingston, Toronto and the U.S. border at Detroit. In each of these cities, fever sheds had to be set up to accommodate the sick and dying.[19] Events at Pointe St. Charles, in Montreal, were typical. *The Gazette* reported the horror on September 5, 1847:

> In the hastily erected emergency sheds the people were dying by the score in the crowded sheds, in the stench and heat, desperately neglected. When there were enough attendants they were hastily tossed into shallow pits nearby when they succumbed to the fever. In all the history of Montreal there is no story so poignant. There are hundreds of orphaned children. Many of the little ones had to be pulled from the arms of a parent who had suddenly died. Older ones were wandering around frantically looking for parents who were already buried in the pits. The scene in the children's shed was beyond description.[20]

The Canadian response varied from hostility to sacrifice. Ordinary citizens gathered to help in any way they could. Doctors and Protestant and Catholic clergy responded, many losing their own lives. The Grey Nuns in Montreal took on the management of an orphanage and arranged for Quebec families to adopt Irish orphans. By June of 1847 there were already 500 Irish orphans in Montreal. The mayor of Montreal himself tended the sick at Pointe St. Charles, fell ill, and died that November.[21]

In Toronto, a stopover for the immigrants on their way to the U.S. border, Bishop Power, founder of the new Catholic Archdiocese, also died in 1847 as a result of his work in the fever sheds. Panic overwhelmed the city, and Irish immigrants met with resentment and violence from a population largely of English descent. Even without Famine fever, the Catholic Irish were un-welcome.[22] According to Murray Nicolson, the Famine Irish in Toronto fled to neighbourhoods such as Cabbagetown, where "they were despised as human vermin, as 'obsolete people' fit only for absorption or extinction."[23]

Black '47 also hit New Brunswick. The community responded swiftly. From quarantine at Partridge Island, about 600 people were taken to the Saint John poorhouse, where they died. Almost 1,000 had already died on the voyage. One report of the time noted:

> So destitute were the people on their arrival [at St. John, N.B.] that the legislature voted £1500 sterling to alleviate the distress and a further sum of £1500 was collected in St. John [*sic*]. The victims of the famine were crowded into emigrant ships while in a low state of health and suffered from typhus on the voyage....In the month of June 35 vessels arrived with 5800 passengers and during the summer about 15,000 Irish immigrants were landed at Partridge Island. The total mortality was upwards of 2000 persons. Their bodies lie in nameless graves and their story is indeed a sad one.[24]

After 1855, Irish immigration to Canada plummeted and the United States became the focus for the second stage of nineteenth-century immigration. At Confederation in 1867, although the Irish were the second-largest group in Canada after French Canadians, Irish immigration had dwindled to an average of fewer than 2,000 a year. During the 1890s it fell below 1,000. In the 1850s and 1860s, prospects for the Irish began to seem brighter in the United States.[25]

The Orange Order in Canada

By 1871, less than half of the Irish in Canada were Catholic. Ontario's Irish population was two-thirds Protestant. The Orange Order, with its roots in the Ulster of 1795, had made great headway. According to Houston and Smyth, in the first three decades of the 1800s, the Protestant emigrants were Ireland's first Orange-born generation. As they settled and established themselves in Canada, so too did the Orange Order. Carrying intact its original ideals, the Orange Order espoused "a politico-religious philosophy which sought to defend Protestantism and the British constitutional monarchy."[26] Indeed, by the end of the 1800s, these ideals had spread beyond Irish Protestants and their descendants: One-third of all Canadian English-speaking men had joined. The Orange Order included Prime Ministers John A. Macdonald, J. J. Abbott, and Mackenzie Bowell, members of Parliament, premiers, mayors, reeves, councillors, wardens and members of legislative assemblies.[27]

The Orange Order soon became an old boys' club where Canada's white male Protestant elite cemented economic, ideological, political-religious and familial ties. Once or twice a month, the local men gathered at the lodge to engage in a secret ritual, followed by socializing. Politics were discussed and jobs promised. Houston and Smyth recount the secret ritual: Members gathered around an altar draped with a Union Jack, an open Bible on top.[28] Presumably, prayers were said and allegiance pledged to the British monarchy. The Union Jack and the Christian Bible were key symbols of the link between colonialism and Protestantism as Britain expanded its empire not only in Ireland but throughout the world.

The Orange Order in Canada engaged heartily in the July 12 celebrations commemorating the defeat of the Catholic Irish at the Battle of the Boyne in 1690. Members paraded through towns and cities, led by a lodge brother on horseback representing King Billy. The men all wore orange sashes, the parade symbolism underscoring the political platform of the Orange Order.

In Toronto, dubbed the "Belfast of Canada," the Orange Order reigned supreme. Bent on preserving monarchy and empire, it looked askance at the U.S. and at French Canadians. The U.S.-based Irish Fenian invasion of Canada in 1866 fuelled the Orange fire. Houston and Smyth contend that "officially, the Order frowned on violence."[29] Its practice, however, was often different.

Murray Nicolson notes that there were violent attacks by Protestants on Irish Catholics on March 17 and July 12. In the Jubilee Riots of 1875 in Toronto, Irish Catholics were attacked by "an Orange mob."[30] Surrounded by a wall of Orange power and privilege, the Catholic Irish were as much discriminated against in Canada as in Ireland, and it was this more than anything else that sent them to the United States.

Irish Women's Work in Canada

If the recent wave of publishing on the Irish in Canada reveals little or nothing about Irish women, it is not because of a dearth of records. Women's religious orders have documented their histories, detailing the work of many Irish immigrant women who founded them. Parish records also reveal that Irish women, Catholic and Protestant, were active in their churches. During the 1830s in Montreal, Catholic and Protestant women were involved in charitable work. Catholic women in the Irish Ladies of Charity worked with the St. Patrick's Orphan Asylum, founded in 1847 during the Famine epidemics. After the Grey Nuns took on the management of St. Patrick's, the Irish Ladies of Charity continued their support for many years. The YWCA, the Women's Protective Immigration Society and the Women's Christian Temperance Union in Montreal were run exclusively by Protestant women,[31] and presumably included Irish Protestant women.

In looking at women's history, we must separate women from their patriarchal surroundings to view more sharply their contributions. So proscribed were Irish women's roles that women could contribute only within patriarchal structures. The Catholic Church is one example. Although the Church relegated women to the private sphere of the home and required a wife's subservience to her husband, women in religious orders, although still subservient to the Fathers of the Church, could and did take part in the public sphere. In the passage that follows, a male historian recounts the life of Toronto's first Catholic archbishop. His comments are fraught with the stereotyping of women and with ambivalence about their role and its value:

> The Catholic Church has always wisely placed her benevolent establishments under the direction and management of these good women who have left the world and its allurements to live and labour for their fellow-men [sic]. These heroines are called "sisters of charity" and their name is legion. They are saints unknown [sic] to the world, the ministering angels who are to be found in hospitals and orphanages and when fatal epidemics occur.[32]

Women's religious orders in Canada played key roles in founding Canada's education and health-care systems. Many of these orders were founded in the mid-1800s by Irish immigrant women. Three of these orders are the Loretto Sisters (Institute of the Blessed Virgin Mary), the Sisters of St. Joseph, and the Sisters of Mercy in Newfoundland.

The Loretto Sisters

At the invitation of Bishop Power, the first Bishop of Toronto, who needed teachers to set up a Catholic school system in his fledgling Archdiocese, five young Irish women from the Loretto Sisters' mother house in Dublin made their way to Canada. They arrived in Toronto in September 1847, at the height of the Famine epidemic. A few weeks later Bishop Power lay dead from the fever he had caught in the fever sheds.[33] The five young women, the founders of the Loretto Sisters in Canada, were the Rev. Mother Ignatia Hutchinson, Sr. Teresa Dese, Sr. Bonaventure Phelan, Sr. Gertrude Fleming, and Sr. Valentia Hutchinson. Within four years, three of the women would be dead, succumbing to tuberculosis and the fever. In 1851, Sr. Teresa Dese became the Reverend Mother Superior of the order and remained so until her death. In

1849, two more Irish women, Sr. Joachim Murray and Sr. Ita Cummings, joined the Canadian convent. In 1851, Sr. Dolorous O'Connor and Sr. Gonzanza Donovan came from Ireland.

Shortly after their arrival, the Loretto Sisters began opening schools. By 1861, under the leadership of Rev. Mother Teresa Dese, the Loretto community had grown to fifty and the number of pupils in its schools to more than 1,500, a remarkable feat in a city where the diocese had only been founded in 1842. An early Loretto curriculum announced: "The course of instruction comprises every branch suitable to the education of Young Ladies":

> Reading, Writing, Arithmetic, Grammar, Geography, History (Ancient and Modern), Elements of Astronomy, Botany, Natural History, Rhetoric, and Logic; English, French, and Italian languages; Music, Drawing, Painting, use of Globes, Embroidery, Plain and Fancy Needle-Work, &c.[34]

The curriculum appealed not only to Catholics. Leading Protestant families also enrolled their daughters, prompting objections in Protestant circles. These objections culminated in the 1865 opening of the Bishop Strachan School for Protestant girls. The nuns went on to open schools in other parts of Ontario, building the foundation for what was to become Ontario's separate school system.[35]

The Sisters of St. Joseph

The four Sisters of St. Joseph who founded their order in Canada came to Toronto in 1851[36] from France, Bohemia, the United States and Ireland. Less than a year after their arrival, the Sisters were asked to join the campaign begun in the 1850s to establish Catholic separate schools in Ontario.[37] The Sisters set up schools across Ontario and in Western Canada.

A 1891 diphtheria outbreak in Toronto was too much for the existing hospitals to cope with, and the city's medical officer of health asked the Sisters of St. Joseph to open a general hospital. In

1892, they set up St. Michael's Hospital, one of the first hospitals in North America to receive approval for graduate and post-graduate courses for nurses and interns. That same year, the Sisters also opened a training school for nurses in Toronto, and they later established hospitals in Winnipeg and British Columbia.[38]

Irish women had an "exceptionally strong" presence in the first decades of the Sisters of St. Joseph and made a significant impact on the work of the Order. Bernard Dinan, who came from the Parish of McCroom in Co. Cork and was one of the founders of the order, was appointed as the Superior of the Sacred Heart Orphanage, established in 1887 by the Sisters.[40] Rev. Mother Bernard Dinan was the Order's Superior General from 1869 to 1874.

Mother de Pazzi Kennedy, born in 1837 in Borris O'Leigh, Co. Tipperary, was Superior General from 1887 to 1899. She is credited with organizing the building of a chapel for the order in Toronto. She also founded a hospital in Port Arthur in 1884.[41]

The Sisters of Mercy in Newfoundland

Three Irish women founded the Sisters of Mercy in Newfoundland in 1842.[42] The founder, Sister Frances Creedon from Co. Cork, had lived in Newfoundland before entering the convent at the mother house in Dublin.[43] In 1842, she returned to Newfoundland with Srs. Rose Lynch and Ursula Freyne. In 1843, they opened their first school. That year Srs. Lynch and Freyne went back to Ireland, never to return, and were replaced by another Irish woman, Maria Nugent from Waterford. Rev. Mother Creedon and Sr. Nugent taught in the school the Sisters had founded and visited the sick in their homes and in institutions.

During an outbreak of typhus in 1847 in St. John's, the two women worked with the sick and Sr. Nugent died. Rev. Mother Frances Creedon was left alone at a critical stage of her Order's foundation. But she carried on[44] and opened up an orphanage for girls whose parents had died in the typhus epidemic. By the time she died in 1855, two more Irish women had joined the convent.

Sr. Bernard Clune from Limerick succeeded Frances Creedon as Superior. Under her leadership, forty women, twenty-five of them Irish, had joined the order by 1870. By the time of her death in 1882, there were seven houses of the Sisters of Mercy in Newfoundland. In 1884, under the new leadership of Ellen Mary de Chantal O'Keefe, of Co. Cork, St. Bride's Academy for women opened in St. John's. In 1895, it became a teacher's college and subsequently played a key role in education in Newfoundland. In 1898, Sr. Mary Joseph Fox from Fermanagh opened the first commercial school for women in St. John's, to prepare women to take part in the business world. The Sisters of Mercy went on to organize more schools in Newfoundland and to found St. Clare's Mercy Hospital in St. John's.

The records show very clearly that Irish women, as founders of religious orders in Canada, contributed notably to the founding of Canada's education and health-care systems. Canada's education system, reflected in the founding work of Catholic and Protestant missionaries, had a devastating effect on the peoples of the First Nations. The Churches collaborated with colonialism in attempting to destroy the economic, legal, cultural and spiritual life of the people of Turtle Island (the First Nations name for Canada). Particularly devastating was the abuse which peoples of the First Nations suffered in residential schools at the hands of Catholic and Protestant religious. Peoples of the First Nations are speaking out now about those abuses.[45]

Working-Class Irish Women

Irish women are not a homogenous group. Their work reflects not only the possibilities afforded their sex; it also reflects their class. Middle-class Irish women could and did take advantage of education. They entered convents, found jobs, or became wives and mothers and worked as volunteers for charities. Working-class

Irish women had to go out to work. That work included service-sector jobs, trades and domestic work.

Murray Nicolson, researching the lives of Irish Catholics in Victorian Toronto, combed the records of births, deaths and marriages and interviewed Irish octogenarians. He notes:

> Irish girls usually left home in their mid-teens and most were gone by twenty-two....In the first decades following the famine, many of them became domestic servants, living in the homes of their employers or boarding in lodgings nearby. As the city diversified industrially, they found additional employment opportunities in laundries, bakeries, tailoring establishments, and as dressmakers, shopgirls and waitresses.[46]

It was by no means an easy life. Canadian feminist historian and law professor Constance Backhouse points out that Irish women in Victorian Toronto who lost their jobs as domestic workers might end up on the streets and then in jail: "Perilously poor and suffering from marked social dislocation, the Famine Irish found themselves prosecuted by the police roughly twice as often as their numbers within the total population would warrant. For crimes such as vagrancy, drunkenness, and prostitution, Irish women represented upwards of 90 per cent of the female prisoners in some jurisdictions."[47]

Backhouse cites Nicolson on the 1860s: "Toronto's policemen were Protestant and were accused of arresting Catholics while Protestants might be warned for the same offence. Judges arbitrarily sentenced Irishmen [sic] if they were residents of any Irish Catholic area in the city, particularly if they lived in the central core." According to Backhouse, the arrest of one former domestic who had turned to the streets "was specifically linked to her being Irish Catholic." On St. Patrick's Day, 1878, "O'Donovan Rossa, an American Fenian and proponent of a free Ireland, had come to deliver a lecture in Toronto. Angry anti-Catholic Protestant demonstrators rioted, and the police turned out in full force. Mary

Ann Gorman was only too familiar to them and she was taken into custody. Charged with vagrancy, this was one of the few occasions on which she managed to pay her $4.25 fine and obtain release."[48]

Apart from domestic and other service work, factory jobs and religious life, there were few options for Irish women in Victorian Toronto. "Because of the dominance of nuns in the separate school system, the lack of a Catholic hospital until 1892 and few Catholic firms in the city, teaching, nursing and office work was effectively closed to Irish girls."[49]

After marriage, Irish working-class women in Victorian Toronto "managed the economies of the home" and bolstered the family's income by taking in washing and ironing or returning to domestic work. When the husband was without a job, women's work "often became a major element in survival."[50]

A study by Suzanne Cross on women in nineteenth-century Montreal points to census returns for 1861 and 1871 showing that most of the servants employed in wealthy Protestant homes to be young Irish Catholic girls.[51] According to Marilyn Barber, between 1870 and 1920 a severe shortage of domestic servants in Ontario instigated a campaign of recruitment for domestics from the "British Isles," then the preferred source of supply.[52]

It is estimated that between Confederation in 1867 and the Depression of the 1930s, more than 250,000 women immigrated to Canada and worked as domestics.[53] Prior to World War I and again in 1920, the Ontario government offered assisted passage to attract domestic workers; this assistance had to be repaid out of their wages. Toronto became the goal for "British" domestics in the 1920s.[54]

For many immigrant women, domestic work was a bridge they had to walk to find freedom, marriage and better jobs. They cooked and cleaned in isolation in middle-class homes and had to learn a new culture. Catholic Irish women faced racism and classism on the job and in the street.

Complaints that experienced Irish domestic workers could not cook led to a report in 1924 which claimed that Irish women were incompetent. Their "experience had been with cooking over a turf fire made on the floor of the house and ... therefore they would be entirely lost if asked to do any cooking on a gas range or an electric stove."[55] Coupled with such ridicule and derision, it was not uncommon to see advertisements in Protestant-dominated Toronto for employment and housing with the warnings "No Irish Need Apply" or "No Catholics Need Apply."

Unless a distinction is made between Irish Catholic and Irish Protestant or English domestic workers, the discrimination Irish Catholic domestic workers faced disappears from the record. But at least Irish Catholic women did not face discrimination based on skin colour. Dionne Brand's collection of narratives of Black working women in Ontario from the 1920s to the 1950s and Makeda Silvera's collection of Black domestic workers' stories reveal the pervasiveness of racism.[56] Additionally, prior to 1962, Canada severely restricted Black immigration, except when Black workers were needed as a source of cheap labour. Only after the post-war industrial boom, when domestics from Europe were difficult to find, did Canada turn to the West Indies for Black female domestic workers.[57]

A look at nation-building in Canada reveals the intersection of sexism, racism and classism. The recruitment of white domestics from Britain and Ireland was more a reflection of the drive to keep Canada's population base white than a result of the shortage of domestics. Roxanna Ng looks at Barbara Roberts's research on the separate spheres for men and women during Canadian nation-building between 1880 and 1920: While men concerned themselves with developing Canada's economic infrastructure, with its nation-wide transportation system and a manufacturing base, women, more particularly upper-class "ladies," concentrated on selecting Canada's population base.

Ng points out that these upper-class women, mainly from Britain, worked to ensure the white character and Christian morality of the nation by recruiting working-class women from Britain as domestic workers and wives. These upper-class women also worked to impose their notion of the practice of "proper motherhood" on working-class families. Thus, according to Ng, "an examination of the history of Canada indicates that class cannot be understood without reference to ethnic and gender relations; similarly, gender and ethnicity cannot be understood without reference to class relations."[58]

Irish Women in Modern Canada

With the exception of the peoples of the First Nations, Canada is a country of immigrants.[59] Over the course of this century, Irish immigration to Canada has dwindled: 6,000 in 1920; 220 in 1940. In the 1970s and 1980s, despite a massive exodus of people from Ireland, conspicuously few Irish immigrants were accepted by Canada. In 1970, about 1,500 Irish people arrived from Northern Ireland and about 2,000 from the Republic. In 1988, only 1,300 were accepted from the Republic and slightly more than 300 from Northern Ireland. The figures for 1991 show just 147 Irish people immigrating to Canada, 79 of them women. In 1991, the top five immigrant groups to Canada, by numerical rank, were from Hong Kong, Poland, China, India and the Philippines.[60]

In the 1986 Canadian census, 670,000 people reported Irish as their single ethnic origin. Another three million reported Irish as part of their ancestry, with more women than men in that group. That census also reported some 26,000 Irish-born immigrants living in Canada, 51 percent of whom were women. The number of Irish-born women increased by 64 percent from 8,575 in the 1981 census to 13,300 in the 1986 census.[61]

What does the present-day Irish immigrant woman find in Canada? Unlike Famine Irish immigrants, unlike immigrant and Canadian-born Black and Asian women, and unlike First Nations women, today's Irish immigrant woman does not have to face racial discrimination. The Orange Order has all but died out, and discrimination against the Irish has given way to discrimination against newer immigrants, particularly against Blacks and Asians. Racism towards the people of the First Nations has prevailed since the first arrivals of the English and the French. The First Nations had sophisticated cultures, legal and political systems, and spiritual ways of life that, beginning in the 1600s, came under attack by both English and French colonizers, who seized First Nations' lands and later forced their children into residential schools where they banned the speaking of First Nations languages and expressions of culture. As the politicians negotiate and renegotiate Quebec's place in Canada's Constitution, the First Nations are demanding their rightful place at the bargaining table, a settlement to land claims and the right to self-determination.

By the end of the wave of Irish immigration to Canada in the mid-1800s and until the 1920s, Canadian women were organizing around various issues, including temperance and suffrage. These first-generation feminists — among them Nellie McClung, who was of Irish descent — won many changes, including the right to vote.[62] Beginning in the 1960s and 1970s, the second wave of feminism also questioned the structure of women's lives and fought for equal pay for work of equal value, access to male-dominated jobs, universal daycare, better health care and reproductive rights. Male violence against women also became a key issue.[63]

However, discrimination exists in the women's movement as in the broader society. Middle-class white women have dominated both the first and second waves of the Canadian women's movement. Moreover, racism and classism continue to exclude women on the margins: women of colour, women of the First Nations, poor women, disabled women, lesbians and working-class women.

Feminist critics on the margins argue that the second wave's initial challenges of the 1970s have given way to an institutional feminism in the 1990s, which focuses on the careers and aspirations of middle-class white women and excludes "other" women's struggles. Still dominating the feminist agenda, some of these women now operate from institutions such as universities, government and business which have exacted compromise in return for privilege and power, advantages which are limited in relation to men but substantial in relation to "other" women.[64]

In Canada in the early 1990s, an Irish immigrant woman's

prospects for paid work are better than in Ireland, where the official rate of unemployment hit 17 percent in the South in 1989 and 13.5 percent in the North in 1991, with Catholic workers two and a half times more likely than Protestant ones to be out of work.[65] But in Canada, the recession of the late 1980s continues into the 1990s — many would say it is now a depression. Here, women earn on average 66 percent of men's earnings. Women, particularly visible minority women and immigrant women, together making up about one-third of all women in Canada, are particularly hard hit.[66]

Poverty is a major issue for Canadian women. The recession is taking a severe toll, particularly on single mothers, most of whom live in poverty. Statistics Canada reports that the average family income increased by a mere 5.4 percent in the 1980s, compared to 26.1 percent in the 1970s and 46 percent in the 1960s. The report also shows that in 1990 sole-support female-headed families had a 7.3 percent drop in average income, to $21,961. And 60.6 percent of mother-led families were poor, increasing from 52.9 percent over the previous year. More than one million Canadian children live in poverty.[67] As a group, Black, Asian and First Nations women continue to find their job prospects and wages significantly more limited than those of white women.

In Ireland, divorce is against the law. In Canada, however, where divorce is legal, low-income pink-collar jobs, combined with inadequate child support from ex-husbands, leave divorced women and their children in poverty. According to a Statistics Canada report, almost four out of every ten marriages ended in divorce in 1989.[68] One U.S. study found a woman's actual income drops by 73 percent within one year of separation; a man's disposable income *increases* by 42 percent.[69] A recent Ontario study showed that 75 percent of men ordered by the courts to pay child support default on their payments.[70] Statistics Canada reported recently that those men who did pay alimony and child support in 1988 paid, on average, $4,600 per year before taxes, which accounted for a mere 15 percent of the income of those families receiving support.[71]

Like other immigrant women and like Canadian-born women, Irish women find limited job prospects in Canada, the result of female job segregation and its corresponding low wages. Over the past fifty years, women's labour-force participation in Canada has risen dramatically. In 1931, 19.7 percent of all women were in the labour force; in 1961, 29.5 percent; and by 1986, 55.1 percent. In 1951 about 4 percent of married women were in the work force; by the 1980s a majority were.[72] A recent Statistics Canada report found that, between 1983 and 1986, 70 percent of the immigrants to Toronto were visible minorities and that 68.2 percent of visible minority women were part of the labour force, compared to 63 percent of other women.[73]

Many white working-class women and women of colour have always worked outside the home. But during World War II the Canadian government mounted a public campaign to bring many more women into the work force, to fill posts in munitions factories and other jobs. This campaign indeed brought more middle-class white women into the public sphere. However, when the men came home after the war these women found themselves pushed back into the private sphere of the home, reinforcing their roles as wives, mothers and homemakers.

Canadian women did not stay long at home. Married middle-class women reentered the work force in large numbers in the early 1950s for practical reasons. Their earnings were essential in creating the higher standard of living desired by Canadians who were weary of depression and war. Women's earnings in job ghettos let families buy houses and cars and send their children to university.[74] Black women and white working-class women had long worked outside the home.

Many middle-class white feminists argue that the campaign to bring women into the labour force during World War II had an emancipating effect on Canadian women. Canadian feminist historian Ruth Roach Pierson argues that although the war brought more women into the work force, its impact on women's work was not as great as some have claimed.

While the war effort necessitated minor adjustments to sexual demarcation lines in the world of paid work, it did not offer a fundamental challenge to the male-dominated sex/gender system. And the post-war years witnessed a return to unquestioning acceptance of the principles of male economic primacy in the public sphere and male headship in the private.[75]

Today the majority of working women in Canada hold jobs close to the bottom of the income pyramid. In 1981 almost 60 percent of Canadian women remained segregated in low-income, pink-collar–ghetto clerical, sales and service jobs.[76] By 1986, women were still concentrated in these three areas, where they made up 79.9 percent of clerical workers, 48 percent of salespeople and 61.3 percent of service workers.[77]

The recent boom in part-time employment is a significant change in the Canadian labour market. In 1987 women made up more than 70 percent of this sector, in low-waged jobs without job security, pensions or benefits. More than one-quarter of all employed women hold part-time jobs.[78]

Canada is also a country that is de-industrializing: "Between June 1989 and October 1991, there was a net loss of 461,000 jobs. Manufacturing now employs only 15% of the total Canadian labour force, likely the lowest level in the industrialized world. For observers of Canada's Free Trade Agreement with the U.S., it is important to note that over 150,000 jobs disappeared before the formal onset of the so called recession."[79] The consequences of free trade for women are job losses and lower wages in manufacturing (a traditional employment area for immigrant women), data processing and the public sector.[80]

The patriarchal structure of the home also limits women's participation in the work force. Recent media reports of women returning to full-time homemaking fail to acknowledge men's refusal to take on childcare and domestic duties as a factor in the return.[81]

Having abdicated childcare and homemaking responsibilities, the majority of men ensure their full participation and advancement in the work force at the expense of women, who are forced to carry husbands' responsibilities in addition to their own.

On average, husbands of women in the labour force spend less than an hour a day on housework and childcare.[82] Thus these wives end up working a double day, with significantly longer hours than their husbands. This unequal division of work in the home affects women's and men's employment outside the home,[83] forcing women to be absent from work more than men are and to enter occupations compatible with childcare and housework.

The Mulroney government's refusal to set up a national daycare program also blocks women's opportunities in the workplace, and underscores the unequal division of work in the patriarchal family. Without adequate daycare facilities, women are forced back into the home, with its patriarchal family relations where the husband's economic advantage gives him power over his wife.

Male violence against women, a fact of life for Canadian women, and the legal structure in place to deal with this violence, have particular ramifications for Black and Asian women, First Nations women and disabled women. The editorial collective of *Diva*, a South Asian women's journal, sums it up this way: "In Canada, sexism, racism, homophobia and class-based oppression has created a difficult situation for many women. Any support developed for women around issues of sexual assault, incest and rape, is not equipped to serve most Women of Colour, including South Asian women."[84]

Recent studies show that one in five men living with a woman admitted to violence against the woman, one in ten women is battered by a male partner, one in four women is likely to be sexually assaulted at some time in her life,[85] eight in ten First Nations women in Ontario have been abused.[86] An average of 100 Canadian women a year are murdered by a male partner.[87] The proposed "no means no" law on rape (Bill C-49) will, if passed, restrict the accused's defence of "mistaken belief." At present he can argue that he "honestly thought" the woman consented. Apart from the alleged offence, it is now also more difficult to question rape victims on their sexual history.

Centuries old, sexual harassment is often part of men's attack on women's participation in all aspects of the public sphere, from the workplace to the education system. The Ontario Human Rights Code did not include protection against sexual harassment until 1981. In 1990, sexual harassment cases were 8 percent of the Ontario Human Rights Commission's caseload, with 157 cases filed, compared to 137 the year before. In 1983, the Canadian Human Rights Commission found that 49 percent of women have been sexually harassed.[88] Under the Canada Labour Code, federally regulated employers, such as banks and telecommunication firms, must set policies against sexual harassment and these policies must be posted in the workplace.[89]

Unlike Ireland, Canada permits abortion. In January 1988, the Supreme Court of Canada struck down the old abortion law that restricted the circumstances under which women could get a legal abortion. Although access to abortion is still limited in many provinces, abortion is now legal in Canada. In Ontario, abortion clinics are fully funded under the provincial health-care system. However, a growth in right-wing religious groups, including those sponsored by the Catholic Church, has led to a major political campaign to recriminalize abortion. Anti-abortion demonstrators have also mounted a cross-Canada campaign to harass clients going into the clinics. In the mid-1980s, this harassment turned to violence when a firebomb aimed at Toronto's Morgentaler clinic hit the neighbouring Toronto Women's Bookstore, which was gutted by the fire.[90] In May 1992, yet another bomb destroyed the clinic.

On December 6, 1990, fourteen women were shot dead on the campus of the University of Montreal by a man shouting that he only wanted to kill women. The Montreal Massacre is symbolic of the deeply rooted misogyny of Canadian society.[91] That this event occurred on a university campus shows that sexism goes to the heart of Canada's universities, where women suffer sexual harass-

ment, are underrepresented on faculties, and are confronted with
sexism, racism, classism and homophobia in textbooks and in the
classroom.[92]

Irish women's immigration to Canada must be placed in the
broader context of global patriarchal and colonial politics. Canada
has much to offer, but sexism, classism and racism pervade every
aspect of Canadian life. In this respect, Canada is no different than
Ireland or the rest of the world. Gita Sen and Caren Grown
advance the global perspective needed to locate women's immigration. The founding members of Development Alternatives
with Women for a New Era (DAWN), established in 1984 in India to
address the experiences and perspectives of Third World women,
Sen and Grown trace how poor women in the Third World have
mobilized against the debt, famine, militarization and fundamen-
talism springing from the current (and long-standing) global
political and economic crises. Given Irish women's history and
given Irish women's immigration to Canada and our connections
as women to all women, the global women's perspective advocated by Sen and Grown is a fitting conclusion to this chapter.
First, addressing the aims of feminism, they offer this challenge to
mainstream middle-class white feminists:

> Feminism cannot be based on a rigid concept of universality
> that negates the wide variation in women's experience. There
> is and must be a diversity of feminisms, responsive to the
> different needs and concerns of different women, and *defined
> by them for themselves* [emphasis in original].[93]

Sen and Grown also present a vision of the world:

> We want a world where inequality based on class, gender, and
> race is absent from every country, and from the relationships
> among countries. We want a world where basic needs become
> basic rights and where poverty and all forms of violence are

eliminated....We want a world where all institutions are open to participatory democratic processes, where women share in determining priorities and making decisions.[94]

As Irish women we know very well that these words reflect our history, our experiences of immigration, our exile. We too must share and work towards that vision wherever we are, at home or on distant shores.

Notes

1. Rosalind Miles, *The Women's History of the World* (London: Paladin, 1989, pp. 12–13).
2. See Robert O'Driscoll and Lorna Reynolds, eds., *The Untold Story: The Irish in Canada* (Toronto: Celtic Arts Canada, 1988; 2 vols.). Of the 73 contributors to the book, only 12 are women. Prominent Canadian suffragist Nellie McClung, the daughter of Irish parents, merits one of the six cameo profiles. Her extraordinary public life is summarized in just eight lines, including the notation, "she became wife and mother of five children." The men profiled in the cameos are not described as husbands and fathers. Index references to"women" correspond to one or two lines scattered throughout the text; as well, the reader looking for "women" is advised to "see also sexual attitudes"!
3. Donald Harman Akenson, one such historian, uses Malthusian notions of overpopulation to account for the Famine. His 1982 review of *Paddy's Lament: Ireland 1846–1847, Prelude to Hatred* by Irish-American author Thomas Gallagher, who linked the Famine with English oppression, contains anti-Irish comments. Calling the book "evil," Akenson declares:

> Bluntly stated, the Irish Famine of 1845–1848 occurred because the Irish peasantry procreated themselves to death....The peasant

farmers adopted a virtual monoculture based on the potato, and their dependence on this single crop, combined with their excessive fecundity, meant that a massive famine was inevitable. The only doubt was when it would occur, and precisely what would trigger it. Thus, when it came, the famine was the product of social patterns indigenous to Ireland and had as little to do with the arrangements for governing the country as had, say, the starvation on the Indian subcontinent in our own time with the achievement of independence in 1947. (*The Globe and Mail*, August 7, 1982, p. 24.)

Geographers Cecil Houston and William Smyth, in *Irish Immigration and Canadian Settlement: Patterns, Links and Letters* (Toronto: University of Toronto Press, 1990), fail to place the Famine within the framework of English colonial policy. Advocating that the Famine be "kept in context and remembered — not as a linchpin, but as an anomaly — in the pattern of Irish emigration to Canada" (p. 60), they ignore the fact that the vast majority of the Famine immigrants were Catholics, in contrast to the Protestants who were the bulk of Irish immigrants in the years prior to the Famine. Further, bemoaning the attention given to the trauma of "the unfortunates" (Famine victims) arriving in Canada, Houston and Smyth attribute the Famine simply to "pauper immigration." They write, "The pathetic year [1847] will remain in Canada's history as the primary symbol of pauper immigration — a deserved distinction" (p. 62). To Catholic Irish, the Famine is very clearly a linchpin of English colonization. To Protestant Irish, it is but an anomaly in immigration patterns. While these historians are entitled to their opinions, they also have an obligation to reveal their standpoint which shapes such opinions. Here we see more clearly knowledge as a social construction.

4. See Houston and Smyth, *Irish Immigration and Canadian Settlement*, p. 20. Like their male colleagues, Houston and Smyth's account of Irish immigration patterns to Canada fail to include Irish women as a group.

5. *Ibid.*, p. 42.
6. *Ibid.*, p. 43.
7. John J. Mannion, *Irish Settlements in Eastern Canada: A Study of Cultural Transfer and Adaptation* (Toronto: University of Toronto Press, 1974). See also Mannion's *The Peopling of Newfoundland* (St. John's: ISER Books, 1977).
8. For references to Newfoundland, see Mannion, *Irish Settlements in Eastern Canada* and *The Peopling of Newfoundland.*
9. See Marianna O'Gallagher, *Grosse Île: Gateway to Canada 1832–1937* (Quebec: Carraig Books, 1984); Marianna O'Gallagher, *The Voyage of the Naparima: A Story of Canada's Island Graveyard* (Quebec: Carraig Books, 1982); Marianna O'Gallagher, *Saint Brigid's Quebec.* (Quebec: Carraig Books, 1981); Marianna O'Gallagher, *Saint Patrick's Quebec: The Building of a Church and a Parish, 1827 to 1833* (Quebec: Carraig Books, 1981); Nancy Schmitz, *Irish for a Day: Saint Patrick's Day Celebrations in Quebec City 1765–1990* (Quebec: Carraig Books, 1991).
10. See Terrence Punch, *Irish Halifax: The Immigrant Generation 1815–1859* (Halifax: International Education Centre, St. Mary's University, 1981); Terrence Punch, *Some Sons of Erin in Nova Scotia* (Halifax: International Education Centre, St. Mary's University, 1980).
11. See Peter Toner, ed., *The New Ireland Remembered: Historical Essays on the Irish in New Brunswick* (Fredericton: New Ireland Press, 1988); William Baker, *Timothy Warren Anglin — Irish Catholic Canadian* (Toronto: University of Toronto Press, 1977).
12. See Bruce Elliott, *Irish Migrants in the Canadas: A New Approach* (Kingston and Montreal: McGill-Queen's University Press, 1988); Donald Harman Akenson, *The Irish in Ontario: A Study in Rural History* (Kingston and Montreal: McGill-Queen's University Press, 1984); John Mannion, *Irish Settlements in Eastern Canada: A Study of Cultural Transfer and Adaptation* (Toronto: University of Toronto Press, 1974); Murray Nicolson, "Peasants in an Urban Society: The Irish Catholics in Victorian Toronto" in *Gathering Place: Peoples and Neighbourhoods of Toronto, 1834–1945,* edited by

Robert F. Harney (Toronto: Multicultural History Society of Ontario, 1985), pp. 54–55; Houston and Smyth, *Irish Immigration and Canadian Settlement*.

13. O'Gallagher, *Grosse Île, p. 47*.
14. *Ibid.*, p. 48.
15. *Ibid.*, p. 51.
16. *Ibid.*, pp. 50–52
17. These figures were given to me by Marianna O'Gallagher in a telephone conversation. The first figure comes from the *Ancient Order of Hibernians Magazine*, circa 1910. The second figure comes from the commemorative appendix to *Quebec Chronicle 1909* in a report by John Jordan. Additionally, Claude Marcil in *Québec Science* 14, no. 2 (August 1976), cites Damas Potvin's estimate in *Le Saint-Laurent et Ses îles* that 12,000 died of typhus and were buried at Grosse Île.
18. O'Gallagher, *Grosse Île*, pp. 51–52.
19. O'Gallagher, *Voyage of the Naparima*, p. 123. O'Gallagher also notes that Mary Ford, grandmother of auto magnate Henry Ford, died and was buried at Grosse Île before her husband William and their children went on to Detroit.
20. *Ibid.*, pp. 124–25.
21. O'Gallagher, *Grosse Île*, pp. 54–55.
22. O'Gallagher, *Voyage of the Naparima*, pp. 128–29.
23. Nicolson, "Peasants in an Urban Society," p. 47.
24. O'Gallagher, *Voyage of the Naparima*, pp. 145–47.
25. Houston and Smyth, *Irish Immigration and Canadian Settlement*, pp. 71–74.
26. *Ibid.*, p. 180. For further information on the Orange Order, see Cecil Houston and William Smyth, *The Sash Canada Wore: A Historical Geography of the Orange Order in Canada* (Toronto: University of Toronto Press, 1980); Donald Harman Akenson, *The Orangeman: The Life and Times of Ogle Gowan* (Toronto: James Lorimer, 1986); see also Frederick Armstrong, "Ethnicity and the Formation of the Ontario Establishment" in *Ethnic Canada: Identities and Inequalities*, edited by Leo Driedger (Toronto: Copp Clark Pitman, 1987) for an analysis of how the Ontario establishment formed from Protestant

English and Irish settlers in eighteenth- and nineteenth-century Canada and consolidated their power in the ownership of land and the accumulation of wealth, as well as through marriage and through connections with British officialdom. The author argues that today's Canadian elite is the culmination of this history.

27. Houston and Smyth, *Irish Immigration and Canadian Settlement*, pp. 180–81.

28. *Ibid.*, p. 183.

29. *Ibid.*

30. Nicolson, "Peasants in an Urban Society," p. 60.

31. D. Suzanne Cross, "The Neglected Majority: The Changing Role of Women in 19th Century Montreal" in *The Neglected Majority: Essays in Canadian Women's History*, edited by Susan Mann Trofimenkoff and Alison Prentice (Toronto: McClelland & Stewart, 1977), pp. 78–79. One reference to the Irish Catholic Ladies, Franciscan Tertiaries of Montreal, on a pilgrimage to honour Our Lady is made by J. G. Shaw, "Devotion to Our Lady at Cap de la Madeleine" in *The Canadian Catholic Historical Association* (Toronto: The Association, 1952), pp. 61–86. One wonders what work these Irish women did in Montreal. Parish records reveal volunteer work — women's work.

32. J. C. McKeown, *The Life and Labours of Most Rev. John Joseph Lynch, D.D., C.M., First Archbishop of Toronto* (Toronto: Sadlier, 1886), pp. 91–92.

    For a discussion on nuns, see Barbara Cooper, "The Convent: An Option for Quebecoises 1930–1950," *Canadian Women's Studies* 7, no. 4 (Winter 1986), pp. 31–35. Cooper, who has also researched nuns in Ontario, notes, "Not all agree on the nature of the contribution nuns have made, but more are recognizing the need to examine the religious life as an avenue that was open to women as an alternative to marriage and motherhood" (p. 31). She also notes that the emphasis in feminist research has shifted from a focus on the piety and heroism of the founders and leaders to interest in the general membership, its reasons for choosing convent life, and its work.

33. Information for this section comes from the history of the Loretto

Sisters, documented by Sr. Kathleen McGovern: *Something More Than Ordinary* (Toronto: Alger Press, 1989), and from the Rev. M. Margarita O'Connor, "The Institute for the Blessed Virgin Mary" in *The Canadian Catholic Historical Association* (Toronto: The Association, 1945). In addition, the Sisters have produced a variety of pamphlets culled from material in their archives.

34. O'Connor, "The Institute of the Blessed Virgin Mary," p. 73.
35. *Ibid.*, p. 71.
36. For information about the Sisters of St. Joseph, see Sr. Mary Agnes, *The Congregation of the Sisters of St. Joseph* (Toronto: University of Toronto Press, 1951); see also Elizabeth M. Smythe, "The Lessons of Religion and Science: The Congregation of the Sisters of St. Joseph and St. Joseph's Academy, Toronto 1854–1911," Ph.D. dissertation submitted to the Ontario Institute for Studies in Education, University of Toronto, 1989.
37. Sr. Mary Agnes, *The Congregation of the Sisters of St. Joseph*, pp. 89–90.
38. *Ibid.*, pp. 169–85.
39. Smythe, "The Lessons of Religion and Science," p. 76.
40. In 1921 this became St. Joseph's Hospital.
41. Sr. Mary Agnes, *The Congregation of the Sisters of St. Joseph*, pp. 129–30.
42. For information on the Sisters of Mercy in Newfoundland, see Sr. M. Williamina Hogan, *Pathways of Mercy: History of the Foundations of the Sisters of Mercy in Newfoundland 1842–1984* (St. John's: Harry Cuff, 1986).
43. Catherine McAuley (1747–1841) founded the Sisters of Mercy in Ireland in 1831. Before her death, she established twelve houses in Ireland, two in England and the one in Newfoundland, which was the first in North America. For more information on the founding of the Mercy order in Ireland, see Sr. Bernard Degnan, *Mercy Unto Thousands: Life of Mother Mary Catherine McAuley* (Westminster, Maryland: Newman Press, 1957).
44. The Sisters of Mercy in Newfoundland commemorate their 150th anniversary in 1992; anniversary pamphlets credit Frances Creedon's "dedication, courage, and perseverance" with the sur-

vival and growth of the congregation in Newfoundland, which has a community of close to 200 Sisters today.

45. See Celia Haig-Brown, *Resistance and Renewal: Surviving the Indian Residential School* (Vancouver: Arsenal Pulp Press, 1988); Jo-Anne Fiske, "Colonization and the Decline of Women's Status: The Tsimshian Case," *Feminist Studies* 17, no. 3 (Fall 1991); and Lee Maracle, *I am Woman* (Vancouver: Write-On Press, 1988). For more general reading on Native people in Canada, see Olive Patricia Dickason, *Canada's First Nations: A History of Founding Peoples from Earliest Times* (Toronto: McClelland & Stewart, 1992).

46. Nicolson, "Peasants in an Urban Society," pp. 54–55.

47. Constance Backhouse, *Petticoats and Prejudice: Women and Law in Nineteenth-Century Canada* (Toronto: Osgoode Society/Women's Press, 1991), p. 229: citing Nicolson, "Peasants in an Urban Society," p. 58.

48. Backhouse, *Petticoats and Prejudice*, p. 241.

49. Nicolson, "Peasants in an Urban Society," p. 55.

50. *Ibid.*

51. Cross, *The Neglected Majority*, pp. 68–69.

52. Marilyn Barber, "The Women Ontario Welcomed: Immigrant Domestics for Ontario Homes, 1870–1930," *Ontario History* 72, no. 3 (1980), pp. 148–72. Barber's misleading references to "the British Isles" do not include Irish women as a separate category. One reference is made to Irish domestics on p. 171. In light of the discrimination against Irish Catholics, as well as the Irish struggle for independence, such a distinction must be made.

53. *Ibid.*, p. 148.

54. *Ibid.*, p. 162.

55. *Ibid.*, p. 170.

56. See Dionne Brand, *No Burden to Carry: Narratives of Black Working Women in Ontario 1920s to 1950s* (Toronto: Women's Press, 1991); Dionne Brand, "Black Women and Work: The Impact of Racially Constructed Gender Roles on the Sexual Division of Labour," *Fireweed*, no. 26 (Winter–Spring 1988), pp. 87–92; and Makeda Silvera, *Silenced* (Toronto: Williams-Wallace, 1983).

57. Agnes Calliste, "Canada's Immigration Policy and Domestics

from the Caribbean: The Second Domestic Scheme," in Jesse Vorst *et al., Race, Class, Gender: Bonds and Barriers* (Toronto: Between the Lines, 1989), pp. 133–65.

58. Roxanna Ng, "Sexism, Racism, Nationalism" in Vorst *et al., Race, Class, Gender*, pp. 10–25. See also Barbara Roberts, "Ladies, Women and the State: Managing Female Immigration, 1880–1920," in Roxanna Ng, Gillian Walker and Jacob Muller, eds., *Community Organization and the Canadian State* (Toronto: Garamond, 1990).

59. For an excellent short social and economic history of Canada, see Patricia Bird, *Of Dust and Time and Dreams and Agonies* (Toronto: Women's Press, 1975).

60. Statistics Department, Ministry of Employment and Immigration, Ottawa.

61. Statistics Canada. From 1901 to 1971, the Canadian Census misleadingly listed the Republic of Ireland under the U.K. Even the 1986 Census's look at population by "Ethnic Origin" places "Irish" in the category "British Origins."

62. For a discussion on early, mostly white middle-class, Canadian women's history, see, for example, Linda Kealey, ed., *A Not Unreasonable Claim: Women and Reform in Canada, 1880s–1920s* (Toronto: Women's Press, 1979); Alison Prentice, Paula Bourne, Gail Cuthbert Brandt, Beth Light, Wendy Mitchinson and Naomi Black, *Canadian Women: A History* (Toronto: Harcourt Brace Jovanovich, 1988); Mann Trofimenkoff and Prentice, eds., *The Neglected Majority*; Margaret Anderson, ed., *Mother Was Not a Person* (Montreal: Black Rose, 1972).

63. See Nancy Adams, Linda Briskin and Margaret McPhail, *Feminist Organizing for Change: The Contemporary Women's Movement in Canada* (Toronto: Oxford University Press, 1988). This book contains a bibliography on the first wave of feminism and on the contemporary women's movement. Again, the focus is largely on middle-class white women.

64. See, for example, Vorst *et al., Race, Class, Gender*; Himani Bannerji, Linda Carty, Kari Dehli, Susan Heald and Kate McKenna, *Unsettling Relations: The University as a Site of Feminist Struggles* (Toronto:

Women's Press, 1991); bell hooks, *Ain't I a Woman? Black Women and Feminism* (Boston: South End Press, 1981); also *Fireweed*, no. 25 (Fall 1987), "Class Is the Issue" (special issue on class); Sheila Baxter, *No Way To Live: Poor Women Speak Out* (Vancouver: New Star Books, 1988); Janet Silman, *Enough Is Enough: Aboriginal Women Speak Out* (Toronto: Women's Press, 1991); Patricia Monture, "Ka-Nin-Geh-Heh-Gah-E-Sa-Nonh-Yah-Gah," *Canadian Journal of Women and the Law* 2, no.1 (1986), pp. 159–70.

65. The figure for the South is from *The World Almanac and Book of Facts 1991*. It gives no figures for unemployment in the North. According to the *Europa World Yearbook 1991*, the North's total work force was 700,400 in 1991, with 95,100 out of work, for a rate of 13.6 percent.

66. Morley Gunderson, Leon Muszynski and Jennifer Keck, *Women and Labour Market Poverty* (Ottawa: Canadian Advisory Council on the Status of Women, 1990), p. 99. For a discussion on "visible minority" women and the role of Canada in the division of labour by race and sex, see Linda Carty and Dionne Brand, "'Visible Minority' Women — A Creation of the Canadian State," *Resources for Feminist Research* 17, no. 3, 1988, pp. 39–42; Roxanna Ng, "The Social Construction of Immigrant Women in Canada," in Roberta Hamilton and Michele Barrett, eds., *The Politics of Diversity* (Montreal: Book Centre, 1986); Roxanna Ng, "Sexism, Racism, Nationalism," in Vorst *et al.*, *Race, Class, Gender*.

67. *The Globe and Mail*, "One million children in poverty," December 19, 1991, p. A4.

68. Jean Dumas and Yves Péron, "Marriage and Conjugal Life in Canada," Statistics Canada Catalogue 91-534E (Spring 1992), p. 47.

69. Lenore Weitzman, *The Divorce Revolution: The Unexpected Social and Economic Consequences for Women and Children in America* (New York: Free Press, 1985). The percentage cited is the average for all divorced women in the U.S.; it does not specify the implications of divorce for Black and Asian women, immigrant women or First Nations women.

70. Alanna Mitchell, "Divorce a Ticket to Poverty for Women, Figures Show," *The Globe and Mail*, June 4, 1992, p. A10.

71. Diane Galarneau, "Alimony and Child Support," *Perspectives on Labour and Income*, Statistics Canada Catalogue 75-001 (Spring 1992).

72. Gunderson *et al.*, *Women and Labour Market Poverty*, pp. 13–14. See also Margrit Eichler, *Families in Canada Today* (Toronto: Gage, 1988). See Table 1.4 on women's labour-force participation 1931–1986 in Gunderson *et al.*, *Women and Labour Market Poverty*, p. 14, adapted from Eichler.

73. Joanne Moreau, "Changing Faces: Visible Minorities in Toronto," *Canadian Social Trends*, Statistics Canada Catalogue 11-008 (Winter 1991), pp. 26–28.

74. See Canadian feminist historian Veronica Strong-Boag's article, "'50s Dream No Guide for '90s Women: It's Time to Stop Penalizing Women for Motherhood," *The Globe and Mail*, May 7, 1992, p. A21.

75. Ruth Roach Pierson, *"They're Still Women After All": The Second World War and Canadian Womanhood* (Toronto: McClelland & Stewart, 1986) p. 216.

76. Gunderson *et al.*, *Women and Labour Market Poverty*, p. 93. See also Pat Armstrong and Hugh Armstrong, *The Double Ghetto: Canadian Women and Their Segregated Work* (Toronto: McClelland & Stewart, 1978). Unfortunately, there is no analysis of race in most discussions of women's work in Canada, including that by Armstrong and Armstrong and others. The intersection of race, class and gender is critical to understanding women's segregated work. Black, Asian and First Nations women face double segregation because of racism.

77. Gunderson *et al.*, *Women and Labour Market Poverty*, p. 100. "Designated groups" "targeted" for protection against discrimination are women, "Aboriginal people," "visible minorities," and disabled people. The latter three groups remain underrepresented in higher-level occupations. An editorial in *The Toronto Star* for April 26, 1992, noted that the federal government trails the federally regulated private sector in the hiring and promoting of "visible

minorities" under the 1986 Employment Equity Act. Only 3.6 percent of federal employees were non-whites, and a mere 2.1 percent of these were in management. The worst culprits were the Treasury Board, which regulates employment equity, the Public Service Commission, which does the hiring, and the Privy Council Office, which is the nerve centre of government. Agreeing that these findings of the Canadian Ethnocultural Council were "scandalous," the editorial noted that the non-white population of Canada is about 9.5 percent of the total population.

78. Canadian Advisory Council on the Status of Women, "Women, Paid/Unpaid Work, and Stress"(Ottawa: CACSW, 1989), p. 31. This paper examines the stresses women encounter in segregated jobs, full- and part-time, stresses attributed to "the larger problem of gender inequality in society" (p. 1). For a discussion on part-time work, see also J. White, *Women and Part-time Work* (Ottawa: Canadian Advisory Council on the Status of Women, 1983). For a discussion on the working poor, see Gunderson *et al.*, "Women and Labour Market Poverty," Chapter 3.

79. Bruce Campbell, *Canada Under Siege*, (Ottawa: Canadian Centre for Policy Alternatives, 1992), p. 1.

80. Marjorie Cohen, *Free Trade and the Future of Women's Work: Manufacturing and Service Industries* (Toronto: Garamond, 1987).

81. *The Globe and Mail*, April 20, 1992. p. A1.

82. Gunderson *et al.*, "Women and Labour Market Poverty," p. 25. For a discussion on women's work in the home, see Charlene Gannagé, *Double Day, Double Bind: Women Garment Workers* (Toronto: Women's Press, 1986); Bonnie Fox, ed., *Hidden in the Household: Women's Domestic Labour Under Capitalism* (Toronto: Women's Press, 1980); Meg Luxton, *More Than a Labour of Love: Three Generations of Women's Work in the Home* (Toronto: Women's Press, 1980); Meg Luxton, Harriet Rosenberg and Sedes Arat Koç, eds., *Through the Kitchen Window: The Politics of Home and Family* (Toronto: Garamond, 1986). Again, there is no race analysis in many of these accounts.

83. Gunderson *et al.*, *Women and Labour Market Poverty*, p. 25.

84. *Diva* 3, no. 2 (March 1992), pp. 5–6. The journal devoted the entire

issue to the perspectives of South Asian women on male violence
against women. For an examination of male violence against
women with disabilities see Jillian Ridington, *Violence and Women
with Disabilities* (Toronto: DisAbled Women's Network (DAWN),
1990).

85. See for example Julie Brickman and John Briere, "Incidents of
Rape and Sexual Assault in an Urban Canadian Population," *The
International Journal of Women's Studies* 7, no. 3.

86. Ontario Native Women's Association, "Breaking Free: A Proposal
for Change to Aboriginal Family Violence" (1989).

87. *The Toronto Star*, March 22, 1992.

88. *Diva* 3, no.2 (March 1992), p. 63. This and other studies are cited
from Ontario Women's Directorate literature.

89. *The Toronto Star*, October 19, 1991, pp. A1, A8.

90. Information update provided by the Ontario Coalition for Abor-
tion Clinics. See Eleanor Wright Pelrine, *Abortion in Canada*
(Toronto: New Press, 1971); and Janine Brodie, Shelley A.M.
Gavigan and Jane Jenson, *The Politics of Abortion* (Toronto: Oxford
University Press, 1992).

91. See Sheelagh Conway, "The Montreal Massacre — Madness or
Misogyny?" in Anne Innis Dagg, Sheelagh Conway and Margaret
Simpson, *Women's Experience, Women's Education — An Anthology*
(Waterloo: Otter Press, 1991), pp. 33–37. For a discussion on
sexism in universities, see Anne Innis Dagg and Patricia
Thompson, *MisEducation: Women & Canadian Universities* (Toron-
to: Ontario Institute for Studies in Education Press, 1988).

92. See Sheelagh Conway, Anne Innis Dagg and Shelly Beauchamp,
Sexism in Universities: The Myth of Academic Excellence. Paper
presented to the Commission of Inquiry on Canadian University
Education, Toronto, 1990.

For insights into sexism, racism and classism as practised in
Canadian universities, see also Bannerji *et al.*, *Unsettling Relations*.
For a discussion on racism and classism in feminism and the
indifference of middle-class white feminist scholars to women
pushed to the margin, see Himani Bannerji, "Introducing Racism:
Notes Towards an Anti-Racist Feminism," *Resources for Feminist*

Research 16, no. 1, pp. 10–12. Bannerji notes: "When I came into the scene the talk of class, if it ever existed in Canada, had ceased to have any serious content....The great bulk of Canadian literature on women and what passes for Women's Studies curriculum leaves the reader with the impression that women from the Third World and southern Europe are a very negligible part of the living and labouring population of Canada" (p. 10). See also Sheelagh Conway, "Campus Critique Leaves Women on the Margins," *The Globe and Mail*, October 24, 1991; this article criticized the report of the Inquiry into University Education for its treatment of women as a homogeneous group. It pointed out, for example, that although women make up 18 percent of the full-time faculty in Canadian universities, these faculty women, as well as women in graduate schools and those who get published, are mostly middle-class and white. These women enjoy a privilege and power that Black and Asian women, First Nations women and poor women do not. As a group, those who are not middle-class or white remain shut out by the university and the new women's elite within it.

93. Gita Sen and Caren Grown, *Development, Crises, and Alternative Visions: Third World Women's Perspectives* (New York: Monthly Review Press, 1987), pp. 18–19.

94. *Ibid.*, pp. 80–81.

It Is New Strung
and Shall Be Heard

Going Off with the Little Bag

Bridget Grealis-Guglich

Bridget Grealis-Guglich lives in the Ottawa Valley, Ontario, where many Irish people settled in Canada.

Going off with the little bag, that was the story of the people in and around Ballycroy, Co. Mayo, where I came from. Life was hard. There was no doubt about that. We knew at a very early age that we'd have to be leaving and taking the bag, like I'd seen my uncle and my aunt do and different people since. In a way we were prepared for that. The government would be down in the west promoting Gaelic speaking, but they weren't interested in providing any education after you spoke the Gaelic. They didn't care where you ended up, working the subways in London or out in the outback in Australia, which happened to lots of people I knew. All gone and lost to the world.

Secondary-school education wasn't free when I went to school. How I managed to get to high school was that a lady needed help with her children, so at thirteen I went to Achill Sound to help this lady whose kids were a bit spoiled. They weren't like the kids I was used to. I worked there and lived-in and that way I was able to cycle to a nearby high school in Achill Sound, set up for underprivileged kids like myself. All the schools were run by the brothers or sisters. But, of course, there were no nuns or brothers down Ballycroy way providing any education — and if I may say so, there were a lot of bright people in Ballycroy. All the local kids swarmed in on their bikes; their parents couldn't afford the high cost of boarding school in Tuam or Tourmakeedy and all these wonderful places where the more affluent people went. We were in our rags and we knew it. The life that I saw ahead of me was working as a maid or a waitress or something like that.

I finished high school in four years, top of my class. In the house where I lived-in, I had two hours for studying at night after I'd got all the work done minding the children and doing the chores. During the summer I had to foot the turf, bring it in and stack it, do the garden and milk the cows. The man I worked for was a nice man. We used to call him the Pension Officer — he had a fantasy of living in the country. I worked in this house for four years during my high school and I was well accustomed to work. It was no stranger to me, coming from a family of thirteen. It was a lovely house. They had water, a stove, and four bedrooms upstairs. He had an office in the house where people used to come, so it was nicely maintained.

My parents had a hard life. By 1945, when I was about ten, there were seven or eight kids. Altogether there were thirteen children over a twenty-year period, from my first sister to my last. My mother made beautiful lace when I was little, these lovely lace gloves and doilies to supplement the family income. She had some buyers, but as the war progressed nobody was buying lace any more. I can remember the gloves because I could never figure out how she'd make the fingers. I used to keep pestering her to tell me. Then she moved over to the Aran sweaters when they came in. She used to knit about one and a half a week. Beautiful. They ended up in the markets in North America. She used to get a few measly pounds for them, as usual.

My father was a farmer and did odd jobs. He got the place.[1] My father was the fiddler. That was great, but it was also bad because he would be off to the parties and they'd have the good times. Everyone called him Jack the Fiddler. The music was good.

After I finished high school, I got a job teaching in Inisbiggle, a little island off Achill Island. I used to be scared going in the curragh[2] because sometimes it wasn't all that safe. It was while I was there, and not having any proper degree or education to qualify me to stay there, I saw the winds of change. I decided I wasn't going to stay. Everybody was leaving; I was very, very conscious of it from a young age. I would be eighteen by that time. But there was nothing in Ireland, nothing for us. That I had to give up my homeland was maybe the saddest thing in my lifetime. It's a struggle and it'll be a struggle when I'm ninety. All the young people who left to live in Boston and California and Alaska and those places — there's some in Australia that I know of — there's no way we could have changed that. We were conscious of the lethargy and the parsimonious talk of the people who had control.

The government — and even some of the older people — would blame us for leaving, but they would provide nothing. They would never even acknowledge the heartbreak for us who left. I can think of people who could have said, "Well, I have a place and you can have it. I don't have any offspring." There were a few people around in those circumstances. I think Irish people tend to be a bit like that. In spite of their other generosity, they can be very tight when it comes to really helping somebody. The big sin was that we were leaving. We were doing it. But there was a breach on the side of Ireland, of Church people especially. The nuns were not down in the poor places like Mayo and Galway. They were in the rich places. You think that we weren't conscious of that? We knew we didn't rate. Speak up Gaelic, though, and we will somehow honour you. That doesn't put bread on the table. And it doesn't put a nice pair of high heels on a young girl's feet. Continue on carrying the turf and lugging it all your life. At first when I was in Achill, I had some hope I could do something with my life in Ireland. But I soon realized unless you knew somebody that was willing to help you, you wouldn't get far. I was bright but I had no way of going to Galway or Dublin to university. We were too poor. When you're bright you see what's happening. And that's the pain.

I went to England. Hiked on the train. Never on a train in my life. I thought: Well, if I'm a nurse at least that'll give me something. So I did my training in the Whittington Hospital in London — a large majority of the nurses in training were Irish. We were all fresh from the country, doing something enjoyable. We didn't find the work hard — we were used to it. I call it hoofin' it. After you've been carrying turf, cutting turf, baling hay, stacking it, and carrying turf home from the bog in pardógs³ from an early age, nursing was not hard.

I was in England about eight years. I had a career going, the companionship in the residence. We had a very active social life. Afterwards I went off and did my midwifery. And I went out to Luton, where I saw another part of English life: NO BLACKS OR IRISH NEED APPLY. No Blacks or Irish need apply for the rooms or the jobs. That would be 1956. I finished my midwifery in the fall of '58 and got a job offer to go back to the Whittington Hospital as a supervisor — it used to be called "sister" in those days — which I took. I had very good marks and the medicine prize for good standing in my classes.

I was vacillating about going to the United States, but I thought I'd stick it out and see what the scene was like. We used to call it "the scene." Hook a nice man. That was the next preoccupation. Before that it was dancing and the talent — scouting around and looking, nothing serious. What kept us going was to have a good laugh. And we had to make our laughs because sometimes there wasn't much to laugh about. Dancing and laughing. That was it. Have a good dance and have a good laugh and have a cup of tea when you come in. Marmalade on the bread. That was about it in London. All you could afford. There's the time you bought your dress and your high heels and your few toiletry articles and put up with the hard work and the long hours and that was all you had: marmalade and toast. A banana, if you were lucky.

It took me two to three years to decide there was really nothing in London. You were always going to be living in this Irish ghetto. You were never going to be part of England. It was a dark dreary day in November and I decided: This is it, I can't put up with this. That was 1960. So down I went to Canada House in London and met very nice people there. Canada House in those days processed the people they wanted: young, white, good-looking people. Away they went — everything was opened up. There happened to be a lot of Indians and other people and they didn't get the same treatment as we got. From November to April, I saved up the money and got myself organized, with my passport and the whole works. I had a job waiting for me at Montreal General Hospital, arranged through the Immigration Department.

We arrived in April 1961 on this terrible day on Air Canada. I had chosen Quebec because of the French culture, the Catholic faith, the space that would be there. And I knew there had been Irish settlements in Montreal. But it was a terrible surprise to arrive in Quebec only to find a Canada in the middle of a political crisis. I loved Quebec. It was beautiful. Montreal was a beautiful city, so much nicer than London. My thought used to be: Why didn't I come here at eighteen? I was impressed by the friendliness of the Canadians. They were genuine and welcoming and would tell you who their Irish ancestors were and just loved to be around you. I liked the French people. This was a very, very different feeling from what I had encountered in England.

One of the first things I did when I had few dollars after working a few weeks in Montreal was to go to Quebec City. I had read somewhere in my history books of Ireland about the Irish settlements in Quebec. I wasn't aware right away of the Quiet Revolution in Quebec, but it was happening. By '63, however, we were well aware of the Quiet Revolution becoming an explosive revolution and it was a bit unnerving. I could see the similarities between Ireland and Quebec. It's very deep-rooted and it's very hard to cure.

I got married in 1964. The man was from Alberta, he's Canadian. I had just been thinking: Well, I'm going to go to university; I'm going to go to McGill and get my nursing degree. Then I met this man. I called my friend Maura and told her. She was tired of New York and I said, "So come up. You'll like Montreal." So she came and settled in and started to work and she married my husband's friend. My husband and I moved to Sudbury when the bombings got under way. It was an unhappy period of my life. I didn't want to leave Montreal. I didn't believe in leaving it but we did. My two children were born in Sudbury. Over the years I've thought about one advantage of my children being born in Canada: I won't have to go through the pain that my parents went through seeing their children leave. At least here your children will be close by. You won't have that terrible pain and hopefully your children won't.

In the last few years — I think since the troubles in the North of Ireland — Irish people are not really welcome in Ontario. I'm not the only one that thinks that, a lot of my friends think that. The first time I voiced this opinion to this friend, she said, "You better believe it!" And I was so startled. I thought I was the only one that held this belief. The power is focused in Toronto and it's of a certain nature. We're living in Ottawa now so we're very conscious of it. One aspect of our lives which is important is the school system. That traditionally had been a battleground between the Irish Catholics together with the French against the big English system, the system in power. So you're very exposed to these breezes that blow in from Toronto when it comes to money and funding for programs.

Did my dream for Canada materialize? In ways. The country will always be here and it's a nice land. I'd like to get away from the big cities, though. Canada is a land of space which should be respected and treated properly. I get very concerned when I see the way people live, the disregard they have for beautiful things. And I'm very disturbed about the way the government treats Native People. I think a bit of introspection wouldn't hurt Canada at this point. They get so concerned with what's happening in China, for instance, and I think we'd better be careful. A bit of introspection would see how Native People are faring. Are they happy with what happened to them any more than we were happy in the west of Ireland? Look what happened to us. There are some similarities.

Some days when I'm in a mood I think this is all too much for me: I can't stand one more glitz. I can't stand people being so disrespectful when they come in to visit the sick. Are people really like this nowadays? Is this what it's come to? When you see people that stretch out with their dirty shoes on a bed you've just made or fixed up. Or they have their kids dancing on a chair that a patient with some surgery would be sitting on. Or they'll take the full breadth of a corridor, straggling in with their drinks and food from the downstairs cafeteria and spilling it. I can't believe it. This immediate kind of gratification and being so smart and having fax machines and all this. I laugh when I hear the word fax: a fax machine with no facts.

My life has been fragmented because the Church has become fragmented. It doesn't know its own direction and has fallen by the wayside, sullied and stained by some modern theologies or modern ideas that aren't well defined. So you get people arguing and doing their own thing and looking for salvation in their own way. Now that's very fine with me; I've no quarrel with that. What I miss is that we don't have a quiet place to go and contemplate and pray or be with God. There is every second some demand that we do this or we do that. Or this is the way we do it and you have to do it this way.

Give the sign of peace. This is an awful hypocrisy — you could do your whole bloody day's business here without speaking to a soul. Those traditions of Christian caring are being broken down and replaced by your so-called social workers. I call them the sharks of society, the sharks of the medical world. Some of them can be very good, but you can't replace that Christian caring, that sympathy and understanding of another person's suffering and pain. There is something about bringing over a dish or a cake or minding people's place or property while they're grieving. You could be dead here before anyone would know or care.

It wasn't like that when I was growing up. God no. We always helped our neighbours. When my father died that's what the eulogy was about. The priest was new and he got up and admitted that he didn't know Jack, Jack the Fiddler — he was a bit of a drinker, we won't say how much but he used to like his pint; I try to remember the music and the lovely songs. When the priest asked people what was Jack like, he was told that Jack the Fiddler was a good neighbour. We were known for being good neighbours. I miss that.

As an Irish woman you have to survive. There's no mother or grandmother or aunts around. There's no one to advise you.

Nothing. You're on your own and the system in Canada operates against women quite clearly. I read with a bit of humour that the Toronto Police Force got a good raise recently. There are nurses out on strike in B.C. right now who work just as hard as a policeman today and they're not getting any $48,000 a year. I advise every young girl: Don't go into nursing. There are days I feel like I'll take this cap off and I'll go away and you'll never see me nursing any more because there's a whole erosion of what you had dedicated yourself to be, whether it was to be a good teacher or a good nurse.

I don't like this challenging of life and death. What we as country people knew was that we had no control on either and we accepted what was going on. If somebody died they were waked. If somebody was born it was great. Life went on. Prolonging life with technology often robs the dying of their dignity which I find very disturbing. I don't like to witness this. People can't deal with death, they have to hide it. They can't deal with birth, they have to make some drama out of it. They have to have cameras and pictures. They can't integrate this and take something out of it without all this performance.

Life is more difficult being a woman. I'm in my fifties. From the traditional way I was brought up in Ireland, I was very conscious that because I was a girl I was not going to get a fair deal in the education system in Ireland. I was stuck with nursing or teaching. That's fine, but then you've got to go out looking for a husband. There was one reason you looked for a husband: to get your house. It's only recently that you could get a house without a husband. Without a man you weren't much. That was the philosophy back then.

Now the world has changed a lot. Unfortunately, I didn't get out of my profession. I didn't un-mother myself. I got kids, a husband, a house, dogs and all this stuff to take care of, and women get to do the work. Women still get to do nursing, typing, standing at the banks, lifting the big grocery bags, and minding the kids in the daycare centre. Meanwhile, men are off with their nice briefcases. They have the fax machines and, I guess, men still have the facts. Not totally, I suppose; the world is changing.

I was fortunate I came with a profession, I came when I was young, and I was free when I came. But I look at the immigrant women coming in today and they're not getting the same crack-of-the-whip as the men are getting. I wouldn't want to be an immigrant woman today coming in from South America or Vietnam. I'm a nurse and I look at people very closely and I see the same pain and degradation and everything else. It still goes on today. Just different people coming in, different waves of immigration, different needs.

It would have been far more serene if I'd have stayed in Ireland, the west of Ireland. I'd have had a much more peaceful life. I'd trade it any day. You see the hardship of the women in Ireland is really the same hardship that the women have here in Canada. But we had our traditions and our songs, our culture, our language, our beliefs. They were eroded, but not totally. There is always something in me that is very Irish when I'm with Irish people, or I hear the music or just sit down by the sea. Every day of my life here I always see where I grew up in my mind's eye. I see the fuchsia, the church and the hills and the sea and the people. I see the people the most and I hear what they used to say and how good and caring they were.

Notes

1. A common term meaning the land or the farm.
2. A small boat.
3. Baskets used for carrying turf.

This Is What It Was All About

Nellie O'Donnell

*Nellie O'Donnell lives in Windsor, Ontario.
Her name has been changed.*

I was born in 1907 in Tipperary, Ireland. I was an illegitimate child. In Ireland in them days having an illegitimate child wasn't tolerated — it was a disgrace to the woman. After I was born, mother had to stay in the hospital and work in the hospital laundry and kitchen for her support and mine. The only time she could see me was to nurse me. Her father disowned her for quite a while, so she went through hell. Mother told me that I reminded her of her sin all the time — it was hard for her to live it down. My mother gave me out to some couple to look after me. Then my mother got married and the people that she gave me up to couldn't look after me because the man was blind and the woman got cancer. So Mother was asked to take me back.

As time went on, I had five step-brothers and step-sisters. As I grew up I didn't know I was an illegitimate child. Before the sixth child was born, the First World War had broken out and my step-father joined the British Army. It was then I discovered there was some dispute about my name. The pension he was getting from the army wasn't enough to keep us going and mother had to take in washing from the English soldiers stationed in Tipperary. She used to go down with the donkey and cart to bring the soldiers' laundry home to wash it.

She was pregnant with the sixth child, when I overheard her complaining to my step-father that she didn't have enough money to feed us. She asked him about claiming me and giving me the right to his name. I didn't know all this. I figured they were my real father and mother. He didn't like the idea, but she was a little bit scared of what might happen to him in the trenches and she wanted to be secure. When I first discovered I was illegitimate it bothered me. In them days, if it got out around, you were discriminated against for being an "outside" child and your sisters and brothers were discriminated against also.

It was terrible when my step-father came home from the war. He had been shell-shocked.[1] He'd go out with the boys to the pub and they'd drink and laugh and be merry. Then, when he'd come home, he wasn't operating with the full deck. He'd beat my mother up and then I used to have to take my young sister and hide her with me. My mother would hide someplace with my four brothers and sisters until he quietened down. When he went to bed we'd come home. We'd sneak in quietly. The next morning when he'd get up he'd see mother with a pair of black eyes. He used to say to her, "Who did that? Tell me who did — I'll fix that so-and-so." I got so tired of listening to that.

Then he started to where he abused me. When I rebelled he told me that I was nothing but a bastard. It was sexual abuse. He would only do this when mother and him would be fighting and mother would leave and go home to her father. She would put me in charge and tell me what I had to do for my sisters and brothers and she'd take the youngest one with her. This time I made my mind up I wasn't going to stay and I told her about the abuse. She had a very stern look on her face and she got kind of mad and said she was going to go and talk to the priest about it. So off we went to see the priest. He took her in first for an interview and they left me sitting in the waiting place he had in his home.

Then the priest came out and he took me and interviewed me. He said that she wanted to have me put away and what was it all about? I said, "I'll tell you the truth, Father. I don't mind being taken away because I'll get educated and I'll get a better standard of being brought up." I wanted something I could face the world with. They were using me as a maid and I wasn't getting to school every day like I should have. My mother wasn't taking my part. I didn't tell the priest exactly about the sexual part of it. He then talked to the two of us for a little while about us getting along. He didn't blame me. He kind of made me feel that mother should be more responsible than she was, that I needed some help.

I made up my mind that I had to get out of there. I ran away from home a couple of times and worked for a farmer in Tipperary. The wages were small and I had to be up at four o'clock in the morning to go out and milk the cows. The farmer himself used to come to wake me up and pull me out by the top of the head. I used to have to go out on that farm with a canvas apron, mark off the land, pick stones, leave them in piles, and move the bushes over. There were no pails or wheelbarrows, but I was so willing to work. No wonder I'm full of arthritis today. I got no proper schooling because my father said girls were not to be educated — they were just meant to be wives and have children, do the housework and cook the meals. Boys had to have training. So I had the idea: I'm a female; I'm just a maid for my husband. I must have a family for him and he's the one that was to work.

It was 1927 when I left Ireland for Canada. I was twenty. We had to take the train from Tipperary to Belfast. My father stayed overnight to see me onto the boat which was leaving the next morning. When I got on the boat this minister came up to me and was lecturing me about going to another country and about my church and about this and that. The things he'd come out with! I looked at him and I said, "I'm Catholic." And he said, "Why didn't you tell me that before!" And he just snatched the papers out of my hand and took off. I thought: Oh my God, is that what it's going to be like out in the world? The boat coming over was packed. Young people, the cream of the land coming out. When we started to separate off the boat everybody got kind of sad because we were all going in different directions.

I arrived in Montreal and then I took a train to Toronto where my step-father's sister lived. The first thing my step-aunt said to me when I arrived in Toronto was that I was halfways across the Atlantic before she found out that I was not her brother's child. I was coming through the Immigration and there had to be somebody in Canada that would sign papers for me. She wanted nothing to do with me. I would have to pay the extra fare — they gave me the impression that I would be deported. I thought: Oh my God, have I brought that all the ways to Canada with me? I didn't want anybody to know I was illegitimate after I got here.

Canada was on the verge of the Dirty Thirties — the Big Depression — when I arrived. Nobody knows what it was like, only them that lived it like myself. They were putting us in awful jobs. Bringing boatloads of us out — farm help and domestic help — from Ireland or wherever they could pick them up. And the Canadians were disgusted. As soon as they'd find out you were an immigrant, they'd swear at you. We had nothing to do with it because they used to put big posters on our railroad stations over in Ireland about the land of the milk and honey over here. All the money! You'd swear to God you just had to get up on a bush and shake it down and pick it up off the ground, the money was so plentiful. I found out that wasn't so.

I found Toronto hard to cope with. I got into domestic work, like most Irish women. Domestic work was a hell of a job in some of these places. I was a maid in one of the big houses where they had a cleaning woman, a laundry woman and a nursemaid. I was the waitress on the table as well as the cook. They made me stand at the table and I had to take the plate from one side and serve from the other. Then I had to stand at the end of the table, wait while they ate, and serve the next course. That job wasn't too bad, but one day I took a fit of sneezing. They watched and when everything was all over and her company was gone the woman of the house said, "You Irish people don't know what germs are like over there!" She let me go. I had to go out on the street with no money at nine or ten o'clock at night. It was during the Depression, when people were working for practically nothing. They knew they could go to the hostel any time and get domestic help.

There was discrimination in Canada back then. I got another job with a doctor answering his phone, but he said my Irish accent was so bad that his patients couldn't understand. He said he had to let me go for that. Even now people think I have quite an Irish accent. After the British were pulled out of Ireland and we got our freedom, they were getting us back to speaking Gaelic, but I was all mixed up then with the Gaelic and the English language. I was in a turmoil. I knew what I was saying but they were complaining about the reception of my voice on the phone. Of course, we didn't have phones in Ireland and I wasn't used to talking on the phone. I thought I was speaking the King's English, but they didn't understand it.

Oftentimes Irish Catholics were called "Dogan." Sometimes they'd call you "a bloody Irish Dogan," when they'd get mad. That's what they called us in Toronto. Later on they called us "Micks." It was mostly Protestants who called us such names, but other people would get it in there too. In Toronto, the 12th of July was a big day for them Orangemen.[2] It was terrible. If you were Catholic you had to keep the hell out of there when the Protestants were marching on the 12th.

Then I got into a lot of problems with the jobs they placed me in because there was sexual abuse in Canada in them days. I worked in one place where the husband was a businessman. Used to have to sleep in the attic. He used to have meetings about once a month and his wife was away a couple of times while I was there. After the men were gone, he used to come upstairs to try to get into my room. There was no lock on my door, but there was one of them big old-fashioned sewing machines which I used to pull up against the door to keep him out. He'd pound, wanting to come in. "Let me in, Nellie. Let me in!" This night I'd had enough of being put in these kind of jobs, so I told him, "You'd better get away from me. I've got my window opened!" We were on Dundas Street in Toronto and I was going to holler for help. He said some abusive word back to me. I left that job.

Then I found a job in a laundry. If you really wanted you could find jobs that the Canadian people didn't want. It was hard work in the laundries in them days. We had to clean curtains, but they weren't nylon like they are today. They were lace curtains that had to be dried on wooden rods and adjusted to the same measurement as the curtain before it was washed. And then they had to be pulled out and folded. Maybe I was getting $12 or $13 a week

ADDRESS:
WOMEN'S BRANCH

CANADA

IN YOUR REPLY REFER TO
No. 2206
KINDLY DO NOT WRITE ON MORE THAN
ONE SUBJECT IN ANY ONE LETTER

Department of Immigration and Colonization

TORONTO-2, ONTARIO, Aug 31st 1927

R.

URGENT.

Dear

      I understand that you came forward under the reduced rate, namely £4.10, and that it was understood you would engage in domestic employment. I am now informed that you are in factory work. If this is the case, we must ask you to refund the difference between the reduced rate and the full third class fare.

      In view of the fact that the reduced rate is given ti girls who will undertake to engage in domestic employment and remain in that occupation for a reasonable length of time, the balance of the reduced fare is given in the form of a Loan. If a girl does not adhere to her agreement to engage in domestic work, she will be asked to pay full third class fare.

      Please let me know at your very earliest convenience if it is ture that you are in factory work, and if so, what arrangements you can make regarding repayment of the difference between the reduced and the regular third class fare.

Yours very truly,

Woman Officer.

Toronto, Ontario.

Letter to Nellie O'Donnell from the Department of Immigration and Colonization.

for working in the laundry. I worked there from eight o'clock in the morning to six o'clock at night, and overtime you just got straight time for it. I was doing very well and my forelady was very, very nice to me. But then I was getting letters from the Immigration authorities, telling me that I hadn't filled my contract because I left domestic service and went into laundry work which I was not supposed to do.

So I got married. The reason I got married was because I was afraid of being deported. I wasn't going to be able to pay the fare. I was afraid that they would contact my parents and I'd have to go back home. That's the last place I wanted to go. I saw myself getting out of it through marriage. My maiden name would be gone and Immigration wouldn't be able to find me, I thought. But somebody, in the meanwhile, reported me for doing it even though I was married. Immigration kept telling me they wanted that money because I didn't fulfil the contract of staying in the domestic jobs. They kept asking me for the extra fare but I couldn't give it to them because the wages were terribly poor.

I married an Englishman — talk about being abusive. He was. He used to hit me. Then I got pregnant. When I told my forelady that I was pregnant she said to me, "You'd better keep yourself well laced up. It's against the law for pregnant women to be hired in factories. Hang in there as long as you can," she said, "and I'll keep you." She thought I was a real good worker, but I had to leave the job when I started to show pregnancy because the matron would've gotten into trouble.

The marriage didn't work out. There were things I couldn't take from him. The beatings. He couldn't hold a job at first, but then he got a job driving pickup trucks from Toronto to Hamilton. He was so jealous that I'd have to go in the front of the truck with him to Hamilton. I couldn't take the driving on account of being pregnant, so I refused to go any more. That got his back up. When the time came for me to have my baby, I was living in an attic apartment where you couldn't get out. There was so many flights of stairs to go down. After she was born he got so flusterated that there was a baby girl instead of a baby boy. He wanted nothing to do with the baby girl. She's yours, not mine, was his attitude.

I couldn't take any more. I met a woman that was from Kapuskasing, in Toronto, and I was telling this woman what I was going through. She told me she could get a job for me with this man who had three children in Kapuskasing. He was a businessman. I took the job in Kapuskasing, under the name of Mrs. Smith so my husband wouldn't find me and the baby. I don't know whether this man's wife was dead or whether she was separated. That never came up. He had three children. The older ones were nice, but the youngest one was just like a son to me. My job was housework, just like a mother. Housekeeper, in other words. But I got very little pay because I wanted to get away from the situation that I was in. The room and board was supposed to be a lot, but I was putting up with more — for less room and board — with my husband than I was working for a stranger.

At first he was very good to me. He would take me to different places, out for evenings. We'd go on picnics with his little son and my daughter. But he wanted more out of it than that. Then he tried to get sexually involved with me but I would brush him off. Usually, he would leave me alone, but this one time he got drunk and he came home and raped me. His daughter called the police and he was arrested. I didn't know what to do. He was in jail and there was a court day coming up. I had to get out of that house. I'd nowhere to go up in that little town in the bush. So I contacted my husband, hoping that maybe he had changed in that time. I felt bad about it but there was nothing I could do. My husband came up to Kapuskasing and he brought another man with him. He talked very pleasant to me and said we'd go back to Toronto and we'd do this and we'd do that. Before we left Kapuskasing, he asked me if I'd go and get a package of cigarettes for him and buy myself a little treat at the drugstore. By this time my baby was starting to walk. He said to leave the baby in the car with him, and I did. When I came out of the drugstore he was gone with the baby. I screamed blue murder. I went to the police station and I had a warrant put out for his arrest.

The judge used to come to town once a week on Wednesdays. When he came he asked me if I had the papers made out that I had custody of the child. I didn't know the first thing about custodies. He said he was sorry, I should've been told that I had to have these papers. The police had to withdraw the summons for my husband. I had a month's pay, very small, coming to me. In the meanwhile, this man's rape case came up and I backed out of everything, because my child was stolen. I didn't want to hurt the man, anyway, because he had a family. So here I was: I had nothing. I had no family to go to. No father. No mother. No sisters. No brothers. And my in-laws didn't want nothing to do with me.

I went back to Toronto and I stayed with this lady I had met from Kapuskasing till I got myself straightened around. She helped me out and gave me some money. I wanted to find the baby. I found out my husband was working for this transport company, so I went up right to where he worked in the transport company delivering ice. Them was the days they delivered ice from door to door — when they lifted up the tops of the ice boxes and put a block of ice into it. I was sitting there, waiting in the office for him to come back to fill his truck with ice. When he saw me, he said, "Well, I don't want the bloody kid, but I sure got you in hot water, didn't I! And look where I've got you — right back where I want you." I held my temper. I knew I had no custody of the child, but the judge also told me in Kapuskasing that possession was nine-tenths of the law. He said, "I'm not advising you what to do, but you can do exactly what he did to you, providing you don't go up on his property. You can still snatch your kid. And it'll just go on: snatch, snatch, snatch."

I knew where I stood then. My husband said, "I'm going out for lunch. Do you want to come out and have lunch with me?" He was smiling because he figured he had me. I said, "Yes, we'll go for lunch. Where is the baby?" He said, "She was with my mother, but she's not there now. Mother couldn't keep her." He had her in some sort of place where they took them in and kept them day and night. All I wanted to do was get my hands on her. When I got to this place, while I was talking to this woman the office door was open and I spied my daughter. She wasn't able to walk any more. She spied me and looked at me, and I thought: Oh my God, I want to go and see her. I wanted to hug her and hold her. The woman there said that the reputation she'd got of me was that I wasn't a fit mother. She was not, under any circumstances, to let me see my daughter. I cried and left there and I came out and sat in the park opposite the building that she was in. I sat there and cried all that night.

I was planning for an opportunity to steal her again. But I was told that under the circumstances — where I had no security, no money and no home — he would have control of the child. He was a man and he could get a job. He was gone one morning looking for a job. It was all arranged. This woman that knew me said if I wanted to get out of there she would pay me my fare to go back to Kapuskasing. A man would pick me up with my baby and a few clothes. And my God, we met my husband out on the street, but he didn't recognize me in the truck because he was reading the paper. I got away. I went to Union Station and pulled out of there right away. People helped me in Kapuskasing. People would help you a little bit then. You'd get somebody to give you a place to stay, even if it was only on the floor. I did little bits of housework for this woman I was staying with.

I met my second husband up there. He decided he wanted to marry me and told me how much he loved me. But he said, "I don't want to have that child. Don't give me an answer right now. I'll give you twenty-four hours to think it over." I'd known him maybe a few months. He was a nice man. I thought he was all right: He had a steady job and I had a feeling that I would have a home and security. This is what it was all about. When he went to walk away I called him back and I said, "It's no use. I don't need twenty-four hours to think it over. My mind is made up right now. I'm going to muster my fare together and I'm going back to Ireland and I'm taking my child with me. Forget about me." So he looked at me for a little while — he felt kind of bad — hugged me a little bit and I started to cry. He said, "Okay, I'll see you tomorrow night." The next night when he came to see me he said, "You know, I admire you for the pluck and the courage you've got. Maybe you made the right decision. You want your baby, keep your baby, and we'll get married anyway." Oh boy! And then I said, "I can have one for you." He said, "That's okay. There'll be one for me." Things went all right and he was very good to that little girl. Oh my God, he'd be after me if I scolded her.

Then we moved into Timmins and he got a job there with the Hollinger Mines. I had another daughter. We bought this piece of land near Timmins and between the two of us we built our own home. We were both working and doing it on our off-hours. It was on the side of a ravine by a lake. I helped him dig the basement out. We had permafrost up there that never thaws out no matter how hot it gets. When you're digging you have to leave it for so many days then go back and dig again, so it's thawing out as you go along. I got a job at a local hotel and he went to Yellowknife and worked there in the mines and then he could only come home once a month. He'd come home to visit over the weekend. A few men would have to charter a plane. Things went very well and the children got grown and the first thing you know they're teenagers. One wanted to take a business course and the other one was still going to school. I had her taking skating lessons and life was beginning to settle down.

The kids were still going to school when we moved from Timmins to Windsor, Ontario, during the Second World War. I didn't find Windsor bad to get work and my husband got a job on the railroad where there was a shortage of men during the Second World War. As the war went on, they promised all the men their jobs when they came back, so he had to leave it and give the jobs back to the men when they came back from the army. Windsor was a place I thought I didn't want to stay in, but I thought that I could work and make some money. We could fix up a house and put the basement underneath. These were the plans we had made. Both our kids were going to school here in Windsor. Then when he lost his job with the railroad he went into construction work. My daughters both married. One was nineteen when she got married and the other was twenty.

I didn't gain that much by coming to Canada. I caused myself a lot of stress and strain because I had no family here, and during the Depression it was terrible. I lost a baby in the Depression, through malnutrition, and I wasted to nothing. Then there was times I had to eat the leftovers so the children were fed so they could get to school. They paid you twenty-five cents an hour if you went out and scrubbed people's floors and washed their walls down. Which I did quite often to get an extra few dollars. I'd be so tired. In Ireland if we had known that it was as tough in Canada as it was we would never have come here. As far as my younger days in Canada — I wish I'd never come. But after I got in here and got my roots and started having my children, then my life was here and my family was dying off over there in Ireland. I would like to go back and see where all my brothers and sisters and father and mother are buried. All my relatives. I would stay in a hotel or something because there are no relatives there any more to go and visit.

Life is all right if you are ready and prepared to tough it. You can't stand back and cry. With everything that happened to me, I had to get back up again. There was nobody there to help me. If I didn't help myself, nobody else was going to. If I made a mistake, I had to rectify it. I had nobody to go to and in them days you couldn't get the help that they've got now.

I went to church a couple of months ago but I didn't go back again. I went there, thinking maybe I would find something there that would strengthen me. I'm going through a depression in my life now because my husband is gone and I'm alone after all my working years. I worked very hard in my life. I thought I could find something to lean on but I couldn't. I found the Church the same as I did years ago when I was in Ireland. I met a nice fellow. We talked about the Church and I told him that I used to belong to the Catholic Women's League in Uranium City — there was a Father Brown up there. I've got pictures of Father Brown with his teams of dogs; they used to get to the services by using a team of dogs because we had a lot of snow there, pretty near all year. This man gave some literature to read. One book he gave me was *What*

Would Hell Be Like. I didn't need to read a book about what hell would be like. I figure what I'd been through in life was hell. And I thought: Oh Jesus, hell is right here.

Notes

1. Known today as "post-traumatic stress disorder," and highly publicized in the aftermath of the Vietnam War.
2. For decades, Toronto's dignitaries turned out for the Orange parade on July 12. By 1920, the city was home to fifty-nine branches of the Lodge. For more on the mood of Toronto, "the Belfast of Canada," in the 1930s, see Cyril H. Levitt and William Shaffir, *The Riot at Christie Pits* (Toronto: Lester & Orpen Dennys, 1987), pp. 29–31. In that work, reporter Jocko Thomas describes the Christie Pits area of Toronto, a neighbourhood known in the 1930s for its anti-Catholicism and anti-Semitism:

   > A lot of Orange people lived in that area....There used to be trouble between the Catholics and the Protestants in that area. Catholic kids going to school used to be waylaid by Protestant children coming home at lunch time and attacked. I used to see those things going on. I got my eye blackened one time by taking the part of one guy, Patty London, who was getting beaten up by some of these Orange kids, who'd come from Orange families. (p. 183)

   The power of the Orange Lodge had long ranged beyond the North of Ireland. Its members abroad pledged to resist any efforts to weaken the British Empire and British influence. In Victorian Toronto, "Through its membership [the Orange Lodge] controlled the militia, the police, civic employment, city hall ward politics and the work place." (See Murray W. Nicolson, "Peasants in an Urban Society: The Irish Catholics in Victorian Toronto," in

Gathering Place: Peoples and Neighbourhoods of Toronto, 1834–1945, (Toronto: Multicultural History Society of Ontario, 1985), p. 65. Orange power would not diminish significantly until after the Second World War.

Faith

Anna Copeland

Anna Copeland, a Protestant woman aged eighty-two, is from Co. Tipperary. She lives in Montreal, Quebec.

I believe profoundly in God and the goodness of God. God to me is somebody that I have a very close relationship with. I talk to Him as if He were with me. Whenever I've had trouble or problems in my life, I'd go to church on Sunday. And I'd talk to God in my own way and somehow the sermon preached that day was meant for me. I'd come home feeling very light.

Many, many times I've felt that God has touched me and said, "Don't worry, all will be well." I've never allowed my faith to be shaken, ever. I've always believed everything's for the best. I'm not fanatical about my religion and I never try to persuade other people. If they have different beliefs, that's their business. My faith is a great comfort to me, so I suppose I'm lucky in that respect.

I believe in the afterlife. I know that when I die my spirit will be with my loved ones again. There's got to be a life after, a better life. It's a great comfort when you don't have the fear of dying, when you know that you're going to a better place.

Memories

Mary Clifford

I met Mary Clifford at the Father Dowd Nursing Home in Montreal when I was there doing the interviews for this book. Mary was born in Catherciveen, Co. Kerry, in 1907. Sometime in the 1920s she emigrated to Montreal, where, I was told, she spent most of her life working as a housekeeper.

When I got to her little room in the nursing home she was sitting beside the window looking out. She was thin and frail. It was her hands I noticed most. Little blue veins meandered under the translucent skin and told a tale of universal time and place.

Mary could not comprehend my presence. I could not comprehend her absence. I would get back a memory or a song completely unrelated to my questions — yet there were moments in the silences when I thought we understood each other completely. Mary's thin voice would rise to the highest notes of "The Last Rose of Summer" and end on a long note of triumph followed by a small sigh and a silence. In the silences between Mary's renditions she looked out the window with that faraway look. In the same silences of long ago between tales we used to look into the peat fire burning in the hearth.

Finally, Mary became impatient with my questions. She looked at me, with her head tilted slightly to one side as though peering out at me, and she said, "Go 'way now, you'll get no more news from me." Then a pause, a further tilt of her head, a twinkle in her eye and very slowly a little smile streaming across her lips, in a soft Kerry accent she said, "Aren't you de little divileen anyway." I put away my tape recorder and my questions and sat still. Then we both looked out the window together in silence.

Mary Clifford died on April 5, 1990, at the Father Dowd Nursing Home in Montreal.

It Would Mellow a Lot
of This Harshness

Síle Ní Bhreanach

Síle Ní Bhreanach lived in St. John's, Newfoundland, at the time of the interview. She has since moved to British Columbia. Her name has been changed.

I was one of five children. My sister was four years older than me and we had two older brothers. One brother was two years younger than me, and there was a miscarriage or a stillbirth. These were not discussed either. They were all the will of the Lord. We were a fairly traditional middle-class Irish family: conservative, kept to ourselves a lot. My mother was deeply religious. She had been brought up by a grand-uncle of hers who was very wealthy and she was educated by the Ursuline nuns, the snob order of the day.

My poor mother was a slave to the Church. She went to three Masses every day and we were all brought along from the time we could barely toddle. She was up at five o'clock in the morning to get the seven o'clock Mass. She'd come home and get breakfast, go back to nine o'clock Mass, come home again and go to ten o'clock Mass and we were brought along. Then we stayed for benediction. She never really looked after herself. She always said her husband came first and the children. Where the boys were concerned, they were spoiled. My sister and myself did all the work, the scrubbing and the washing and the polishing.

My father was a good ten years older than my mother, not uncommon in Ireland at the time. He was somewhere in his forties when I was born in 1942 and my mother was thirty-three. Of course, they never discussed age — that was taboo. My father was fairly easy-going. He read all day long, smoked a pipe and had his favourite chair in the dining room. He worked with a local company in the accounts department in the town where we lived. My father rarely went to mass on Sunday. He had been head of the Vincent de Paul and he had been head of the Stella Maris, a club for visiting sailors from all over the world who came into port. But he had some kind of a run-in with some of the clergy — that was never discussed.

The years went by and my father died suddenly of a heart attack when I was seventeen. My mother died six weeks after my father. It was a very strange relationship. I never saw them embracing or hugging or kissing — that wasn't done. We always had to kiss our father good night going to bed, and my mother likewise. But there was no warmth or affection.

As Irish women we were always told that we should be seen but not heard. That was always drilled into us from the earliest of times. Consequently, I lived in a world of fantasy and I never had a full grasp on what was going on outside in life until I went out into life myself. I look back on my mother — she really had no life. I look at my aunts who were not married, and they seemed to have a better life. I look at educated women who are teachers or doctors or professional photographers — many of whom could never make it to the top, while very mediocre men were getting positions above them.

I did realize there was something radically wrong. Nevertheless it never bothered me to have a major role as a woman in society. I never wanted to see myself going to the top. I saw myself always as having influence from the back seat: giving advice and helping people and having a lot of influence without getting my name mentioned. I never wanted the limelight. Yet I would like to encourage other women to get to the top and I would use my own influence from behind the scenes to get them there.

Eventually, I decided to go and do nursing. I did my training in a Dublin hospital, then trained as a psychiatric nurse. I loved working in psychiatry. Then I got a position at a private psychiatric hospital for "wayward clerics," of all people! I was one of the first females to be appointed.

I couldn't understand from Adam what was going on. They were all alcoholics, as a result of deep-rooted sex problems. There were transvestites, drug addicts, perverts — everything you could possibly think of. A lot of them were child molesters. That was never discussed because once they were put there they were kept silent. They were put there to keep them out of the way and they were disowned by their bishops.

I remember Cardinal Conway, the Cardinal of the day, coming down to open a new alcoholic unit at this hospital. There were a number of his priests from the diocese of Down and Connor. When we heard Cardinal Conway was coming, everything was bedecked in grandeur and splendour and all these poor fellows were out in their best Sunday suits, waiting. We were under the impression that the Cardinal was really going to visit. So they wined and they dined him and they had the best of everything and the media were there and, lo-and-behold, Conway left and never even as much as asked how one of those priests were.

There was one priest who was a compulsive gambler and an alcoholic, but a very likeable man. He spent his day down at the bookie's office. Red in the face, he'd walk maybe five miles into the city to put a bob[1] on a horse. And he'd come back stoaters drunk. He let out a string of curses when Conway had gone. I said, "You're perfectly right. Say what you feel because Conway's an absolute disgrace." To think he never even bothered even to ask about them! That really opened my eyes to the so-called Christian charity they were preaching to others. That changed my whole outlook on Catholicism in Ireland, and I started thinking very deeply. We had accepted our religion because we were born into it and never questioned anything; we were told we didn't question. As I saw it, we were never brought up to be Christians; we were brought up to be Catholics. There is a very big difference.

This "wayward hospital" for about 100 clerics then decided to allow female patients to be admitted. I never thought I'd see the day they'd have an integrated ward with male and female and clergy thrown in. There were about twenty in that particular ward, with just little screens between the beds, so you would have a female in one bed and a male in another bed. They were all in the horrors and the DTS. They didn't know who they were or what they were. Nuns were using language that I never heard and priests were calling them all sorts of names: whores and sluts and even stronger words. The nuns in turn called the priests bastards and whoremasters. I'd hear Father So-and-So say, "You bloody bitch. You were whoring around all night long and you're wearing a habit all day long."

I was sixteen years old before I realized that a nun was a woman like myself. I thought they were another sex, that you had male, female, and nuns. I never saw them as being feminine because of the way they were dressed, because they were devoid of any femininity. It was only then in this hospital that I realized they are human beings. They are women and they must have emotional and sexual feelings like all of us. In this hospital they were under the influence of a drug because they were addicted to it and then all of a sudden they poured out their hearts and used language that we don't associate with the clergy.

The priests were really expressing their true feelings about women. That's when I started thinking. It wasn't that I couldn't be shocked, but I kept saying to myself: This is exactly how we have been treated. The priests, when they were under the influence of alcohol or drugs, treated the nuns and women in the place with contempt and disdain.

I remember one lady who was pregnant. She'd had a psychiatric crisis and she was admitted to the hospital. Now, there was this alcoholic priest from the west of Ireland and he was a real old parish priest and very, very conservative and obviously had great influence and great power. She was passing his bed one day and he was always leering at her over his glasses and he said, "You whore! What are you doing in here with the clergy?" Then I heard him berating her from a height. "You're not fit to be here! You have to wait until you're fit to deal with the likes of me! Do you realize who I am?" I thought: Maybe he's not of his right mind. But there was an element of truth in what he was saying because that's exactly how they treated the women. He didn't feel inhibited at the time saying it. I had to reassure this poor woman not to pay any attention, that he didn't know what he was saying.

There was another lady who was very liberated for Ireland at the time — that was around 1965. She had come from a very well-to-do family in the west of Ireland and she had a double-bar-relled name. She was alcoholic. This particular priest knew her family. When she was going down the ward one day — the long wards that they had in Ireland — she said, "Oh hello, Father. How are you?" He said, "You speak to me? You're a whore and a slut! Be more in your line to go home and look after your children!" She took him on and I was really delighted. "Who the hell do you think you are? Just because you wear a Rome collar doesn't mean you can lord me around," she said. He really got red in the face; I was sure he was going to get a stroke. He deserved every bit of it.

I had the onerous task of searching some of these priests for drugs and they would deny it. They would lie, face-to-face with me. In the breviary I would find the Seconal, a barbiturate, tipped out of the capsule and put through the leaves. When they were reading their office, flicking over these pages they would inhale it up their nose. A Dominican theologian looked straight at me one day and said, "How dare you question me! Do you realize who I am?" I said, "Yes, I'm perfectly well aware of who you are. You're a goddamned liar." I found the drugs nicely packed in the hemline of his coat. It was very sad, but society in Ireland had them the way they were. They had the power and the control. They were never questioned or challenged and now they were in a helpless situation. Yet they were fighting to the bitter end: They were still right and we were wrong. I didn't take any of the nonsense. I stood up to them.

The Church has always looked on the female as being dirty and only there for the pleasures of man or just for procreation. Confession really turned me off. I haven't been to confession, I'm sure, in thirty years. I'll always remember one priest asking, "Do you have wet dreams?" Now, I never knew what wet dreams were. My mother was always going to confession, and I'm sure she felt so guilty every time she had sex without having a pregnancy that she was going to be damned. I remember one priest said to her something about getting pleasure and that really upset her; she was in a state of guilt for months on end. The Church had tremendous influence over women and everything was done out of fear and out of dread. And there was no real happiness, no real love. Everything was a duty. This hospital really started bringing all this to mind to me.

I never saw myself as one to get married; I was very particular about male company. I had plenty of male friends but I always liked older men. When my husband came along, he turned out to be a year and a half younger. I'd always said I'd never marry a younger man. I had no time for them. I felt they were immature and we wouldn't have much in common. But he turned out to be a great talker and really got the best out of one. So I was married within twelve months of meeting him and we went to Leeds to live, because he was doing his master's degree in science at Leeds University. Thirteen months after we got married, my first baby was born, and she was three and a half when our second baby was born. A year later a third baby came along.

As a mother I saw myself detached in some way. I could never put a finger on it. I did everything I should as a mother, but I could not see myself being close and emotionally involved with my children. I did my duty and I was strict and I would talk to them like they were adults, not like children, but I couldn't see any warmth in myself. Maybe it was because I was suppressed for so many years and not able to express myself emotionally or as a woman. It took years before I could get comfortable with that. I felt I was talking down to them all the time.

We came to Canada in 1980 and arrived in Vancouver. From the moment I set foot in Vancouver, I felt a whole new person, as if I had had a whole weight lifted off me. The countryside was beautiful. We stayed six weeks there. At that time they couldn't offer a job because you had to be a landed immigrant before they could offer any specific jobs. Within six weeks of coming he had a government position. We had to go up to a city in northern B.C., a logging town of about 10,000 people, and I got a job at the local hospital in the psychiatric unit there. A lot of the patients there were Native People and I saw how they were treated by the white people. They were looked down on in many ways. When they'd come in for admission, the staff would say, "Well, we're getting so-and-so in. You'll have to lock them into the quiet room." This is their land. They're just pushed aside as being nobody.

We came to Newfoundland in late 1981. We had always known that Newfoundland was very Irish and that the Church played a major role here. I remember learning about Newfoundland way, way back when I was at school. Talaimh an Éisc, we used to call it in Gaelic: the land of the fish. St. John's had an affinity with Waterford because the emigrant ships usually left Waterford en route to St. John's. In one of the churches in Waterford there's a registry showing all the people who left Waterford for Newfoundland way back even to 1784.

Coming to Newfoundland was exciting in one sense, but the Church in Newfoundland is a good thirty or forty years behind Ireland. I thought Ireland was one of the most conservative countries where religion was concerned, particularly the Catholic Church. Ireland in the sixties was more liberated than Newfoundland is in the eighties.

Sex abuse by the clergy had gone on but was never publicized by the media; the Church in Ireland kept a good lid on that. But once the media got hold of it here, that was it: Everything was exposed. Listening to the sermons sometimes here in the churches, they're still talking down, talking at the people. They think we are simple-minded people, that we're not educated, we don't understand certain aspects of theology. The sermons are not inspiring.

I just go to Mass, that's it. The sex scandals of priests abusing children here in Newfoundland haven't affected me at all because of my experience in Ireland. It doesn't surprise me really. I'm sure that was going on in Ireland all the time, but it never got into the public eye. It has shocked an awful lot of the traditional Catholic families in Newfoundland. They just can't come to terms with it. I know quite a number of elderly ladies who are devastated. But they say, "God is good, time is a great healer" — all the old clichés. "We have the faith. The Church is not based on the priest alone; the people are the Church." They're rationalizing all of this and they're terrified. I think there won't be a priest left here in the whole province the way things are going. A lot of Catholics see very weak leadership from the hierarchy and they feel also that the priest has too much power and too much control.

The woman is emerging as a very major power in the Church. When I go to Mass on Sundays, I look up on the altar and see the extraordinary ministers. You may have six of them and usually four out of six are female. Or you may have a complete six who are female and the only male will be the priest. If there are altar boys, they're males. It's the females organizing everything, but they're not yet getting the full recognition. Often you find the chairman or the president is a male on most of these parish councils. There are quite a number of women saying that it's a waste of time having anything to do with the parish council here because they have no say. The priest has his point of view and that's it. You could spend hours upon hours raising money, but when it comes to matters of Church and discipline and change, it's not a matter for the laity at all. A lot of Catholics are disillusioned.

I never saw myself as having a role in the Church. Never. I'm not interested. The mystique and the mystery when we had the old liturgy — that Latin which was very powerful — it had a special meaning then. But with Vatican II everything changed. I loved the mystery, and the mystery was gone. The religion started to wane as well and maybe that had something to do with it.

I certainly would encourage other women who are interested in getting involved. Certainly women have a role in the Church; they're very important and they could have a very stabilizing effect on the Church if they were involved in it, in decision-making in particular. I think the clergy should be allowed to marry. What do these men do when they have nobody to talk to? It must be frightening if you have something major to discuss and you have nobody to talk to except another clergyman. To have another sex involved in the Church would be very healthy.

The clergy are holding on desperately to this male-dominated organization. We hear all these clichés rather than facing that they're not able to cope with it. In Newfoundland they're leading a false lifestyle: They're molesting behind the scenes and they're saying Mass. They're telling women they can't use birth control and they can't seek a divorce. The Church has to come clean and everything has to come out in the open because people are losing respect for them. They've brought it on themselves, there's no doubt about that.

Women must be ordained. Women are very capable and intelligent. They've got a different outlook on life and they have the feminine disposition of caring and nurturing. That's what the Church needs. It would have a very softening effect and it would mellow a lot of this harshness.

Note

1.   A shilling.

They Were the Dirty Thirties

Edith Pringle

Edith Pringle was born in Belfast in 1906. She lives outside Vancouver, in Maple Ridge, British Columbia.

My husband Andrew and I got married in 1931, just as the Great Depression started, and we lived in Calgary until 1934. As the Depression deepened, building construction came to a halt. Andrew was glad to find any type of work, and the usual wage for odd jobs back then was only twenty-five cents per hour. People everywhere were begging. They used to come around to the door and I'd make them up a sandwich or something. They could get a flop-house bed for twenty-five cents in some places. Sometimes they just froze to death. Many became transients, riding the freight cars. They'd jump up and ride on top of them — it was awful. They were the Dirty Thirties.

In the spring of '34 the provincial government and Calgary launched a back-to-the-land scheme. Grants were given to families to relieve the unemployed in the city. The federal and provincial governments as well as Calgary provided $200 each, amounting to $600 per family. My husband Andrew and I applied and our application was approved. The grant was divvied up as follows: $50 had to be a down-payment on a quarter-section of CPR land — very rough and heavily treed; $75 was to build a house; $200 was given in trust to the local grocery store for each settler and $8 per month for the first two years. Eight dollars! No luxuries.

They had even stipulated what we could buy: flour, sugar and tea. The balance of the money was used to purchase a team of work horses, one cow, harnesses, tools, an axe, a shovel and a milk pail. We bought a team of horses in Calgary and an old coal and wood stove for $14, all cast iron. It saved us from freezing to death in the winter. We then made arrangements with two other families

161

to rent a boxcar on the railway to ship our horses and other goods to our destination, the district of Lousana in central Alberta, about 110 miles from Calgary. About eight other families went to that district. Most had young children but we were not blessed with any.

When each family reached their piece of land they set up their tents and made makeshift shelters. Some spent the first day sleeping in wagons or hayracks. We set up an eight-by-ten tent in a suitable spot, sheltered and close to the rough road we had to travel to reach the main road to Lousana, four miles away. The tent was furnished with a Winnipeg couch, an old trunk and my precious sewing machine that I had bought for $10 at an auction sale in Calgary. It served us faithfully over the hard years, mostly patching and trying to make old clothes look like new.

The old stove, a homemade kitchen table and a few chairs sat outside for a few days — until we built a crude shelter around them with small trees and an old piece of linoleum as a roof. That lasted several weeks until one of those Alberta hailstorms struck. Hailstones as big as golf balls made holes in the lino and broke nearly all the dishes, blew down the tent and soaked us. But we were young and strong and soon set it all up again.

Alberta has many changing moods. It can be a beautiful day that can just suddenly turn into thunder. Or it can be raining with chinook winds and then turn into sunshine again. One night we went out to a neighbour's while we still lived in the tent and we had another one of these awful storms. When we came home the tent was blown down. At the time we had acquired two wee pigs and we had made a pen for them. We were soaked with the storm, so I had to get into my old tent trunk to get out some dry clothes and a couple of dry sheets. After we got everything ready and we were in bed, we heard: Honk! Honk! The two little pigs had come into the tent and had gone under the Winnipeg couch to get out of the storm. Andrew said to let them stay there. All I could do was laugh — they used to tell me the Irish keep a pig in the kitchen, but here we had two under the bed!

We had to carry our milk pail and the tea kettle full of drinking water from the farm, nearly a mile away, every day! Our nearest neighbour did not have a well, but there was a small lake on a road half a mile from their property. The water was the colour of tea. Farmers around drove their cattle and horses to water there. In winter they sawed a hole through the ice.

That first summer we got a cow from a neighbour and she produced two large pails of milk daily. We had to buy a creamer can, so we could get some cream for butter and, until a kind neighbour gave us a calf, we had more milk than we could use. I was learning how to milk a cow, but she didn't enjoy me practising on her, so after she kicked the stool and left me, I gave up that year. I did love feeding that calf, so one day I decided to take it for a walk. He was secured on a long chain and I was alone, my husband was busy felling trees for the buildings. Did that calf ever take me for a run! He was so happy. In just minutes he was dragging me on my knees until I had to let drop the chain. My hands and knees all scratched.

Later on a friend gave us six hens. My husband, being born and raised on a farm in Scotland, knew how to make a nest for the first brooding hen. I was so excited when the day came and the eggs hatched. He was away nearly all day — our horses had gotten out because we hadn't got fences put up — so I kept vigil over that old hen. I couldn't understand why the chicken didn't pop out. A little head came out and this little thing was wobbling around.

I thought that poor little chick was weak, it couldn't get out. I picked all the shell off and naturally it died. Every time another little head came out, I did the same thing. When my husband came home I was in tears. There was one egg left and he said to leave it alone until morning. And in the morning there was Mrs. Hen so proud, walking her one chick around. I was teased all summer about my hand-picked chicken.

A woodsman from Ontario taught my husband how to cradle the corners and trim the trees. The cabin was eighteen by twenty-six feet and cost $75. The only material we bought was shingles and sheeting for the roof and floor, a second-hand door and three small windows. We gathered moss from around the trees to chink between the logs. I tried to beat off mosquitos and hornets because they loved my Irish blood. Finally, we were able to move inside our cabin around the end of September. It was such a joy to have a roof over our heads and a door to close and to be able to cook inside. Never in all the fifty years later did I enjoy camping again.

After four attempts digging a well, we finally struck water at thirty feet. Not a great supply but enough for household use. A man who lived in the district used a water diviner to find the spot. We built a barn with poles and straw, so the animals had some shelter, and we had to buy straw and haul it all winter to bed them. We bought a low set of sleighs at a farm sale.

My good man cut trees all winter to trade for feed, grain and so on. Five hundred long straight poles were traded for a team of old horses, but one didn't survive that winter. Fifty large poles were traded for two turkey hens in the spring. My most precious possession — a nice quarter cut-off dining-room suite we had bought in Calgary at an auction sale in 1932 — was traded to a farmer for three milk cows. Cows were selling for $25. We needed them to buy a cream separator and sell cream at thirty cents a gill[1] to the local dairy creamery. In 1935, after my husband had earned a few dollars on a threshing crew, we went to a local farm auction sale and bought two cows for $15.50. I did learn to milk cows that year.

Life wasn't all gloom and doom in those days. People were wonderful. Neighbours helping neighbours. We had social evenings at the old schoolhouse. The women cooked the food. There were a few musicians in the district. A good accordion player always provided Scottish reels for square dancing. Two brothers usually gave us an exhibition of tap dancing, and there were a few violin players. We also had bridge games during the winter at each other's homes. Sometimes the prize was a bar of soap. Nevertheless, the competition was keen.

We also had a one-room school. The lone schoolteacher would have her pupils trained for a concert around Christmas. How much we owed to those brave schoolteachers in the early days in this country. On the prairies they had to wade through snow and freezing cold to get the old wooden coal heater going before the pupils arrived. Most of the young teachers married farmers' sons from around the district and settled there.

We struggled through the first six years, breaking land with horse power, making walks and routes, and cutting hay. We always had a good vegetable garden, and we picked wild raspberries and saskatoons for jam. We had good homemade bread and butter. Of course, I could get Eaton's catalogue — that was the only way we could shop for anything. We would sit and dream of all the things we would like.

We bought our first car in 1938 — a 1927 Chevy — for $90. Repairs were cheap. We patched so many old inner tubes for those old tires. We enjoyed it for a year; then we were offered a trade. A neighbouring farmer had a power tractor and breaking equipment and offered to break ten acres of land for the car. We picked rocks on those ten acres but never really had a good crop of grain. It was poor soil and very rough land with hills and valleys. It wasn't even good pasture.

I was happy throughout those days because I had a good, kind husband. One year we had no income. About a week before Christmas, we had nothing to sell, but we had vegetables in the cellar and everything. And Andrew said, "How much money have we got?" I said, "Three cents." "Oh," he said, " I should never have married." I said, "Well, I'm happy."

The next morning he butchered a heifer to get some money for Christmas. He hung a hind quarter up for us and he put three quarters on the sleigh and off he went. He was gone for hours. When he came back the sleigh was empty and I rushed out and asked, "How much money did you get?" "Not one cent," he answered. "What!" "Well, I met one of our neighbours, and you know, they've got those two little kids and no money. They needed meat so I gave them some. Then I went to another neighbour and he's almost an old man and they had no money and they needed meat."

To get our next sack of flour he took the hide — you could get two or three dollars for a hide — and he cut the hair off the horse's tail, worth fifty cents a pound. He went into town with the horse hair and the hide and he got us a sack of flour and a pound of tea. That's the way it worked.

But it really was tough. I never got a new coat for seven years and I used to think back to the tailor's place where I first started to work. I used to make my own clothes and every winter I would get a new coat. One for Sunday and the other for work. I'd say to mother, "I'm going to wear my other one now. You can give this one to somebody." She'd say, "You'll see the day, my girl, when you'll be glad of a good coat like that." When I brought out this same old coat for seven years long, I used to think: I'm glad my mother can't see me now.

The Depression hit us really hard — we got so little for the produce. However, in the city food was very cheap. Flour cost $1.70 for 100 pounds in a good cotton sack. Meat was very cheap. Hamburger, sausage and liver were all five to ten cents a pound. Butter was twenty-five cents a pound and eggs were twenty cents a dozen. But farmers only got $1.50 for five gallons of cream. Five gallons! We bought a cream separator and we had to make payments on it. The cream was picked up twice a week, and if we shipped two cans a week, we got three dollars. That was our money to live on.

In 1946, I persuaded my husband to sell the farm. We had worked for twelve hard years with very little future. We put the farm up for sale and we got $3,000. A neighbour bought it for his son-in-law. Altogether we sold 320 acres with a house and a drilled well and outbuildings and about eighty acres that my husband had broken with the sweat of his brow. It was terrible. We'd wasted the best years of our lives out there.

Note

1.   A quarter of a gallon — 2 pints.

I Have a Love/Hate Relationship
with This Country

Maria O'Kane

Maria O'Kane lives in Toronto, Ontario.

When I first came to Toronto in 1983 I was very unsettled. I thought it would only be a matter of time before I settled in, but I'm here six years now and I'm more unsettled now than I've ever been. I'll be twenty-seven in two weeks. Every time I go home to Ireland, I want to come back to Canada, but every Christmas and every long weekend in Canada, I want to be at home. I have a love/hate relationship with this country. I love what it has to offer me in education and choice, but as far as security and family, Ireland is the better place to rear children. In Canada, if I had children, I would worry about what would happen to them if something happened to me.

Anybody who comes abroad does so for a reason. If you're happy, why would you leave? You leave because you're discontented. Something on the other side of the ocean is drawing you — a career, a different attitude towards life, or money. A lot of people come to Canada for money. That wasn't my reason, ever. I left Ireland because I was tired of the chauvinism, tired of women being tied to the kitchen sink. Even from the time I was fifteen or sixteen, I had made up my mind I wouldn't be one of those women. I will not be pushed around. As a kid, I resented that my brother got to play with cars and dinkies and I had dolls. I wanted to play with cars and dinkies, but I didn't have that choice. I would've been regarded as a tomboy.

When I came abroad it was refreshing to find women plumbers, women carpenters, women doctors, women lawyers. Women were allowed to do more in other countries. It was exciting. I thought for the first time in my life: I have the brains, I may not have the money, but in Canada there are possibilities. I could go to school and make something of my life and that's what drew me to Canada. And maybe the prospects of meeting a man who would love me for me — not because I was a wonderful little cook or a wonderful little domesticated woman.

But as time passes I'm beginning to realize that money and prestige will never mean anything to me if I don't have somebody to share it with, if I'm not going to be educated and if I'm just going to be an underdog for the rest of my time here. If I'm just going to work in an office or something then I might as well stay at home and be poor and be with my family. You know, if I could get an education in Dublin, I'd be gone tomorrow because I believe our schools are some of the best.

I would very much like to get involved in social work, to get my master's degree in social work and eventually specialize in gerontology. However, that is several years away for me at this stage. Initially, I had intended to go to school full-time, but my situation has changed over the last couple of months. I just split up a long-term relationship — five and a half years — so I decided to go to school part-time, for the first year. But I do intend to get an education. If I'm not going to get that, I really would rather go home and spend my time in Ireland and be with my family and make the most of the situation there.

I heard Canadians and Americans loved Irish people, so I thought I didn't have to do anything other than be Irish to be liked. I was at a bus stop coming home from a nanny job one night — it was at St. Clair and Mt. Pleasant in Toronto — and this little old lady was standing at a bus stop with a bunch of bags. Back home, it would be polite to ask if she needed some help. She didn't seem to be forthcoming with a reply, so I repeated myself a second time and said, "You look a bit bogged down, love. Would you like a hand?" She said, "Go away! Leave me alone! Mind your own business!" And I thought: What's wrong with her? What have I said wrong? I realized shortly afterwards, several months down the road, that she must have been a little bit frightened. Maybe she thought I was trying to rob her. I really didn't understand why she was getting so excited and so annoyed. It was very different from the reception I would've got had it been at home in Dublin. But this was Canada.

Toronto is a cement jungle. It's very easy to get swallowed up. People over here are very polite, very responsible individuals. But they find it hard to find time for laughter and it's sad because they're so educated and they have so much money and they have so much prestige. You have to have time to smell the flowers, you really do. You have to have time for the little things. You never have time for that in Toronto because it's such a fast-paced city. You're always chasing your tail. If you're not studying, you're working. If you're not working, you're working out. If you're not working out, you're doing laundry. If you're not doing laundry, you're cooking. There's never a lot of time to sit and relax and think about why you're doing all these things.

I've watched friends of mine, young women who came here from the same sort of background I do — working-class people from Dublin. They come over here and they do well for themselves and they move on in their jobs and they forget their roots. You have to remember where you came from to appreciate where you're going. Often, I find myself of a Sunday morning sitting in my room, looking out the window, thinking: My God, what is it all for? I'm still no better off and I can't exactly say I feel whole and satisfied and complete.

In October 1990, Maria O'Kane returned to Ireland with a one-way ticket. Later I received a postcard from her. "I remember now why I live abroad," she wrote. "Dublin's booming, lots of work, but I don't want to stay for good. I made a mistake. I'll be back, maybe even before Christmas." Maria O'Kane returned to Canada in December 1990.

You Cannot Go Back

Maura Keohane

So then everything changes and we change as well,
I am sure it's the truth you too will now tell,
Far away in some far beloved land in our dream,
Is the road by the river that flows through Raheen.

— *from an old Irish immigrant's song*

Maura Keohane lives in Nanaimo, British Columbia.

Growing up in the thirties on the River Suir was just the most wonderful childhood. My family lived in Ferrybank, on the banks of the River Suir just outside Waterford, in such a beautiful quiet place where you could take lovely rambling walks. We used to play in Ray's Stream, near the River Suir. That stream has a real place in my heart. That's where we went to fish for little minnows. Back then, it was covered with overhanging branches of enormous beech trees. Further in, it got deeper and greener and the sunlight filtered through the trees creating a most beautiful atmosphere.

I loved being surrounded by green. The banks of the stream were covered with moss. We'd go in there with our jars, trying to catch these little minnows. When we got tired of that we'd come out and sit on the banks of the stream which was covered with wild irises and daffodils. I can remember lying down there with these flowers surrounding me, looking up at the clouds scudding by. The stream ran under a little bridge and sometimes we would go in under it and come out into a field. I remember the terror we'd experience going under that bridge. And the delight when we'd emerge at the other end into the meadow. Sometimes we used to go through the fields and estates of Lady Garroway, one of the landed gentry. We would spend hours climbing trees and paddling in streams there.

My paternal grandfather, Padraig de Breit, was one of the founders of the Irish-speaking college in Ring, Co. Waterford, and recognized as one of the best Gaelic speakers in Southern Ireland. He was also an alderman in Waterford. He died while I was young, but he certainly was a presence in our lives. There were ten of us in the family. I came after five boys — one died of muscular dystrophy. Then there was a gap of a few years before my sisters were born.

As Catholics, we are given Mary to emulate. But it is my mother that I emulate. I feel very close to my mother still. It is my mother that I always think of when I think of what a woman really is and should be. My mother was a bulwark through all of our troubles. We were never hungry despite the fact that money was very scarce. I remember my mother bringing in the tinkers who would come around. My mother was a wonderful seamstress and made all our clothes with an old-fashioned treadle sewing machine. I can see her working away there and making those lovely dresses with the frill around the collar and the big bow in the back. She employed her gift to make clothes for these tinker people and their children.

One day some of these people came to the door and we were sitting down to roast beef and gravy and all the trimmings. I could hear the voice outside saying, "Oh what a lovely — is that roast beef?" And my mother said, "Come in. Bring your children." We were moved up away from the table, and they were all sat down and fed. It has never left my memory. I came home another day and here was this fella ensconced on our sofa, lying back with a big bacon sandwich and a bottle of stout. He was on his way to New Ross and my mother was giving him sustenance before he continued on the journey. He was some poor man down on his luck.

My Dad worked as an engineer with Clover Meats Factory in Ferrybank. During that time, two acts of his had a profound and lasting effect on me. Firstly, during a strike at the factory, he came out in sympathy with the men. Because he was a salaried worker and not a union member, he received no strike pay. This was a rough time for our family. At one time he was on strike. Things were really bad for us and my father was using his bicycle. Secondly, during this time, he somehow got talking to this man down at the railway station who had missed the train to New Ross, fifteen miles away — a heck of a distance if you have no means of getting there. The man desperately needed to get there because his job depended on it. My father gave him his bicycle.

The bicycle meant a great deal to my dad in those days. It was his means of transportation, but he was convinced that the man would send it back. Sure enough, the bike came back on the train from Rosslare the next day, addressed to my dad. These examples of solidarity and trust helped shape my view of others. Happily, my father got hired by Henry Denny's Bacon Factory, where he stayed, as a valued member of the staff, long past retirement.

I met my husband James at a rowing regatta in Waterford one afternoon in June 1952. He was vice-captain of the Lee Rowing Club from Cork City. We got talking and he invited me to the dinner and the regatta dance in the Olympic Ballroom in Waterford. There was no romance, but we were very good friends. A year later he wanted to go to Canada, in search of adventure as young people will, and he asked me if I would like to go to Canada with him. I knew he was the kind of fella you could go anywhere with and have no worries because he was just a perfect gentleman. But I said to him, "Canada!" Canada was the last place on earth that I wanted want to go to. I was very happy in Ireland and really had no desire to leave.

So James left. He had been gone maybe eighteen months or so. I was still working in the office at the Henry Denny's Bacon Factory in Waterford. About three days before Christmas of 1955, he arrived home from Canada. We got engaged on New Year's Eve. I had said I would never go to Canada, but we planned that I would go for maybe two or three years. James felt that maybe he'd make his stake in that time. The plan was that I would come out to Canada and be married out in Canada the following June.

But then my mother and family prevailed upon me to get married at home.

I got married in Ireland in February 1956. Ten days later James left for Canada. He was working in the big Eldorado Mine in Uranium City, up near the Northwest Territories, about 500 miles northwest of Edmonton. I think it was the biggest uranium concern in Canada. Of course, in those days we never understood how dangerous it was.

I didn't go out to be with James then because it was wintertime and the temperatures in that area were 44 to 60 below and consequently you could not build. It was his plan to have a home built for me starting in April, when the thaw would start.

In July 1956, I left Ireland from Cove, Co. Cork. I was 22. My mother and father drove there. It was my first time in Cove and I knew a little of the history of it. This is where so many Irish immigrants left and never came back. A lot of our Irish music is about emigration, especially the heart-rending songs. That day I went into Cove, I really could feel the tears, all the tears that had ever been shed there, and my own tears were mingling.

That morning I left the day was grey. The sea was grey and the sky was grey. It was early in the morning when we were going out on the tender to the ship. And the ship seemed huge to me. I had never been on a ship this big in my life. I got on the ship and I can remember thinking that the best thing I could do is have a good breakfast. I hadn't eaten that morning — I couldn't swallow with the lump in my throat. So I had a big breakfast and even ate porridge, which I never eat. When I got on board I was very fortunate to meet a girl about my own age who was going to the States and we became very close right away. My God! I was fine for those first few hours while we were eating and there was that initial excitement. But when the ship started to pull away, I looked back at Ireland. I couldn't see the place for the tears.

We arrived into New York and it was 90 above and humid. It was so hot that the wax earrings of fruit I was wearing started to melt. James met me in New York and we stayed with his aunt for about four days. I felt I was two people. There was somebody talking and acting for me, but inside I was crying all the time. I was anxious to get away from New York. I just wanted to be alone and felt if I could only make those first five days, if I could only make them move — it was agonizing trying to talk.

We flew to Edmonton, where we stayed the night. The next day we took off for Uranium City. At that time they used old army planes, so we were flying fairly low and I was able to have a good view of the land. As the plane left Edmonton, the farms and the homesteads petered out and we were now flying over a lot of muskeg and water. I was amazed at the amount of water I could see below and the vast tracts of land. We arrived in Uranium City in the early afternoon.

The welcome I received was absolutely unbelievable. This was my first meeting with Canadians and they showered me with kindness. That evening they had put on a big welcoming party for me in the mess hall — Uranium City had a lot of single men working and there was a huge mess hall for eating. The recreation centre was festooned with welcoming signs for me — they really surrounded me with absolute kindness.

My first impression of Uranium City was: Dear God, what have I gotten myself into! It was such a contrast to Ireland. Ireland was so green and I had now arrived in a place devoid of greenery. The air was extremely dry. The temperature on that day I arrived was 100 above.

I felt that I was in absolute wilderness. Flying in, I had seen only a vast land with no signs of habitation. Suddenly, I was in this little place that was honed out of the wilderness. Our house was the only house that was finished. James would leave to go to work at six-thirty in the morning and he wouldn't arrive back home again until quarter to six or so in the evening. There was no radio. The water and sewage wasn't hooked up, so I had my first experience of an outdoor toilet.

I started to suffer from dreadful homesickness. I stopped eating. I weighed 98 pounds when I got married — and because I was eating so little I lost weight rapidly and was feeling so bad the doctor hospitalized me. The diagnosis was homesickness.

There were two other doctors in Uranium City, but one I would not go to because I had heard that his feeling on women was that we are all neurotics.

I wasn't neurotic. I was suffering from being sad for Ireland. I missed my family. I liked to go to plays, the opera and the library. I loved to walk in the country and walk by the river. And all of a sudden that stopped. The doctor said that I could have died from it. This is where I became afraid. I left the hospital, accompanied with a huge jar of nerve pills. I got home to the house and I looked at those nerve pills and I said: No way. If I'm going to recover, I will recover without those. This is where my faith comes in. All along, what was keeping me going was my faith and my mother's example of faith in God. I prayed and I knew everybody else was praying for me. But never, even in the very bad months that I felt my worst, did I inflict any of that on them at home in Ireland. I kept it to myself. And I knew deep down that God would help me.

I got over the homesickness, but it didn't happen easily. In Uranium City, I had three children — which didn't give me any time for having homesickness. I loved them dearly and my life — because of becoming involved in the various activities in Uranium City — settled down. I joined the Catholic Women's League, where I met other Irish women; there were a lot of Irish women in Uranium City. We received a plaudit from the national head office of the Catholic Women's League for the work we did. At the time, there was a lot of trouble going on in the schooling system. I had young children, but they weren't going to school yet. A lot of Indian children there were suffering discrimination in the high school. There was an arrangement to teach catechism after school to the Catholics by the Catholic priest and to others by the Anglican priest, but it wasn't working out. We Catholics got together and we went through the government to open up a school. It was all approved.

Very soon, the two years had gone by. I wasn't that anxious any more to go back to Ireland. But I did not want to stay in Uranium City and neither did James. We had a friend in Uranium

City who came from Kaslo. Ben was one of the older men in Uranium City, whom we had adopted as a grandfather to our children. He wanted to return our kindness, so he took us on a trip to Kaslo, in the interior of British Columbia on Kootenay Lake. It is the most beautiful place — like Heaven compared to Uranium City. We sold our house in Uranium City and bought a store in Kaslo in 1963. Our son was born there. In Kaslo, we were very much part of the community. James was an alderman and I was on the hospital board. I was also in the Catholic Women's League and the historical society, and I worked for the Guides and Brownies. Nevertheless, back in my mind was that desire to go back to Ireland.

We went home to Ireland in 1972, on a holiday. Everything was booming there and it seemed to be the time to make the move. Our children were young, ranging from fourteen down to nine. Finally, in June 1973, we returned to Ireland. We settled in Cork and we were there for seven years. James got a job as manager of a furniture store in Cork. I did not work those first years, but I joined the Irish Country Women's Association and the education committee of the school my son attended.

But as time went along, I became very disillusioned. I found that Ireland had become very materialistic and had changed drastically. I can understand that materialism to some extent. For years Ireland has been so down, and when people did start to get things, you could hardly blame them for getting caught up in them. And I realized that you cannot go back. Without realizing it, I had changed very much myself. I had become very attuned to a Canadian lifestyle and had come to love Canadian people and Canada. I did not realize how much I loved Canada. Being away from it, I could see all of the wonderful kindness that had been extended to me in Canada when I moved there and when I moved to Kaslo. When we moved into our first house in Kaslo, the women came to clean it and made it habitable and did all the cooking for me that first day. I encountered none of that in Ireland. Instead, I found myself a stranger in my own land.

When I would bring the subject of Canada into the conversation, it was as if a shutter were coming down over my listeners' ears. Saying something about Canada, particularly if it were positive, was somehow interpreted to mean that I was running down Ireland, which was not what I was doing at all. This attitude was definitely brought home to me when we decided to return to Canada. I was stunned at the amount of people who turned to me and said, "What's wrong with Ireland?" And then I realized something in those seven years at home that I could never put my finger on: There was a resentment that I had left Ireland in the first place. It was very subtle and very wounding.

Seven years went by. I was no longer able to connect. Something was missing and I was beginning to get homesick for Canada. My children started to feel restless. My husband was happy where he was working, but I noticed him gradually talking about Canada and then I noticed he was mentioning it more frequently. Sharon, our eldest daughter, had done a year of university in Cork. One day she came home and announced she was Canadian and wanted to go back to Canada. Soon we were talking about returning. Finally, in July 1980, we returned to Canada. When I got off the plane in Vancouver, I was filled with a sense of surety that we had done the right thing. I was coming back home.

Ireland will never leave me. This is why I decided to join the Irish Celtic Association here in Vancouver. I love Irish folklore. I love the mythology of Ireland and I also love singing the songs. I spent a great deal of time travelling around Ireland with James while we were back for the seven years. We used to go down into the little coves that nobody would frequent. I would sit there, and the wind would blow through the sally grasses, and the water would come in and the clouds. The Ireland of our youth and the Ireland we loved — the mystical Ireland — is still there underneath this gloss of materialism.

As time goes by, I see more and more that the Ireland I had gone home to was an Ireland that existed purely in my mind. It was an Ireland of my youth and it had gone. The places I loved to play in were all gone. Ray's Stream was covered over with cement and houses. The irises and daffodils were gone. Traffic was everywhere. I looked at it and I was very saddened with what I saw. But I realized Ray's Stream will always be with me. It is the symbol of everything that was wonderful when I was a child. That's where I used to sit and lie on the banks of the stream and think as a young child about life, about God. I felt very close to God in Ray's Stream.

Am I Really Working for This?

Connie O'Sullivan

Connie O'Sullivan lives in Woodbridge, Ontario.

I'm from Six Mile Bridge, Co. Clare. I was born on December 4, 1956. There were eleven children born. One died at eight months old. He had spina bifida. After him, there were four children born, including me. So I ended up with five brothers and four sisters — ten of us altogether. I'm eighth in the family.

My mother died when I was eleven and a half. She was only forty-six years old. My older sister was telling me it wasn't until my brother was born with that disease that her health went downhill. They had it very hard. My father didn't earn much money and they had to feed all us kids. Once my mother's health got bad, things just started to disintegrate. Towards the end she got very sick. I remember going to the airport when one of my sisters was emigrating to Canada and friends came with us. When you're that young, you're so selfish. The only person you think about is yourself. I remember being in Shannon Airport and one of the women remarked how pale my mother looked. But because she'd been sick four or five years before that and she'd been away from the house a lot, it didn't dawn on me. It was a year after that she died. My second-oldest sister had emigrated to Canada just three weeks before she died. My father was left to raise a family of nine kids.

I came to Canada in September 1976 and worked for a social service agency. It was the best job I did, from the point of view of getting to know Toronto. I worked for a little agency. What they did was help people in the community. They had access to all different government agencies. Most of the things they did were helping people to work out problems, immigration and marriage counselling and children and all that type of stuff. After about four months — I knew nothing about the Canadian system or how things worked here — they threw me in the deep end. As I was helping people with their problems, I had to find out which agency would help them. So I had to get to know the agencies.

It was the best thing for me, even though I was really scared at the beginning. I was dealing with all different nationalities — Italian, Polish, German, French, Jamaican, people from Trinidad, all different countries. Within six months I had got to know the system, how things work here in Canada. I stayed with that agency for about a year.

After that, I worked for a daycare agency for about two years and then I worked as a live-in nanny for a year. I looked after a little baby. That's when I really started liking the idea of working with kids. I was talking about this one day to my employer and she was saying, "Why don't you consider daycare, if you want to continue working with children but don't want to live-in?" So I went to the Canada Employment Centre. I had very little money at the time and I knew they sponsored certain programs. I talked with a counsellor who gave me some options for careers, including daycare. A few months later, I applied for one of their programs and they accepted me. They said they would pay me for going to school. I was told to contact George Brown College in Toronto and I took a course in daycare there. That was in 1979. I got my first job in 1980 and I've more or less worked in daycare ever since.

The biggest problem in daycare is the low wages. It's mostly women. Men won't work in daycare — not that they don't love children. But they wouldn't work for the money. Somebody has to do it. There are some very good daycares where the wages are very good, but on the other hand there are very bad daycares where women are still being paid $200 a week with no benefits. Some daycares are badly built. They're a health hazard. Food is extremely bad. Proper precautions aren't taken to meet safety regulations. And there is overcrowding with too many kids and not enough staff. After a few years, women get burned out because they're putting a lot of themselves into the jobs and they are stressed to the limit.

Daycare workers are not getting any help from the people who should be helping them: the government and the social service system. There are many great bosses who do everything they can to help the staff and they write letter after letter after letter. And the government says they're doing all they can. But they're not.

Last year, the government said they were going to give so many millions of dollars to daycare. Eight or nine months later, at budget time, they turn around and say they can't give as much money as they promised because they don't have it. To someone like me, that's a slap in the face. You're out there working and raising a next generation, with no money coming in because looking after children is not considered a valuable job. If I was out there working as a mechanic fixing cars, I would be getting at *least* $18 an hour. Some daycare teachers are getting $6.50 an hour. How can any woman possibly support herself on such disgracefully low wages? You have to ask yourself: Am I really working for this? Women are coming out of college after spending two years studying childcare and they are going into jobs where they are getting $16,000 to $18,000 a year. In some of the better daycares the most you can earn is about $25,000 a year, with benefits and holidays.

The biggest laugh is that the government has a program where they give grants to daycare workers every year to compensate for the low wages.[1] Then they tax the grant. By the time they've taken all the taxes, you get half of what you were originally supposed to get.

A lot of young Irish women like myself come here thinking because things aren't so good in Ireland, they will be better off in Canada. They think they'll get a job in Canada with decent wages. But it all depends on the job you get. If you work in daycare, after a while you realize if you spend your life working in low-paying jobs here in Canada, you're no better off than you were in Ireland.

I wanted to do some volunteer work, to help people but also to have something to do at nighttime. One of the things I got involved with was the literacy program. I found out about it through the library. I went to this meeting, where facilitators were explaining the different types of illiteracy. At first, you have this dream: I'm going to take somebody and I'm going to teach them to read; this is going to be my project. You get an awful shock — you find people who can't fill in a form, people who don't know how to fill in a bank deposit slip. Being able to learn to do all these things is such an achievement. I did that for about one and a half years. I had two students. I met them at their houses and they told me what they needed to know.

I started doing this because I can never remember a time when I couldn't read. To see people not being able to read, to see the struggle for something I had taken for granted, made me realize literacy is a gift. I didn't have that struggle and I realized that I had a gift to pass on to other people. People are here to help other people.

I also started doing volunteer work in prisons about three years ago. I had so many misgivings. But I began to think about how I might feel if I was in prison and in a strange place — the loneliness I would feel if no one were to come and see me. And I remember thinking about that quote in the Bible: "I was in prison and He came to visit me." And I remember going to that prison on a cold January night. I kept thinking and praying, praying. I was scared, really scared. God had to guide me because I couldn't do it myself. It wasn't what I had imagined at all. There were no high walls, no bars. It was a beautiful building — Metro West Detention Centre in Toronto.

We were taken on a tour of the prison and at the end of the evening my first fear was conquered. I had gone in. I had met the people who worked in there. About two months later, I went to meet my "match-up." She was a young woman and she turned out to be very nice. I remember going into a little room and the door locking and thinking: Oh my God. I'm in this little room — nice little room — and, of course, there was glass in the door. If there was any trouble, you pressed the button and somebody would come and open the door for you immediately. I remember being very nervous. This woman came in and she sat down and we introduced ourselves. Straight away she started talking to me. She was putting me at ease. So we started talking and before I knew it the two hours were up. Two hours of non-stop talking to this woman. She told me why she was there and I explained who I was and where I was from and what I was doing. She was an American. It really brought it home to me then how it was to be in prison in another country.

I continued visiting her for a year and then her case came up and she was dismissed from court. She was allowed to go home. I was really happy for her. When you do something like that, you really get to see another side of life that most people don't ever think about, but when you first think about it, it's very frightening.

I have very mixed emotions about the Catholic Church. Up until a few years ago I went to Mass every Sunday. Then for a few years I stopped going and then I went back again. And then I thought: Here we go again. It's Sunday morning. You go there. The priest stands up and gives his sermon. Then I started to believe in inner faith. I definitely believe there is a God and a reason for me being here on this planet. It was up to me to find out what it was. It wasn't going to be delivered to me in a flash of lightning. It had to be taken step by step. Getting back to the prison system, one of the reasons I became involved was because I believed that this was part of the plan too.

I have a certain resentment for the Catholic Church because women becoming priests is a problem. Years ago, people said women shouldn't become priests--it wouldn't look right. Of course, it wouldn't look right for a few months. It mightn't look right for a year, but like everything else people would get used to it. It may not happen in my generation, but I do hope there will come a time when they will accept women in the Church as priests. Jesus Christ had such great respect for women such as Martha and Mary. Yet the Church, which is supposed to be teaching love and peace and harmony, still won't accept women. I get so mad and so resentful sometimes. Yet I continue to go to Mass on Sunday because I think by going and praying that you do get stronger and more accepting.

The Church is an institution like everything else. And like every institution, there are things you agree with and things you don't agree with. I don't really fully accept it, but I would like to continue going. And now, with being pregnant, I think I would like my child baptized in the Catholic Church. But when the time comes, I may feel differently.

The Church in Ireland was very unfair to women. Especially my mother's generation. She had all those kids. I don't know if they would've used contraceptives if they had them, or if they really wanted to. But there were families like my mum and dad — with nine, ten, eleven and twelve children — and they'd go off to Mass on Sunday. The priest, who lived in his own house with a maid, would get up and talk about having big families. And these parents would have the father working — if he was lucky — bringing in a meagre wage. With eight, nine, ten, twelve or sometimes fifteen children, there would be barely enough money to feed these kids. And the priest would go home to his house and his maid and have his lunch.

I'm now four months pregnant. I've been feeling lonely lately. It's this yearning to go home and talk to people. You know what it's like when you drop in and have a cup of tea with somebody. You don't have to make arrangements. You're walking down the street, and you meet somebody, and then you walk past their house and they say, "Oh, come on in. Come in for a cup of tea." And you go in and one cup of tea leads to another. Then you leave their house and get waylaid by somebody else and they also want you to go in for a cup of tea. I don't know what it is that I miss most. I think it's the countryside right now. Going for walks. The hills. The village I live in is sort of in a valley. When you look out of the house you see all the hills around it. It looks beautiful. It's all different colours, all different greens and everything. It's very tranquil, very quiet. And it's the humour too that I miss. Right now I'd love to go even for a week to Ireland. It could be because of the baby. It could be a yearning to be with all those other women who have kids too.

Connie O'Sullivan no longer works in daycare.

Note

1. Following years of pressure from unions representing daycare workers and daycare advocacy groups, the Ontario government brought in these supplements in the latter part of the 1980s. At the time the supplements were introduced, increasing wages was but one priority for their use, and not all employers would pass the money on to the workers.

The Winnipeg Polio Epidemic

Nora O'Grady

Nora O'Grady was born near the Curragh of Kildare in 1913. During World War II, O'Grady was Nurse Matron in charge of the first-aid post at the Shannon Airport Flying-Boat Base, where she held the rank of Captain. She lived in Winnipeg, Manitoba, at the time of the polio epidemic and now lives in Vancouver, British Columbia.

I arrived in Winnipeg in the winter of 1951 and I was hired as an R.N. to work in the municipal hospitals. I was head nurse at the Princess Elizabeth Hospital, but during the polio epidemic I worked at the King George Hospital. I was being paid $150 a month time and they deducted one dollar a day for room and board. In 1952, Winnipeg had the first of two terrible polio epidemics. That year we had 800 cases. We were swamped.

The following year we had 2,200 cases of polio. One of my jobs was to train the domestic staff to put Kenny packs on some of the polio patients. These were blanket squares put into a steamer and applied warm to an infected joint to prevent it from stiffening — that way it would be easier to do physiotherapy. We had some excellent physiotherapists from England, Ireland, Scotland and Wales who worked on those patients. By the summer of 1953, it was just too much. We had three extra generators going at the hospital and we were being swamped with patients. We couldn't cope. Finally the Manitoba government called in the army, navy and air force nurses, orderlies, doctors and practical nurses to help, and we all worked side by side under what was probably the world's most desperate polio epidemic.

It hit whole families. A wife would wait for her husband to come home because one of the kids wasn't feeling well. By the time he got home he'd be flushed with the fever and she'd be sick too. No taxi would come if they knew they were going to the municipal hospitals; they wouldn't take polio patients in the taxis. It was just a terrible situation. Neighbour helping neighbour, but nobody wanted to have anything to do with polio. The nurses weren't allowed even to go to a movie. They didn't want us getting on the buses going downtown. They said we were covered with bugs. But none of us got polio. I really don't know why.

The polio hit mainly young adults in the prime of their lives. Why? We have no idea. It wasn't the water supply; it wasn't mosquito bites. The victims were all young and very healthy when they were hit. Whole families were hit. You just had to go from one patient to another and steel your heart against tragedy and give everything that you had. I was younger then. You can do that when you're young.

On one occasion, I was on the afternoon shift in admissions. We had four little cubicles going, operated by four doctors and four medical students who were working as orderlies. I remember coming flying down and seeing a whole family there — a husband and wife and two children. The children were about five and eight and they all appeared to have polio. I said to the doctor, "Do you want to do a spinal tap here or go upstairs? I think the lady has to go into an iron lung." He said, "Get them upstairs right away." We had some other patients who hadn't got bad polio. They helped me get the family on stretchers to take them upstairs. I got the woman into an iron lung right away and they got some doctors to go and do the spinal tap upstairs. I don't remember what happened to the family.

I really don't know the proportion of deaths that occurred. A goodly proportion did get somewhat better, but others were left permanently damaged. We had very few cases in 1954, and by about 1955, the polio vaccines were in general use and we haven't had a polio epidemic since.

I had to prepare myself for retirement in 1972, after I had worked in Vancouver as a nurse for several years. So I got involved in politics federally and provincially, and I joined the Liberal Party, the Norwegian Club, the Chinese Club, the Irish

Club and a few other clubs here in Vancouver. When Mulroney de-indexed the seniors' pension in 1984, I was very upset because I knew that within ten years my pension would really be worth very little.

The media phoned me and wanted to know if I'd get forty or fifty seniors and go down to Pat Carney's office and maybe set fire to it or do something! But I said no, I have no intention of making Pat Carney a martyr. Instead, I made a huge poster, just as big as the nurses are wearing on the streets now.[1] The front said "SOS, Save Our Seniors." On the back, I had a little ditty:

> A sober old senior from Kitts
> Developed seizures and fits,
> When Brian Mulroney reduced her to penury
> By slashing her pension into bits.

I carried a fan I'd made from pantyhose cardboard — white cardboard. On the fan I had written, "If seniors have no bread, let them eat strawberries." Then I haunted about half a dozen of Pat Carney's private Tory strawberry teas for her supporters. I tried to gatecrash all her strawberry teas but I was thrown out. I had inside information about where all these strawberry teas were taking place. They cost $10 to go in. So of course I arrived with this sign and the fan. I didn't ever wear a hat because you can look ridiculous in a hat. It was very, very hot weather and I was plastered with that anti-sun stuff. I wore a very simple pair of sandals, plain light blue pants and a light blue sleeveless top. And here I was, fanning myself with the fan.

In my left arm I had a clipboard with petition sheets and a pen on about ten rubber bands — so nobody could walk away with my pen. I'd go up to these Tory ladies I knew from different organizations and say, "Excuse me M'am, would ya sign me petition to save me old age pension." It nearly drove them up the wall. None of them would sign the petition, but I would then parade around and let everybody read what was written on the front of the poster.

I also went down to Robson Square where everybody sits on the steps during lunchtime. Robson Square is right downtown and all the people come down from the surrounding highrise offices to have their sandwiches. I knew a band would start playing at noon, so I'd be there at eleven-thirty, collecting signatures. When the band would start I'd turn my back on everybody sitting on the steps and I'd conduct the band. This gave them enough time to read my poem. Then I'd weave up and down the steps with my petition. I got at least 1,000 signatures in ten days. This was June 1984.

For me, it was a one-woman show. My petition had one line of French and one line of English because it was the same petition going from the Atlantic to the Pacific and anybody could sign. I would tell everybody, please don't sign unless you know what you're signing. Only on two occasions did somebody say, "I won't sign no froggy language." So we have it out here — the bigotry against the French Canadians. However, my campaign was very successful and I made the pages of our little local newspapers. I didn't make the big newspapers, but I sure got people talking.

Not only that, I was thrown out of a shopping centre here in Vancouver. They sent five guards after me. I told them, "If you lay a hand on me, I'll fall on the floor and have fits and seizures!" I went to their main office and everybody in their main office signed my petition. I took the long way out, got more petitions, and finally I got out of there. I also went to the Granville Island Market and I was thrown out of there. I got my last petition taken by special courier to Ottawa on the Tuesday. Michael Wilson climbed down on the Thursday and Parliament closed down on the Friday for that summer. He had backed off on the Thursday and then disappeared for three months. So Brian Mulroney and his Tories did not de-index the old age pension.

I'm a minority only when I open my mouth and say my name is Nora O'Grady. Other immigrants are having a tough time. This is why I'm a member of this Chinese club. We should help other minorities to try and make it in this country. They're absolutely entitled to come here — this doesn't belong to Britain. Canada is

Canada and I think that anybody should be able to emigrate here — Canada needs more people.

I never look back, I look forward. You paddle along and try and make a living and have fun. I mean I've always had fun. I've gone to the Irish clubs and gone dancing when I was able to dance. I've gone out at night because I've always had a little car. That's what makes a woman liberated: to be able to drive a car.

Note

1. At the time of the interview, B.C. nurses were on strike for better wages and working conditions.

A Slip of Culture Happens

Joan Bridget

Joan Bridget lives in Hamilton, Ontario. In 1990, she co-founded Legit, a group that lobbies for landed immigrant status for same-sex partners who wish to immigrate to Canada. Legit is also a support group.

I left Limerick at eighteen in 1967 and went to Dublin where I taught art at a secondary school for two years. I would still say that it was the job I most enjoyed in all my life. They were very working-class kids and a little wild. They were between twelve and sixteen, and I don't think that it ever occurred to many of them to expect much in life. Some of the teachers were very disrespectful towards the children and expected nothing from them. It certainly didn't occur to a lot of their teachers that part of what they were supposed to do was not just teach them English and French, but educate them and open their minds.

I loved teaching them and learned as much from the kids as they learned from me, for sure. The head nun was wonderful. When I asked if I could take the kids in my class to look at art galleries and museums she said yes, as long as I didn't lose any of them. In those days, that wasn't done. Some of these kids had never been out of Artane. They didn't know what was available to them to do in the city. We went and looked at stuff and they planted little gardens as part of their civics and art. I used to combine as many courses as I could because they had the idea that art was something that you did for a free half-hour. But I was trying to say to them: No, it's everything you do. The way our clothes are designed, and the way you put them together and the things you use — it's all art.

I got pregnant and I wasn't married so working in a nice

Catholic girls' school run by the nuns wasn't on. So myself and my fella, Gregory, decided we'd go to England. Around June of 1971 we left for England. We went by boat. I can remember being on the boat and pulling out of the harbour and thinking of all the people who got on that boat and pulled out of the harbour to emigrate. Given more choice, I would've stayed. I don't think it was something I did lightly or easily — it just about broke my heart. Some essential tie to the country broke. I can remember clearly thinking how going away like that would change you anyway, even if you came back. You don't come back the same person; you change and the people left behind change. Then it's like a slip of culture happens.

England was a whole other education. I would phone up for apartments with my Irish accent and they were all gone. And Gregory would phone up with his Canadian accent and he'd get to see the very same apartments. He said that people would even say to him, "As long as you're not Black or Irish, come around." It was certainly there — great bolts of discrimination against Irish people. Outright racism was rampant in the city towards Black people and towards Irish people. At that point, they didn't have the race relations board they have now, and it was still reasonably common in parts of London to see signs up saying, "No Blacks, No Irish, No Dogs."

I decided not to get married until after the baby was born. The birth was pretty ordinary. I remember holding my son the evening after he was born and realizing inside myself that every single person deserves to be loved just because they are — you don't need to do anything. I don't think I ever really realized that before. In 1972 we returned to Limerick; my daughter was born in July 1973. But Gregory couldn't get a job because the economy was down in Ireland at the time.

We decided to leave Ireland, and in July 1975 we came to Canada. I wanted to go to British Columbia, but Gregory decided we should go to Ottawa because he thought I would have less culture shock there. In retrospect, I think he was right. There were some serious disappointments for me in Canada. One was that

Canada gives you the impression there isn't much discrimination against women or against anybody, but this is blatantly untrue. I got a job working in a senior citizens' home in Ottawa when we first arrived in 1975. I went into the office the first morning and there were lots of nursing attendants — all kinds, all nationalities, all colours.

There was one young woman, sitting on a bench in the hallway when I went in. I was shown my job and everything else, but hours later this woman was still sitting on the bench. Everybody was bustling by her. People were ignoring her to the degree that I thought she had done something she shouldn't have and was being called up on the carpet. So I asked somebody finally, "Why is this woman sitting here so long?" And they said, "Oh, she's just starting today. She's waiting for somebody to show her around." She was a Native woman. She had started her job an hour and a half before me, but hours after I was shown what I had to do, she was still sitting there, waiting for somebody to show her what to do.

Worse than that was when she got her first paycheque. I was in the office and used to do the schedules and the paycheques. I had a man call me from the bank to verify that she was working before he would cash her cheque. Right away I knew that this was not the land of equal opportunity. Absolutely right away. The residents in the home loved her because she treated them like they were human beings. She would take them for walks and do all kinds of things for them that the other staff — so busy being official care-minders — didn't do.

There's this appearance of women being equal, but it's only an appearance. Any woman who had a job also did 100 percent of the work in the house as well. I was very disappointed about that. Any old guy could come over here from Ireland — from anywhere — and work in an unskilled job and make twice the money I made. The construction business was booming then and they could get a job making twice as much as any women who came over here.

My husband's salary supported the household and my salary supported the daycare. That's what happened in the beginning, but our situation was not very typical. His salary and my salary were not very far apart because he worked doing artwork for the government and it didn't pay that well. Our salaries were not that far apart, but whenever the kids were sick, I was the one who had to stay home, and that really annoyed me. Whenever the laundry needed to be done, I was the one who hauled it off to the laundromat. Of course, I could nag him enough to take it to the laundromat, but I really got to resent having to nag.

Then I knew there was a thing called women's liberation. And I thought: Well, surely there's some kind of an organization or something around Ottawa. I was so silly and naive. Up on Parliament Hill, outside the National Arts Centre, they had an information booth for all kinds of things. So I went up to this information booth and said, "Is there a women's centre or something like that in the city?" One of the women got very busy under the counter, shuffling pamphlets. The other woman kind of looked at me and said, "Yes there is. It's on such and such a street."

The other woman popped her head up and said, "The women up there are kind of radical, you know." And I thought: Oh good, this is just what I want. I remember them then being very, very nervous, and I was thinking: I wonder what they're so anxious about? So I went to the women's centre and I found out what they were so anxious about. The women there were very radical women and they were mainly lesbian women. I helped them organize one of the very first lesbian conferences in Canada.

I always knew at the back of my mind I was attracted to women. I also knew it was not okay and that my friends knew it was not okay. So I didn't deal with that at all. It just sat there at the back of my mind — something best forgotten. The first time I got any inclination I might be lesbian was when I was about fourteen. My two best girlfriends and I were coming out of a coffee shop in Limerick that teenagers hung out in. Being me, my allegiance was probably quite clear that I was on the side of my girlfriends all the time. My girlfriends were going steady. I had my particular male friend, but I wasn't going steady in the same way. As we were walking out of the coffee shop, one of the guys standing around called out something.

I'm slightly deaf, but I knew by the reaction of the guy I was with that it was at least something interesting. So I said to him, "What did they say?" He said, "Oh, nothing." "Come on, tell me what he said." "He said that you're a lezzie." And I said, "What's a lezzie?" "You know, a lesbian." "No, I don't know. What is it?" So he told me and I said "So what's wrong with that?" "Well, you're not supposed to, you know." And I thought: Oh, I guess I'm not supposed to. That was the first idea I had.

Eventually, I met Gregory and married him. But as the marriage progressed I was quite aware that whatever it was that marriage and sex was supposed to do for me, this one was not quite doing it. It had nothing to do with being fond of Gregory. There was a basic personality incompatibility. There was the unequal sharing of the house, and quite frankly I felt like I was taking care of three children instead of two. I didn't think that that's what I had signed up for. I thought I had signed up with a partner.

The breakup with my husband was extremely difficult. I had no family here. I had some wonderful women friends at the time who were as good as they could be, but there was still no family support. No sister I could call on and say, "Would you mind the kids for the afternoon?" or anything like that. It was the way most marriage breakups are: painful and messy. Then there was the added problem of Gregory telling his mother that I was a lesbian and her getting in contact with the Children's Aid Society to check out if the children were all right.

Then the Immigration people calling me in for an interview. Everybody only had incomplete information. Immigration had no idea that I had children and they were calling me in because they thought I married him as a ticket into the country. As soon as they realized I had children, everything was fine with them. The Children's Aid contacted the daycare to check up on the welfare of the children, but they got the thumbs up from everybody. In fact, the Children's Aid worker told me the daycare had said the children came from a "culturally enriched" background! That's just the Canadian climate — I'd take them to the museum or art gallery for the air conditioning!

It's what many women go through, and some women go through far worse. It's particularly hard when it's not your home country because you don't know your way around the system in the same way you might if you grew up in a place. It was shocking to me to have Children's Aid and Immigration contact me within hours of each other, simply because of my sexual orientation.

I was in Canada about a year when I kidnapped the children from daycare. Gregory's sister said that she'd see to it that they would take them away from me — I didn't actually kidnap them because I had as much right to take them as anybody else. I took them with the help of some friends and got quite a long way away. Then one night I was talking to the kids and I realized that my troubles with their father were not the children's troubles. I knew if I took them away I would deprive them of any contact with him. And I didn't feel I had the right to do that. If his family wanted to do that, that was a decision that they made. I would cope with it in whatever way I felt was necessary, but I didn't feel that I had the right to make that decision for them. So I came back.

They were very young, three or four. It was an awful time, really. I had problems with my health and wasn't allowed to work for quite a few months, eight maybe. And then it was August and September: the winter was coming and I had no money. I was on welfare and looking for a job desperately. I thought: I can't provide for these children here in the winter. How am I going to get them snow shoes and snowsuits and all those other things they need? My parents said that they would pay my fare home. I wasn't very happy with that at all, but I didn't feel I had much choice about it at the time. So I talked to their dad and said I was thinking about going back. He said he would go back too. Then he said that he wanted to have the children.

We got there and he left them with his parents for a while in Ireland while he went to London. Then I returned to Canada. I was planning to get on my feet and then return for them a year later. He had them for about three or four months when he was living in London. When the year was up I went over to England to get them, but he refused to give them up. I went out for my walk and thought about it.

I realized I could fight for the children, but it would be the children who would get hurt. They didn't deserve to be pulled back and forth between the two of us. It wasn't their doing. They said they wanted to be with their friends and they liked their school and could I come and live there. They were only five or six at the time — quite young. But I said no. I promised them if they ever wanted to live with me, I would come for them. The only time they asked was in very recent years. My daughter now wants to come to live with me. She's coming the end of August 1989.

It's been very difficult. Very, very difficult. I talk to my daughter about coming. We don't really know each other; part of her coming is that we will get to know each other. It's very frightening. It's not like bringing up a child, where you take each other's foibles for granted. She's sixteen — it's getting to know an adult. But I'm very happy that she wants to get to know me.

When my mother-in-law told my sister that I was lesbian and my sister asked me if that was true I said yes. Only once did she really talk to me about it. "I don't understand it. How were you married?" I tried to explain to her that it was a question of an emotional and sexual preference — it's not that I hate men and can't stand them in any shape, make or form. But my emotional allegiance is with women and this is where my sexual preference is also. I don't think that she quite understands that, but she accepted it. She's been to visit me. I lived with one woman for quite a long time and she met her and knew her quite well. My sister told everybody else in the family. My father said he didn't want my mother to know because she couldn't handle it. And I just accepted that. I don't think that I'm very interested in bringing all of that up with my parents. I don't live close enough to them for it to matter.

I worked with LEAF, the women's Legal Education and Action Fund, an organization that challenges the legal system under the Charter of Rights and Freedoms on behalf of women. For example, they have fought for the right for girls to play hockey on whatever team they qualify for. They have also fought for the right of choice for abortion. They are fighting for the rights of women prisoners. They have fought for the right of women to be informed about crimes against women in communities — that the police should notify women at risk. I have not been out there in the front lines of it. I don't think temperamentally I'm suited for that, so I worked in the administration and did the finance work.

I now work in administration for a community legal service, a poverty law clinic in Toronto. I'm the office manager and I work in finance and personnel. I'm happy working in the non-profit sector. It doesn't make me as much money as working in the private sector would, but I feel that I make a contribution to society that I would not make working in the private sector. It's a very deliberate choice I've made to do that, even though it will probably keep me poor forever.

When I came out as a lesbian, I came out with a strong awareness of lesbian issues because I did it in the context of the women's movement. It was a question of it being as legitimate a choice as any other that a person can make. I certainly suffered from internalized homophobia. It took me a long time — long after I was practising it — to name myself as a lesbian. It took a much longer time to be more public about it and to tell people I met, if it was appropriate. What I mean by appropriate is that I don't tell people for the sake of telling them, but I won't talk about imaginary boyfriends. If it comes up in conversation, or somebody says to me, "Do you ever want to get married again?" I'll say, "No, I'm happy the way I am." And if they ask me what the way I am is, I tell them. I certainly make no secret that I'm very committed to my partner, Ali. But that didn't just happen. It was a slow process.

It's important to fight for our legal rights. It's important to be able to have family benefits apply to your partner or to be able to claim bereavement leave if your partner dies. I have as much right as anybody else to display my affection for somebody, within the normal bounds of decency — if I want to hold hands, why shouldn't I? If I want to have some public ceremony acknowledging my relationship, why shouldn't I?

That's all fine and well when I work in a job where it's okay to be gay. Nobody gives a damn as long as I do my job well. It's fine, but there are jobs where that's not possible. I know people who have done it and had people bringing unfair charges of sexual harassment against them. It happens. One woman I know came out at work and very soon she had a co-worker charging that she had approached her sexually.

Lately, I've been thinking about Ireland again and being an immigrant. My partner is from Scotland — there is definitely a cultural bonding there for me that does not happen with Canadian people, no matter how close I get to them. There's that common background and common understanding. Our position as satellites to England is a deep understanding we share. We know what we're talking about when we talk about the Sassenachs.[1] We know exactly what we mean when we say it. Sometimes it is quite ironic that I left a nation dominated by a bigger more powerful one to live in another nation that's dominated by a bigger and more powerful one. There's a big threat to Canada from the United States, what with free trade and the whole lot of it.

Coming to a country that's not my own and fighting for social justice, fighting for the advancement of women, I think: What am I doing it here for? Why am I not doing it at home in Ireland? What is Canada to me that I would want to do that here? I have no conclusions about it, but it's definitely something crossing my mind of late. In Ireland, there's the status of lesbians and homosexuals which is illegal at the moment. I'm sure that lesbian and homosexual Irish people will live their lives the way they always have, but nonetheless that is a dreadful infringement of their rights.

There is also the divorce question. Divorce is against the law too. You just have a poor person's divorce in Ireland: You move out and stop living with that person, but that affects so many things — inheritance, your name. Then there is the question of a woman's right to choice about abortion — also against the law in Ireland. I would not like to be in a position of having to face the choice to have an abortion. Abortion is a woman's choice. I don't believe that anybody else should have the right to make that choice for her. There are a lot of issues.

And there's class. People have this idea in the back of their minds that if people are poor, it's because that's what they've made of their lives and it has nothing to do with education, opportunity or expectations. It sits in the back of people's minds because it's a very comfortable way to think. They know they don't have to do anything about it. If people are poor it's their own fault. That's the attitude.

It's my notion that part of having a social conscience is from being brought up Catholic. Some people don't agree with that, but they weren't brought up by nuns in Ireland. When I was brought up it was emphasized by the priest — and particularly the nuns I went to school with — that part of being a Catholic was that you were concerned about society. I'm not sure they would quite approve of the bent my concerns have taken, but that's certainly where I got my concerns for dealing with these issues. I certainly don't think I would be happy in a big job on Bay Street.

I don't go to church, but I certainly believe in a supreme being. I haven't quite worked it all out because it's only in the last few years that I started feeling a strong need for a spiritual component in my life. When I think of a supreme being, what I think of is a connection to all living things — animals and plants, the essence of life. It wouldn't occur to me to make major decisions in my life without a sense of questing. But I don't see it as God the Father, by any means. I don't see it as God the Mother either. I see it as connected to the strong, positive life force, as much in me as it's out there. I pray after my own fashion.

It wouldn't occur to me to go to Mass or confession. I don't think it was hard for me to give up the Church in that sense. Most of what I rejected was the damnation and hellfire. I don't believe in it. But I do think if you don't learn from your experience and keep in contact with some sense of spirituality, you will kill your soul and make for yourself a pretty empty life.

When I was in school I had a teacher who encouraged me to write. I wrote mainly poetry for about fifteen years, but after I left the children I stopped writing — I just had to close away a whole emotional part of myself. You can't write and have a whole emotional part of yourself closed away. But as they got older and we talked more, I started writing again. And then I started writing short stories.

I've written poetry and short stories — published in Canadian and American anthologies. But there are many, many obstacles in the way of a woman writer. I'd decided quite consciously that I would write about ordinary women's experience — the doubts or questions or struggles or delights of women's lives. They're all I have. I went to Carleton University and took a poetry writing workshop one winter. I remember the instructor sitting down with me one day over a beer and saying to me, "You know Joan, you really are quite a fine writer. And when you broaden your subject matter you'll do just nicely." I was furious! What is this broaden-your-subject-matter all about? What's the matter with my subject matter? Of course, the matter with it is that it relates to women's lives. The instructor was male. I feel quite comfortable writing about women's lives and lesbian lives. I wouldn't say I write exclusively about lesbian lives, but I'm very comfortable doing it and that's what I want to continue doing.

Joan's daughter came to live with her in September 1989 and the arrangement has been working "wonderfully."

Note

1.   A Gaelic term for the English, usually derogatory.

War Bride

Brigid Ryan

Brigid Ryan lives in St. John's, Newfoundland.

I was twenty when I left Loughglynn, Co. Roscommon, in 1932 and went to England to do nursing. When the war started I was nursing in a fever hospital in Ealing near London. We had mostly children in the fever hospitals then, and every night when the sirens went off we had to wrap the children up and take them to shelters. Then we had to black out all the windows with cardboard and dim the lights. We weren't even allowed to use a flashlight. It was really bad. For years we were going back and forth like that to the shelters.

Later on, I got a job nursing in Bournemouth and I had some Irish friends in Poole near Bournemouth whom I used to visit and we used to go to church together. Often we met sailors at church and would invite them for tea, especially the Newfoundlanders. One Sunday, I went to visit my friends after mass and I met my husband there. He was a sailor on a boat with the Royal Navy and he was from Newfoundland. When he first went to England, he was in the forestry but then after about six months he joined the Royal Navy because he had lots of experience of sea and the boats here in Newfoundland. We were friends for a while and then he was transferred to another part of England. When he came back again to Poole, he phoned me to meet him at a friend's house. That was 1941.

In 1942 we were married in Falmouth, where we lived for a while. That's where our daughter Theresa was born in 1943. In Falmouth, there was bombing every night because the Americans were there building a hospital — that's where one of the convoys left to invade for D-Day.[1] My husband got ill. He couldn't go to sea any more so he was transferred to the barracks at Lowestoft, in the east of England. So we went to live in Lowestoft, which was worse because there was hardly a house there that wasn't damaged with the bombs. The naval barracks were there, and there were as many as 6,000 sailors at a time waiting to be transferred to boats or barracks or wherever they were needed. The Germans knew it, so every night they'd be bombing to try to get it. They never hit it for all that. Before we left, the flying saucers were coming over.[2] They were the worst because they used to make those queer noises before they dropped.

In 1945, my husband was sent home to Newfoundland. He got phlebitis in his leg. It was the end of April and the war was still on. He left on a Sunday. The next day I got word that we had to join the boat leaving from Liverpool for Montreal. At nine o'clock in the morning we had to get the train from Lowestoft bound for Liverpool. We spent all day travelling because the lines had been bombed and the train had to detour so many times. When we finally got to Liverpool it was about two o'clock in the morning and there were two other women who were also war brides waiting to get the boat. Their husbands were also from Newfoundland. One woman was from Scotland and the other was from England. There was no place to stay that night so we all had to sleep in the railway station. I took off my coat and wrapped my little girl in it. In the morning we had to go to the office to confirm that we could join the boat. We had our vaccinations, medical tests and immigration papers, and everything was ready to go. It was May 1945. My husband was on his way home, convoying ships to Canada.

We left on the *Manchester Port*, which travelled in convoy, trying to avoid the U-boats.[3] One of the ships near us was sunk one night and then there was a thick fog. We were at sea when the war in Europe finished on the 8th of May, 1945. The engineer and the captain got word and they told us. Before they left England, they knew it would be over shortly, so they had taken food and drink and everything for a celebration. The captain gave a big party one night. We sang and danced until all hours and the next night the engineers gave a party. Everyone on board was invited.

The chief engineer was from Limerick and he took to my daughter Theresa. He used to carry her around in his arms. When we were leaving he gave her boxes of Irish and English candy.

We got into Montreal. We were first class coming over. The navy paid for everything. We were sent to this guest home in Montreal and then taken to the train in the evening, going on down to Moncton, New Brunswick. We had to change there and go down to Sydney, Nova Scotia, where the boats cross over to Newfoundland — the boats used to cross over twice a week then. When we got there the boat had just left for Newfoundland so we were put up at a hotel there from Friday until Tuesday. It was beautiful. The people made us so welcome — said how brave we were coming over. A year before, the *Caribou* was sunk coming from Sydney to Newfoundland and they were all lost. It was torpedoed, so it was still so much in their minds.

We landed in Port aux Basques, Newfoundland, where we got the train bound for Clarenville. We were on the train halfway to St. John's when I had a telegram from my husband that he would meet us in Clarenville, the nearest station to my husband's home. My husband met us at the station. After we had gone through so much during the war, we were so happy to see each other again. When we got to his home in Plate Cove, Bonavista Bay, the neighbours knew we were coming and they had flags out welcoming us home and they had a big party in the school for us. They presented me with a cake and him with tobacco. He used to smoke the pipe then. It was a great welcome.

We lived with his people then until November of 1945. Then we moved into our own house which we built in Plate Cove. It was isolated, but the people were so nice. My husband went into fishing with his brothers and then he went to working on the high road when they were putting new roads through. It was hard work. Our son was born there and both our children went to school out there. I looked after the house and children. I didn't do any work after I came out here. There wasn't work out here anyway. There was only the fishing and the post office. We managed.

I did some work looking after the church, cleaning the altars and the floors every two weeks. So many women did it on their turns. I used to visit the sick. I also did some knitting — sweaters and socks for Pat's brothers. The majority of people where we lived were of Irish descent. They had the Irish custom with dances and concerts going on all the time and there were the usual superstitions and stories. After people died, they thought that they saw them afterwards if they were out late at night or out drinking. They made their own moonshine. They baked their own bread. They'd be churning the butter and they did a lot of knitting and sewing and mat-making. But apart from that, life was just normal and there wasn't much excitement. I always liked a quiet life anyway. I always liked to stay home. I still do. When our daughter entered the convent and our son went to university we came into St. John's to live.

Canada met my expectations. My children were given scholarships and grants to go to university. When the teacher saw that they had the intelligence they were promoted. The government helped them as well. That's why I love Newfoundland — they had such opportunities to get ahead. Now I've a grandchild and that's the crowning glory of all these years. My son I never thought would get married — he was considered old here at 41 when he got married.

The church is the most important thing in my life and in our family. Everything else fades, even good jobs and good money. But that Irish faith has meant so much to us. Sunday, we're up early ready to go to mass. I read somewhere that the Catholic Church will have trials but it will be caused from within the Church, and it's true now. It's Catholics that are destroying the Catholic Church. It's not the outsiders — it's the priests and Catholic people that are persecuting it. But it will rise up again stronger. One of our priests talked one Sunday about the sad times we are going through with the scandals and the abuse of children by priests in Newfoundland. He said it's only that the bad ones are being picked out and a strong church will emerge. But laypeople will take a bigger part in doing that.

My daughter is with the Sisters of Mercy. Theresa entered the convent in the fifties. She always liked working with people, even when she was a youngster. When they were allowed to choose another way of life besides teaching she said she'd like pastor work. She was appointed over on Bell Island, a little island off the coast there, where she worked for a few years while the priest was away. She visited the sick, and took communion to those that were not able to get out, and she'd do shopping for them. She was given permission by the bishop to perform marriages and baptisms, and if the priest couldn't get in to bury the dead, she would do it. She was really doing the work of a priest, except for saying mass. People were really sorry that she was leaving. I was delighted that she was able to help people. She is still doing pastoral work. She is now at St. Fintans, a little fishing village on the west coast of Newfoundland, near Port aux Basques where I first landed.

I see a dramatic change in the role of women in the church in Newfoundland. At one time, the priests came from Ireland, but now there's a scarcity in Ireland. So it may come about that they'll have to ordain women. Not that I'd like that. Women can work without being ordained. They can still work, like the women in our Lord's time, who did the work of the church. They washed the linens and everything like that; they looked after the church.

Brigid Ryan's husband Patrick died on April 2, 1990. She now enjoys visits from her two-year-old grandson every afternoon.

Notes

1. The Allied invasion of Europe, June 6, 1944, in the last phase of World War II.
2. Perhaps a reference to the German V.2 rockets that peppered southeast England during the war.
3. A German submarine.

Power Arrangements
and Double Standards

Patricia Willoughby

*Patricia Willoughby lived in Montreal, Quebec, at the time of
the interview. She moved to Ottawa, Ontario, in 1990.*

My mother and her four daughters lived for the most part by
ourselves. Dad was away at sea most of the time. When I talk to
friends about it now, they say it sounds like *Little Women*. Because
my father was away so much, my mother had to be both father
and mother to us and our attachment to her was very strong. His
coming and going affected us deeply. My memory is of always
waiting for him to come home, longing for him to come home. You
never knew for sure if he'd be there on important occasions. But
my mother was always there.

She was very devoted, very involved in our lives. It was very
intense being in an all-female family. It's hard to describe. Females
are by training taught how to relate and how to care for each other
in the family. We were being taught to look after each other, but
perhaps we were not encouraged to think for ourselves, or do for
ourselves, or make choices. Being the eldest, I had to look after
everybody else. In a way, I took my father's place by trying to be
another parent.

Though my mother's sisters and her family lived in our village
and were supportive, it was very tough for my mother having to
rear us without her husband. In an Irish village she had no social
life — it just wasn't done for a woman to go out on her own. She
had to make all the decisions. She was the only one there when
problems or emergencies cropped up. I don't know how she stuck
it. I can remember going to bed at night and she would be sitting
up, listening to the radio or reading the paper on her own. Yet she

was very fulfilled by her family and didn't question that it should be any other way. There was another side of her that she didn't have much outlet for. She would've made a good politician; she was very good with people.

With me, it wasn't so much a decision to leave Ireland as a decision to travel. I was very influenced by my father's stories of being at sea, travelling around the world, gifts over the years. I was in Dublin working in the civil service and then I got called to work for the airline after I'd been in Dublin about six months. I moved back home and started to work for this airline in Cork.

I was finding living at home very restrictive. My mother tended to be too involved in my life and who I was dating. It was time for me to have my own life, but it just wasn't done for you to leave home and get a flat in the same city. The plan — if my mother had a plan for me or if I had had a plan for myself — would've been to meet a man and go steady and get married around the age of twenty-three or twenty-four. Part of me wanted that, but part of me wanted to travel and explore and have different experiences.

So I did date various men, but I didn't have any serious relationships. There was one artist who I was interested in because we were able to talk about art and something other than dancing. At the time, I thought I wanted to marry him, but he said he wouldn't get married until he was thirty, and we were twenty then. There was no way I was going to hang around for ten years.

The airline sent me one summer to Kennedy Airport, in New York, and when I came back at the end of that summer I was extremely restless. I just couldn't settle into home again and Cork again. I'd had exposure to a huge, cosmopolitan city and I was able to do the kinds of things I wanted to do in New York. So I made up my mind that this was the solution. This would get me out of home and I could travel more. I asked to be transferred back there permanently. But I didn't see it as emigration; I was going to be with the same company doing the same kind of work that I was familiar with. It was an Irish company, kind of a safe way of leaving.

My mother was very upset and didn't want me to go to America. We had arguments. The two sisters coming after me were also branching out. They had gone to Dublin after she had moved to Cork to make a home base in the city for them. Young people have to spread their wings. So here was I pulling out also and it was a difficult time in my mother's life. She was going through the menopause and was depressed. My father at that time was out in deep sea, on trips that kept him away for months at a time. I felt very guilty for leaving but I had to. I didn't want my mother vetting the men I was going out with — whether they were suitable or not for marriage. I wanted her to have a life of her own but she didn't have one.

Money was a problem. We never had a lot of money, so she couldn't do the things that might've helped her make a life for herself. She couldn't look for a job, because a fifty-year-old woman didn't do that in Ireland. When my father came home on leave he expected her to be there for him and she wanted to be there for him. I did feel very guilty for leaving — that's partly why I denied emigration.

The work I did from Kennedy Airport was very difficult. It was a very stressful place working shift work, night shift mostly. You'd go to work around three and finish at eleven. It made social life a bit complicated, and yet I had a good time. I was sharing an apartment with an Irish friend from Cork, also a stewardess, and a couple of other stewardesses. We had enough money to go into the city if we wanted to. I was exposed to all kinds of different cultures and I did a lot. I went around the world on a trip as well as down to South America because I was able to take advantage of the reduced-rate travel.

I still got back to Ireland a lot. When I thought of New York, however, I just didn't think of staying there permanently. I was starting to get bored with the airline work and had the feeling that I was only valued for my Irishness. Being Irish, I somehow belonged to the company. I was being used as a marketing tool.

Then I started going steady with a man. I assumed we would get married and start a family, but we didn't, for various reasons.

He was someone I met through work. That was a big disappointment. By twenty-seven it was definitely time to begin thinking of getting married and settling down. But it didn't work out and I didn't want to be in New York any more. Then I saw there was an opening in the Montreal office of the airline, so I applied for the job here and I got it.

I knew nothing about Canada — I'd come here by default. But as I got to know Canada a bit and began to see the differences between what I knew of American culture — basically New York — and what I was discovering about Canadian culture, I just started to feel much more comfortable here. I left the airline and went to university full-time. This gave me another chance to think, especially in the women's studies courses. It's like taking the blinkers off. When you see things as they really are and you examine them historically, you're full of rage and you don't know what to do about it. It takes a while to work through those feelings and to start figuring out what you can do. You're overwhelmed by how long sexism has been going on and by how insidious it is.

In women's studies they filled in women's history, the parts that women have played and that have been left out of history. In some of those courses I was able to focus on Irish history and Irish literature. That was very exciting for me. For example, back in Irish history, in Celtic times, the women had a very powerful role in the religion. Those Pagan women were vibrant and powerful in their own right. Women like Maeve, Queen of Connaught, the Celtic Goddess, Brigid, and the many women poets inspired me. It was like a second birth. But in another way, it raised my expectations.

One of the biggest disappointments to me — having tried to re-enter the work force after taking time out to do this degree — was that discrimination still exists against women in Canada. I feel as a woman that I have lost out. If I were an Irish immigrant man with a B.A. and work experience, I would be more valued in Canada. There would be more doors open and I wouldn't have to start at the bottom, what with the old boys' network in the Irish community. More than half the students when I was at Concordia

University were women, but to read their magazine you'd think that a woman never set foot inside Concordia. It's all focused on what the male graduates are doing and on male life. There's nothing ever about family or issues that might also interest a career woman.

The feminist movement changed my life. For the first time I started to think of my own life, my experience, my self. The women's movement was just starting up in New York in the late sixties when I got some of those ideas. There were parades. There were exciting books coming out — I'd never read those kinds of books before. I've always been a voracious reader, but it was more literature I read. These new books were about the self. Women were starting to talk about themselves and to talk to each other, to spend time together discussing issues. Not just filling in between men.

In these discussions and exploration of self, sex became a big issue for me. In Ireland, sex was always down-played. Nobody ever talked about it, yet it was there. It permeated everything. I had a normal drive and a normal curiosity, but I wasn't able to satisfy it. I couldn't get any information about sex, so I didn't even have the vocabulary. When I was growing up there was a separation of feelings and body — almost like the body didn't exist. It was a nuisance. You had to take care of it, but it wasn't something you cherished or you were fond of. You were divorced from your body. Looking back, I think Catholicism produced the attitude there was something evil about the flesh.

There was something wrong with exposing your limbs, but you didn't know what it was. I can remember as a little girl, aged about nine or ten, getting a lecture every summer before the school holidays from the nuns: It was a sin to wear shorts and sleeveless tops. It was a sin to sunbathe. And I remember coming home and telling my mother what the nuns had said.

My mother said, "Well, if those nuns think I'm going to iron four dresses every day, they have another think coming." So of course we wore shorts, and of course we wore sleeveless tops. But I can remember running and hiding when the nuns were seen walking up the village street because I was wearing shorts. And they had their spies in the village. Yet we lived in such a healthy place. Rosslare Strand was a little seaside village and we spent all day on the beach. The feeling of the sun and the wind and water on your body was very sensuous, but those feelings were wrong. You were supposed to ignore them.

Women's troubles — you could tune in any time you wanted, any time my mother was around other females. But it's hard for a little girl to relate to something that's going to happen sometime in the future. You don't connect all of that with the feelings that you're starting to have in your own body. It's as if they separated the act of sex from the result of sex. Children materialized, but nobody dwelt on the behaviour that produced the children — there was just a great silence about it all. That was the big sin a few years later when they started giving lectures about purity. It's all you ever heard of. But I never thought it was a sin to touch yourself. They told me so, but it was my body, so part of me listened and part of me didn't. I was a divided spirit.

I started hanging out with boys when I was about fourteen or so, just like everybody else. There was a natural curiosity, but you never talked. I don't know if kids of fourteen or fifteen these days talk to each other. Back then it was just groping and heavy breathing. Then that burden: You, the girl, were in charge of both your purity and his. Not only did you have to worry about your own responses, but it was your job to keep him in check too. I remember one guy — we weren't doing anything more than kissing, but he actually told me it was my job to keep him pure! He was free to feel his feelings. A fellow couldn't control himself, nor was he expected to. He was a lusty animal — that way he didn't have to take responsibility for his actions.

My mother didn't talk much about sex with us, but she did convey that the body was natural and had its own little systems. It was to be trusted. One example: When I came back from a shopping trip in London, I had bought one of those female hygiene products, vaginal deodorant. My mother saw it in my room and said, "What's this?" "Well, that's supposed to keep you smelling fresh." She smiled and said, "You don't need that. The body has its own way of cleansing itself out."

When I was working and starting to date guys it was very hard to establish how far you could go if you still wanted to be considered a "nice girl." I never could figure the limits out and I probably exceeded those limits, whatever they were. I remember one conversation I had with a young woman I was working with — I was about nineteen at the time. I dated a guy she used to date and she was friendly with him. He must've said something to her because she brought it up one time over a coffee in the cafeteria. All this hinting and innuendo — you had to be careful, keep yourself to yourself, especially when you were going out with guys casually.

I was sitting there mortified, not sure exactly what she was referring to, which guy had told her what, and just convinced these were rules that everybody else knew, but I didn't, and that somehow I was inadequate. That's the way it was: You were fighting to keep your virginity because you were supposed to be a virgin when you married, like the Virgin Mary. But everybody was dying to get rid of that very virginity because it became such a burden. Men could do it whenever they could get away with it; there were no sanctions for them. For women, sex became a commodity. As long as you were technically a virgin, you could do everything else. There were consequences for women but not for men. In the end, I resented being a female. Quite apart from the fear of getting pregnant — really the big deterrent — it was part of life I was having to hold off on.

Going to the dances at home in Ireland, I resented that you had to dress up and make up and put a lot of effort into your appearance. You would arrive at the dance about nine o'clock and the guys wouldn't show up until the pubs closed. They would roll in half-drunk, and after one dance expect to drive you home or walk you home, and expect you to — not sleep with them exactly, but "co-operate." We used to call it "the inevitable half-hour." You might just want to talk to a guy and have a discussion about a book or something, but you also had to go through this struggle with him.

Soon after I got to New York, I went on the pill. My stewardess roommate and I got the name of a gynecologist who dished out the pill like they were Smarties, with a pat on the back. It was very sexist, but I needed that approval to be allowed to be sexual. The "nice girls" standard still applied to women. Now that I was finally free to have sex, guys judged me afterwards, and I became the "bad girl." I thought I had left all that behind in Ireland — that sexism and double standard and virgin/whore dichotomy.

When I look around me, I don't see that men have made much effort to change themselves or to meet women halfway. This is another double standard: The women have been doing all the changing and the men just stay there and don't look at themselves at all.

The power arrangements bother me. So much of women's work is devalued. Under the existing arrangements, a man can go out and have a career and work every day, but he doesn't acknowledge that he can do this only because he has a wife who will take care of the domestic work as well as the children — and often this woman has a career of her own as well. This sexism, this patriarchy, is just as insidious here in Canada. Men have most of the power, even here in this society. The impression here is that people can buy whatever they want, and sex is one of the commodities available. At least in Ireland, we didn't have this selling of sex. It may have been denied, it may have been repressed, but you had the feeling that it did have value. In North America, it's just another commodity. Very often at women's expense.

Part of my dream in coming here was that I would meet somebody and marry and have that security and support. I have had relationships, but they didn't work out for one reason or another. I never imagined that I would be living alone like this. Nothing could've prepared me for the loneliness. When I first came here it was easier because I had a group of single friends, but that group dispersed as the language issues in Quebec flared up. A lot of those people moved on so I have fewer friends than before. I find it hard to make friends.

Life sometimes feels very barren without a child — that continuity is broken. Most of the women in my family married and had children. I now feel cut off from that female handing-down. I have a lot of freedom and that's important to me as a single woman living in a big city in Canada. I only have to think of myself. I'm only responsible for myself. I could come and go. But I find that life gets harder without a partner as you go on — hard in not having someone to share the difficult times with, as well as the good times, not having someone to talk to. I can go for days without talking to anybody. In my upbringing that wasn't ever part of what I was led to expect. Sometimes I feel guilty having all this time and leisure. It's just so different.

But at my age, where priorities are different, I would only consider a relationship in which I could be equal with the other person — in power and in the sense that my activities are as valid as his. I don't want to end up having to mother somebody. I lived with someone briefly; the minute I got into that domestic set-up, I tended to take over and take on responsibility for feeding him. So I became the wife, even though we weren't married.

In the traditional family, the man has to have this kind of cocoon around him. He has to be nurtured and supported to enable him to be a man. The woman is also going out to work outside, but she doesn't get that kind of nurturing. There are so many needy women in marriages where they're giving, giving, giving and doing, doing, doing. Nobody is attending to them. What I want is very different. Frankly, I'm not very hopeful that I'll find it. But I do resent that I put so much energy into changing myself and I turn around and I don't see the men working on their nurturing sides. We're out of balance.

Whatever You Do, Mary, Never Settle for Second Best

Mary Broderick

Mary Broderick lives in Georgetown, Ontario.

I come from a small little village, Derrybrien, in the west of Ireland. Derrybrien is nestled in the Aughty mountains close to Gort, Co. Galway, and not too far away from Coole where W. B. Yeats used to spend his summers. That's where he wrote his famous poem, "The Wild Swans at Coole." At one end of our village was O'Brien's Wood — in Gaelic it's Doire Uí Bhrían — where the trees made an arch as they do in Coole Park. In the springtime it used to be so green, that lush green that you only get in Ireland. The other end of the village was where my family lived, in a little thatched cottage where the forest started.

My mother ran the household, but she also did a lot of work outside. My mother was known by the neighbours as a woman who could do a man's job any day. Kathleen Broderick was known for that. She worked with my father, side by side, cutting the hay and footing the turf. My father was a farmer, but his real heart was in story-telling and reading — he was a seanachí, the Gaelic for the local bard or story-teller. Before television this was how people passed the evenings by the fireside. In those days, because the farms were very small, it didn't make sense to buy machinery. They couldn't afford machinery anyway, and it wasn't really necessary because the farms were very small, about twenty acres or so. Everything had to be done by hand. It was very hard work.

After working in the fields, my mother would come home and do the cooking. My father, while he was a good man in many ways, very kind in spirit, his interest was more or less in the books. He wasn't that interested in farming, but having a big family, farming had to be done. He also worked for the forestry as a labourer on a part-time basis to supplement the family income. My father did his annual thatching to keep our cottage up. It had two rooms and was the original house that his father lived in and his grandfather before him.

My father really didn't want television at all. He sensed it would interfere with story-telling and, maybe more important, reading and people's own self-education. He was a self-educated man. If he had opportunities, he could have become a writer or a poet. He could write a poem about people in a matter of minutes — he would sum up the situation and write about it. While he never had the opportunity to play a musical instrument, he had an ear for music and he was able to put music to words. In the last ten years or so he's been interviewed by the Irish Heritage Society, a society interested in maintaining our heritage and capturing the stories of the west of Ireland before they're lost. So he's been interviewed in the bog, and by the hearth telling stories and yarns.

Being the oldest, I had to look after my brothers and sisters. There were eight of us altogether. I was born in 1947. When I was nine years of age I baked my first apple pie. I was quite proud of that and so was my mother. We used those old iron pots and ovens — the food has never tasted the same since; there's something about cooking over an open fire. One of the big jobs I remember doing was the weekly washing. Because we didn't have running water in the house I had to draw all the water from the stream, which meant I had to carry pails of water up a hill and then boil it over the fire. It took nine pails of water to do the wash, and then I would have to take the clothes down to the stream to rinse them. Drying was another challenge because in Ireland it rains such a lot. There's little opportunity to dry clothes if you have to catch them between showers.

One of my earliest memories was when my father or a neighbour, Mairteen Connaire, would tell myself and my brothers and sisters stories every night. Mairteen was an old man and a great story-teller. He would tell us about hearses with lights coming on and off and headless horses — we were scared to go to sleep at night — but every time Mairteen would come we couldn't resist the stories.

The story-telling was big in our part of Ireland and our house was always open for people to drop in for a cup of tea at nights. The teapot was forever brewing on a few coals to one side of the open hearth. My father was very interested in talking to strangers so he would sometimes bring people or tourists home for dinner. My mother was very good about this. She never knew when somebody new might drop in and we would always share the food around. I thought that pretty normal until I came to this country. Now I find this was unique to our culture.

At the pub people would get together, and after mass on Sundays my grandmother and father from time to time would go in for a little drop of something. My grandmother said it was for medicinal purposes — if anything, she liked it a little bit more. But it didn't hurt her. The pub was always a place that my parents would take visitors from the States or wherever. Mac's Pub was a little hole in the wall of one of the village houses — in the earlier days it was thatched. It had one counter and a few chairs, so it could only hold a few people. It was very small and quaint and cosy. All the villagers went there. Later on it became Carey's.

Sometimes after hours it was commonplace in Ireland to have a visit from the Gardaí — the police. Then people would be invited into the parlour to share some spirits there. But that would only work for a while — the Gardaí would get wind of this and they'd be down to give a summons.

I went to a convent school when I was fourteen; that was when I first left home. I went to live with my great-aunt because my parents couldn't afford boarding school. This was where I had my first experience of discrimination against country people. I got very good marks the first term and because of that I skipped a year. The head nun never let me forget this. She would ask me the most difficult questions — questions somebody at a higher level would not be able to answer. Naturally, I wouldn't know the answers.

Her comment was, "Oh, Miss Broderick, down from the

mountain, you're getting more and more stupid every day." I didn't realize the impact of this until my first job — I found that my ability was greater than my confidence. I was fortunate to have a good manager for my first job in Ireland who helped me see this. She went to the same school and was a couple of years ahead of me. I swore that if I ever had a daughter in Ireland, I would never send her to the nuns. They were very, very cruel.

I decided to leave Ireland — I wanted to have some control over my own destiny. If I had stayed in Ireland, I would've gotten married like most other women, and I would have had at least eight kids like my mother. I had nothing against marriage, but I didn't want to have the life my mother had. The other reason was I always wanted to go to university, but the cost would have been prohibitive in Ireland.

Before I left, I worked as a lab technician for Irish Base Metals, a subsidiary of a Canadian company, which opened the Tynagh mines near Loughrea, Co. Galway. Our lab was on a beautiful setting by the lake in Loughrea. We used to go out in the morning and have our coffee break overlooking the lake. I left home early in the morning to get to work. Passing the lake, I would notice that shimmering effect over it. It was very tranquil. There were some Canadians at work and they talked about snow-capped mountains and lumberjacks. To me it was a fascinating place.

The senior geologist was very easy-going, very personable, and always very supportive. While I didn't report to him directly, he knew me quite well, and he used to show me some photos of Toronto. That was the beginning of my decision to choose Canada as my new homeland. I was fortunate I ended up having a job to come to in Canada — I wrote to this man out of the blue, a personal letter saying I was planning to come to Canada. I had already applied to the Embassy and was coming, whether I had a job or not. To my surprise, he wrote back saying there would be a job for me in Toronto.

I don't remember too much about leaving, but it was a happy experience. I felt that I was leaving only for two years and this is what I told my parents. They weren't surprised that I would leave

— many people leave Ireland and go to England, America and Australia. I was going to Canada — a slightly different place — and people were quite interested in why I chose Canada.

I had been just about eight months in Canada, and I was very, very lonely. Relationships with men were very depressing for me and I was beginning to wonder if there were any decent men around. A lot of the men who approached me were married, but it wasn't apparent to me — I was so naive and green. I was being followed by men everywhere I went and even had to stop swimming lessons because I was frightened to come home at night. I didn't know what it was.

In the first months in Canada, I felt out of place. Standing in the middle of Toronto, walking down Bloor Street or Bay Street in the thick of traffic with this horrible incessant noise, I used to think back home to Derrybrien. I was lonely for my family. I was lonely for the rolling hills of home, the green hills, the ocean, the heather — everything that's Ireland. Brown bread and jam, blackberry jam. My father's story-telling. And the tea sitting on the hearth. Mairteen and my girlfriends that I grew up with. I used to wonder if life had stood still for them.

I was just lonely for the warmth of people. I was also longing for the decency of the men I had left and I looked on them in better eyes after some of my earlier experiences here in Canada. The bright lights of Toronto got to me. I grew up mostly in candlelight — we didn't have electric light. Now I longed for that candlelight — sitting by the fire looking into the burning cinders at home, listening to the kettle singing on the hob and listening to the grandfather doing its tick-tock on the wall. I missed going out in the evening and looking at the moon and the stars; they were so bright that they just lit up the sky and cast shadows through the mountains. I missed the bog too, always a very special place for us — just being there, so far down in the earth, very spiritual in some ways.

Travelling on the subway in Toronto, I almost got killed because I was walking so slowly. I was at the usual normal pace I would walk in Ireland, but in Toronto people were walking on my heels, so I had to start running. I had to pick up the pace and there was a real hustle and bustle about it all.

Not long after I was in Toronto, I got laid off. I'll never forget my first job interview. I was asked what skills I had — the implication being I didn't have any secretarial skills and might not be worthwhile as an employee. I was very prompt to reply that I didn't have those skills and had no intention of acquiring them. I didn't want to be stuck in a pink-collar ghetto, whether it was this country or Ireland. I didn't want to be stuck with low pay and little opportunity for advancement. To my surprise I was hired.

It wasn't a very good place to be. There was a lot of unhappiness among the women in the company. The managers, who were mostly male, expected the women to provide coffee every day and work all kinds of overtime for little or no pay. For some reason, the women came to me and we decided one day we would not provide coffee for the managers, to make a point. The point was well received — there was some concern among the upper management about this behaviour and a meeting was called; this was discussed as well as some of the other problems. However, a lot of people are a little bit scared to really speak up in such a situation. They're scared for their jobs. I didn't have a lot of support among the group for those reasons. I eventually ended up leaving the company because of pay and because I could see myself going nowhere.

I had other eye-opening experiences. I was openly told by an agency that I would not be considered for one job because I was a woman. This really bothered me. I had to do something about it — not just for my own sake but for the sake of other women — so I complained to the Ontario Human Rights Commission, which was just at its beginnings then in the very early seventies. And to my surprise they really took this quite seriously and they investigated the company very thoroughly. The company may have learned a lesson that they cannot discriminate.

Along the years in various companies, I have worked very, very hard. I had to work a bit harder as a woman — to prove myself and to make the plight of other women a bit easier. Women in business were relatively rare in the mid-seventies. It's all in the past ten years or so that women have made some inroads here. I've had a couple of career changes since the early seventies and have reached a point in middle management. I have found some discrimination along the way, but I have taken a fairly positive approach about it all, trying to work from the inside by showing that I have the ability.

One of my major reasons for leaving Ireland was to get an education. I have realized my dream. In 1977, I went to night school at York University to get a degree in business. This took me several years. I did get a degree and I'm very happy about this. It took me seven years of night school, two nights a week — this was particularly tough because I always had busy jobs with a lot of overtime. I used to get home from work and university very, very late at night. My weekends were always tied up in studying and it did have a dampening effect on my social life. But it was very important to me to get the degree so I made a lot of sacrifices and got there. Right now, I'm very happy in my current job. I'm in a position that I really like, working for a large company. Several years of struggle have been really worthwhile.

When I first came to Canada, I was very disillusioned with relationships with men. I came during the early seventies, when Toronto was going through the sexual revolution. But I wasn't even aware that it was going on. I came from Ireland very, very green, very naive and innocent, very trusting. Men weren't interested in any kind of a serious relationship at all. I wanted a meaningful relationship and marriage, but most of the men I met were separated so they weren't available. And those that were available found me a little bit independent. I didn't want a traditional relationship. I was looking for more of an equal partnership and that became apparent as time went on in the relationship.

My experiences in Canada — having to fight for myself in the workplace and prove myself there — probably changed me a little bit too from the way I used to be. I became much more independent and assertive and a little bit more careful in the type of partner I wanted to meet and end up with. In my late thirties, I was becoming very disillusioned altogether with men. I'll never forget my father advising me as a young girl, before I left Ireland: "Whatever you do, Mary, never settle for second best in anything, especially a man." I had listened to him well. I began to think I would spend my life alone and had come to terms with that — I was not prepared to consider a marriage where the man was not going to consider an equal relationship.

One night I happened to be at a classical-music–appreciation night and quite out of the blue I met Patrick, my husband. He invited me out on a couple of occasions, but I didn't have any interest. However, he was persistent and a couple of months later we ended up on a date — we went for a walk in the woods. There was something very gentle about his nature. I played him some Irish music — very "poignant" was his word, and I thought: There's some possibilities with this fellow. I wasn't really thinking romance. We talked a lot and saw each other again at the weekend. I took him to an Irish event he enjoyed very much. There was no pressure, which I appreciated. After about three weeks, he told me that I was "hard on the heart strings," a bit of a surprise to me. We went out several months before I even considered the relationship because I had been hurt many times before and I was being very cautious. We got married just a few weeks ago. We went home to Ireland for our honeymoon — this is the first time after leaving Ireland that I feel very good about returning to Canada.

My dreams have been fulfilled: I got my degree, I'm very, very happy with my career and I have a relationship I have no reservations about. For those who've had rough times, don't give up — it's worth the struggle. When I left Ireland, I looked towards Canada as the faraway hills that are green. I had a very romantic image of the country. As a young woman, I had a great spirit of adventure leaving Ireland. I had no fears. After coming to Canada, for a while the faraway hills weren't so green at all. Now at last they're a bright emerald.

The Troubles

Barbed Wire and Barricades

Máire gan Ainm

*Máire gan Ainm lives in Winnipeg, Manitoba. She decided to
be nameless — gan ainm — for this story because she fears
reprisals against her family in Ireland or in Canada once
her story is public. She also changed dates and places
to avoid detection.*

I was born in Armagh in the North of Ireland in 1950. There were
four children in our family, two boys and two girls. My father was
a storeman. My mother never worked — the mother never
worked. We weren't well off at all; we just managed to get by and
I often wondered how we did. My mother had TB and was in
hospital for a year. My sister also had TB and was in hospital as
well. So I remember at that time in my life — I was only about
five, I guess — being very worried that my mother was going to
die.

We were Catholic. When I was seven I went to primary school,
run by the Sacred Heart nuns who controlled the three major girls'
schools: the convent, the intermediate and the grammar school.
We had Mass in the school every Friday and we went once a
month to confessions. We were very caught up with the Church
in our lives because that was the way our parents were. Funny
enough, the Catholic schools were all at one end of the town and
the Protestant schools were at the other end, so there really wasn't
anywhere that you would meet anyone your own age who
would've been a Protestant. You might meet them on the street,
and you would know by their uniform that they were from the
other school, but you wouldn't talk to them or anything.

The Civil Rights movement started around 1968.[1] I first became aware when there was going to be an election and the local
Civil Rights group were trying to make Catholics, in particular,

aware of the gerrymandering that was going on. I remember going into the city hall where they had pinned up on the wall this great big map of the Armagh area and it showed you all the electoral boundaries. They had it all chalked up in the most ridiculous pieces. It was the funniest shape you ever saw in your life.

To ensure there would be a majority Protestant local Council, for instance, they had divided up the area so that they would take, say, a Protestant estate in the very north of the city and they would put a boundary around that. Then they would count how many houses were in there, and if they didn't think they had enough to win the election, they would take another Protestant estate and put it with that one. Or else they would cut the Catholic estate in half and put the smaller half of the Catholic estate with the larger Protestant one so a Protestant would be the representative. When the Protestants were in the minority they set up this way.

The man that my father worked for happened to be a Protestant landowner — just an ordinary man like my father — but he was a Protestant and he owned his own home and the land that went with it. He also owned a store in the town as well as the mill where my father worked. He had three votes in the election because he had three separate properties. My father had only one. The Protestants had the stance and the position and the land and the property. The wealth that was in the country belonged to them and not to us. They had put us where we were, and no matter how we worked or strived or tried to improve, we could never ever reach what they already had handed to them.

When they started to march for Civil Rights it became popular to become a member because there were lots of people quite outraged. There was a march through the town one day, and without telling my parents, myself and my friend Anne participated in this march. We were trying to show the British government and the Council in Armagh that we knew what was going on about gerrymandering of the votes and that we weren't going to take it. It was a protest march, that's what it was. The line for the day was "One Man, One Vote" as we walked along the streets in Armagh, very narrow old streets.

It was a peaceful march, but when we got to a certain part of the town two lines of police were blocking the top of the street — there was no British Army there at that point — holding back a Protestant crowd which had come to jeer. They were shouting "Papists!" "Pope lovers!" "Dirty Catholics!" "Fenian bastards!" Then they started throwing rocks and bottles at us. To retaliate, the Civil Rights crowd starting throwing things back and soon placards were flying with poles on them all up and down, all over the place. It just went mad. The police ended up protecting the Protestants. I remember being really scared and my friend and I got away around the back streets. We were panting, running and running down the streets. Running for our lives. I don't know what we thought was going to happen to us.

One of the first murders in Northern Ireland happened to a man called John Gallagher who lived in a Catholic estate in Armagh. He had been in a Civil Rights march — I wasn't there that night but there was a friend of mine who was and he told me about it. As they marched along it was nighttime. The "B" Specials[2] — who had come down into the middle of them — started to shoot into the crowd.

Everybody just scattered. This boy that I knew ran towards the Catholic cathedral: He knew that if he could get into the grounds and down the back, he could get out onto the road and away. He scaled the church gates — about ten feet tall with prongs and spikes along the top — in his haste. But this man John Gallagher was shot dead by the police while he was trying to get away.

The next day you could feel this horrible atmosphere in the town — it was almost like a sense of waiting. John Gallagher's body was to be waked at his home. He was in his late thirties or early forties, and a family man, and nobody could believe that he had actually been killed. The day of the funeral nearly all the Catholic stores and businesses closed and I remember going to watch the funeral which went from his home right up through the town and up to the church.

People were standing maybe six deep all along the way. This man would never have been noticed in his life. He wasn't any more remarkable than someone else, except for the way he was killed. After that, I think the IRA movement in Armagh gained a lot of allegiance from people who might never have become involved in it, just because of what happened and that this might happen to anyone else.

When the British Army came into Armagh, they tended to provoke people in lots of ways. One night my husband's sister was going out and she asked if we would babysit. She lived right in the middle of this housing estate. We got the children to bed in the front room and we were just sitting watching television when all of a sudden we heard this commotion outside. We went to the door and looked out and there was a British Army patrol coming through the estate.[3] As they were coming along, they were taking their guns and pounding them up and down the fence in front of the house, rattling it away. They could've just gone and done their business and left.

It was dark. Up one of the side streets, some children were out playing. The Army was going past and the soldiers shouted at the children to get off the streets and the children shouted back that they were just playing. One of the soldiers shot a rubber bullet up into the darkness into the middle of them. Nobody was hurt, but somebody could've been killed. I remember feeling so angry and my husband Patrick having to hold me back because I was going to go out to them.

It was common where Patrick lived to have army patrols search your house, usually when you'd be in bed — say, 11:30 or 12 o'clock at night or later. It wasn't necessarily somebody that they thought had anything to do with the IRA, it just was anybody. Great big burly soldiers walking in with guns and faces blackened in the middle of the night was terrifying. They would even go into the children's bedrooms. If you were asleep, it wouldn't matter and the rooms were searched from top to bottom as well as the whole house. Then they would leave and they would drop in on somebody else.

The night before we got married, Patrick was questioned. Did he know this one? Did he know that one? Did he know where they were? They knew that he was getting married the next day and they knew who he was getting married to. They knew the whole ins and outs of everything. Finally, they let him go — it was just harassment. You could be stopped right on the street. You could be told to line up against the wall, straddle, put your arms against the wall, extend your legs, for men. And they would search you from top to bottom.

Shortly after being married one morning I was going to the Catholic school where I worked. It was raining really hard and I thought I'd take a shortcut up a hill and round a back street. I had this great big umbrella, I remember. It was a driving rain, and I had the umbrella tilted in front of my head as I went up the hill. When I put the umbrella up to see where I was going, I saw the whole street was full of soldiers. We had been told to walk, put your head in the air, and just walk past them. You just didn't talk to them. They were shouting at me because there was no one else on the street which was just a side street. I just kept walking and my heart was thumping.

When I got to the end of the street, this one soldier came up to me. He was just a very young man and he was very rude. He asked me where I was going. When I told him which school I worked at he knew that I was Catholic. He said, "Open your purse." So I had to open this purse and shift the umbrella in the pouring rain. He checked through the purse and he closed it up and he said, "Now open your coat." I knew that women weren't allowed to be searched — they had women soldiers to do this.

It got my ire up. And I said, "No, I won't." And he said, "You will, you know." And I said, "No, I don't have to do that. You can't search me on my person." And he said, "Well, we'll see about that. Do you want to go and talk to the sergeant?" I really was frightened. He was just tormenting me. Just at that moment Patrick, my husband, came to give me a ride to work because it was raining. The soldier didn't pursue it, but I was really upset. A lot of times the soldiers would shout at you, "Are you not going to stop and talk to us?" and "Come on over here!" Or they'd whistle.

We decided to go to Canada for various reasons. One of them was the political situation. We didn't like the idea that our children were going to be brought up in a society where you were going to be searched on the street at somebody's whim. Those things were normal to us and we knew that somewhere those things didn't happen. There had to be other countries where it wasn't like that. We decided to see if we would be accepted for coming to Canada. Much to our amazement we were. We didn't have anybody here to come to, we didn't have any jobs, we didn't have much money and we didn't have anywhere to live. We really hadn't anything going for us.

We were called for an interview. In the middle of the interview the man who interviewed us, who was Canadian, took out this great big French book, put it in front of us and said, "Translate these two pages." I took the book because I had done more French, and the man said, "Not you. Your husband has to do it." And I said, "But I have more French than Patrick." He said, "It doesn't matter."

So Patrick stumbled through this. Then he kept asking Patrick about his job and different things and I said to him, "Well, you know, I have studied and worked as a journalist and I've done...." And he said, "Well, we're really not interested in you. This whole interview is based on the husband." It was as if I didn't exist. And I said, "Why is that? I just think this is so unfair." He said, "Well, the general consensus is that you will go to Canada and you probably will not be a member of the work force. You'll probably have children. We have to base all our decisions on the husband's credentials." I didn't know why he had even invited me to the interview if I was of no importance.

It made me think: God, what am I getting myself into? Maybe it's just going to be as bad over there as it is here. Is this normal in Canada that women are not going to be accepted for what they are and considered valuable members of society? Is it going to be just the way it is at home? I was angry with him and I told him so. Nevertheless, I thought: I'll just get there and once I get there

I'll just do my own thing regardless of this man. I didn't care what he thought.

I remember Patrick and I lying in bed at night talking about emigrating. We were so excited. We were so young making all these plans and just so anxious to get away. And I'll never forget — we were on the third floor of this house lying in bed one night and all of a sudden we hear this knock-knock-knock on the window. We pulled the curtains and here's this fireman, Paddy MacLaren, standing on a ladder. So we opened the window up and he said, "You're having to get out!"

About two doors down there was a pub and an incendiary device was found in it, set for a certain time to cause a fire. The fire had already started and they were evacuating these houses on the hill. I remember putting on my housecoat and taking the brown envelope, and it didn't matter about anything in the whole place as long as we had The Brown Envelope with all our things in it for Canada.

We left Ireland on January 15, 1973. We packed our suitcases and we left from my parents' home. My mother insisted on putting the teapot in the suitcase and two cups and homemade butter and homemade bread. All this just in case there was no food in Canada! Off we went and we got to the airport. All the families were there to see us away and everybody was crying. I remember we got all these letters and we opened them up when we got on the plane. Nearly every one of them had St. Christopher's medals inside. For safe travel!

We got to the airport at Winnipeg — and we could see from the airplane that it was all white and there was lots of snow — but we didn't know that it was as cold as it really was. We came through Immigration and there was a young man on the desk who took our passports and looked at them and he asked us if anybody was meeting us and we said no. He asked had we anywhere to stay and we said no. And he took his little stamp and went bump-bump-bump and said, "Good luck," and handed us the passports back. I thought: God, what do we do now?

We took a cab to a hotel downtown. We just went from the doors of the airport to the cab. As we drove along, this great big snow storm — they had just ploughed and so on either side of the road there were these mountains of snow piled up. It was like going through a tunnel, a big white tunnel. And Patrick was on one side of the cab and I was on the other and the both of us had our mouths open looking out of this window. It was about a quarter to four in the afternoon and the children were coming home from school and they were all wearing snowsuits and scarves wrapped twice around their heads. We looked at them and we thought we'd landed on Mars.

We got to the hotel and got ourselves settled. We'd promised that we'd send a telegram to say we had arrived. The CN telegram office was just about two blocks away, so we thought that would be a nice walk. We hadn't been outside yet. I had a long coat and I had a hat and scarf that matched it and I had boots. Patrick had bought himself a new corduroy three-quarter–length jacket, but he had no gloves, no hat, no scarf, no long underwear or anything else. So we started off down the street.

We had been talking, and all of a sudden I turned around and looked at him — his whole face was covered in frost. It was like he had been chiselled. He couldn't talk, he was so cold. We had enough sense to run the rest of the way and when we got into the telegram office I remember the man saying, "My God, have you no hat on you!" We had to give him the telegram message and of course when he was reading this telegram, "Arrived safely," he said, "Oh, you've just come!"

The contrast between Ireland and Canada was very vivid and real right away. We had been used to seeing a lot of bomb-damaged areas and streets cordoned off, with barbed wire and barricades, in Armagh. The town itself always had this cloud hanging over. In winter it was always very grey, damp, wet. There was no future. After living in the Troubles in Northern Ireland, it was refreshing not to meet a patrol of soldiers with guns on the street or to have somebody come to your door to search your home.

We both got jobs in Winnipeg and it didn't matter whether we were Catholic or Protestant or what we were. Nobody was interested. It didn't matter to our landlord when we filled out our forms for our lease: He couldn't care less who we were or what we were as long as we could afford to pay for this room. Well, it felt wonderful, you know.

One of the things we noticed most was the different nationalities. In the space of a day you would meet all sorts of people. You could get on the bus and would hear people speaking German or Chinese or whatever. You couldn't understand a word they were saying, but you'd be smiling to yourself because it was good that it was like that. People tended to be very friendly because they knew we were from somewhere else and they sort of enjoyed hearing us speak and were willing to be helpful.

The lay of the land was so different. Winnipeg was so big and spacious and open — that flat prairie land that was endless gave the feeling of openness and freedom. Even if it was snowing and it was six feet deep, I'd look out my window when I wakened up in the mornings and see the sky, so blue and so bright and sparkling. It seemed almost like we were going through another door into another life.

Notes

1. Demands included an end to discrimination in local government, the allocation of housing by a points system to prevent favouritism, the repeal of the 1922 Special Powers Act and the disbanding of the "B" Specials. The Special Powers Act suspends habeas corpus and abolishes inquests into suspicious deaths, lets the police search homes without warrants, and permits indefinite imprisonment without trial. On the "B" Specials, see note 2.

2. Part-time members of the Royal Ulster Constabulary — the RUC — set up in 1920 to combat the Irish Republican Army in the

North. "By the middle of 1922 there were more than 50,000 full and part-time policemen in Northern Ireland: one to every six households in the province." See John O'Beirne Ranelagh, *A Short History of Ireland* (Cambridge: Cambridge University Press, 1983), p. 247.

There were also "A" Specials, who served full-time for six months, and "C" Specials or reserve forces; both groups were disbanded in the 1930s. At that time, the "B" Specials became permanent forces of the RUC. On August 1, 1969, none of the 8,900 "B" Specials were Catholics. The Northern parliament disbanded the "B" Specials in 1970 and disarmed the RUC. In 1971 the RUC was rearmed.

3.   For the first time in fifty years, British troops took the streets of Derry, in the North, at five o'clock in the evening on August 14, 1969, after fierce rioting followed an RUC siege of the Bogside area.

And the Blue Sky Made
It All Seem Possible

Maggie Thompson

Maggie Thompson lives in Vancouver, British Columbia.

My family, the Thompsons, emigrated from Scotland to the North of Ireland in the late 1600s, as part of the Plantation of Ulster.[1] During that time Ulster became the power base that Britain has managed to maintain until this day. Most of the farmers in the area that I grew up in were Protestants, and most of the smaller holdings were houses on lots where Catholics lived — there were some Catholics in the district but they tended not to be farmers. My family was Protestant and relatively middle-class. We were Methodists while most Protestants in the North were Presbyterian. There was a bit of chauvinism between all the Protestant denominations: The Methodists thought they were the purer breed; and, of course, the Presbyterians thought they were the purer breed.

I was born in Belfast in 1958, the second of four children; we were all born within five years of each other. Mum and Dad married late, in their early thirties, so I suppose they were in a hurry to have a family. Being the second girl, I was probably a disappointment to them. Most farmers want to have a boy early in the sequence. I became the boy of the family, on the farm a lot with my Dad. My brother who was next in line after me was always in the kitchen with my Mum!

Our farm was between Crumlin and Antrim, in a little place called The Diamond, on the shores of Lough Neagh, very close to the power base of the Protestant Loyalists. It was also a very beautiful, tranquil place. When I was growing up there was a big, big beech tree — two or three hundred years old — at the very end of our garden. At the foot of the garden there was a road. Across the road there was the shoreline of Lough Neagh.

I used to sit under that tree and look out over Lough Neagh. Whenever I got into trouble with my brother and sisters or Mum and Dad, which I often did, I would go for solace and lean against this beech tree and just talk to it. I felt comforted by it. The last time I was home, in 1986, that beech tree still had a very grounding effect on me.

I was ten years old when the Troubles really flared up. As kids we used to build a pile of sticks and light fires in this little area of a field that was kind of hidden from the road. One day we lit a fire and left it unattended for a short time as we were gathering more sticks. When we came back there were two soldiers standing up on a wall above the fire, pointing guns at us. We knew we weren't really supposed to have lit the fire in the first place and we knew we weren't supposed to leave the fire unattended, but we couldn't understand why someone would want to kill us for doing that. We were really, really scared.

Right beside us, about two or three hundred yards down the road, was a pumping station that pumped water from Lough Neagh to Belfast. It wasn't a major supplier of water, but it was a pumping station nonetheless and a target for people who would want to disturb Belfast's water supply. So after 1968 there was a twenty-four-hour military presence at this pumping station. Our land went right to the edge of it. Sometimes as kids we would be playing around in the fields and be yelled at by these soldiers. When we were in bed you could hear cars screeching up and down when they would change the patrol at midnight. The soldiers were always afraid that they'd get booby-trapped somewhere; they were on the lookout for mines and ambushes. There was never any real serious trouble in our area, but there was always the threat of it.

In 1972, when Britain had joined the European Common Market, my Dad's main source of income on the farm was beef and apples. However, after Britain joined the Common Market, it became increasingly difficult to sell either beef or apples. So it became hard for us to manage economically. The Troubles from '71 to '74 made it a very unsettling time. It was during this period that the North went through the initial fallout of the Civil Rights marches in Derry in '68 and '69. In Belfast, the IRA and Sinn Féin were going through internal reorganization and the Loyalist movement was beginning to more publicly flaunt its vicious paramilitary side with the rise of the UDA.[2] It was a very dangerous time. I didn't know all the details when I was growing up, but I could feel that it was scary.

'Sixty-eight was the beginning of the Civil Rights campaign when many people, predominantly Catholics, began demonstrating. Northern Ireland, in 1968, was still operating on the basis that people gained the right to vote primarily by their ownership of property. If you owned a number of properties, you might have three or four or even five votes, but if you didn't own property or didn't have any kind of land rights then you didn't have any vote. So the call in 1968 was the same call that people in much less developed areas of the world were calling for: "One Man, One Vote."

While Northern Ireland was under the overall administration of Great Britain, it had its own parliament, Stormont, and its own prime minister, Terence O'Neill. He was a Protestant and a Loyalist and lived in a mansion in Antrim close to us. He was prepared to make concessions to the Civil Rights campaigners and to give one man one vote — very reformist, moderate concessions. But the possibility of concessions of any kind caused an upheaval among the Loyalists of Northern Ireland. Extreme Loyalists were saying: We shouldn't give them anything, they don't deserve anything, they don't deserve decent homes, they are all a bunch of Taigs.[3] This threat of concessions split the Unionist Party into the Official Unionists, headed by Terence O'Neill, and the more extreme Unionists, headed by Ian Paisley.[4]

The fact that things were becoming very polarized and that my father's friends were much more likely to join a militant, bigoted Unionist party was probably why my father began to think about leaving. In the seventies, not only were things becoming economically and politically rough, but both he and my Mum were worried about us going in and out of town every day. There were bomb scares at school and very, very, very vicious bombing attacks by both the IRA and the UDA. A lot of reprisals. Tit for tat.

We were always told — and who told us this I can't even remember — that you could tell the difference between a Catholic and a Protestant because a Catholic's eyes were closer together and Catholics usually kicked with the left foot when they played soccer. Catholics were less well dressed. There was a lot of classism in the way Protestants were taught to view Catholics, but it was never defined as class. Because of class the opportunities for Catholics to get a decent education or get a decent job were much slimmer than for Protestants. Most of the major companies had policies against hiring Catholics. Disgraceful. And they still do. Still do.

I was very interested in what made the world divide itself into all these religions and I began to ask questions about the Catholic Church, which most people didn't want to answer within my own community or at home. The idea of going into a Catholic chapel was outrageous: If you were seen walking into a chapel you were a marked person. When I asked people how Catholicism differed from Protestantism, I was told that Catholics worshipped the Virgin Mary; Protestants only worshipped God Himself. They pay priests to save themselves; we ask for forgiveness directly from God Himself. We had a direct line; there were all these intermediaries with the Catholic Church. When they die they don't go straight to Heaven, they go to Purgatory. It was always us and them. Good and bad. Black and white.

I was fortunate because I went to a Quaker school. I think that's where my sense of egalitarianism and desire to be involved in my community came from. While the Quakers are considered Protestants, really they're not. They are probably best described as Universalists, but in the North of Ireland you're one or the other, so they are seen as Protestants.

When I was thirteen I became disillusioned. That would have

been 1971. The world was in turmoil. Vietnam was happening but we didn't know much about Vietnam. We just knew that things in Northern Ireland were pretty awful. The parents and old people in our church had asked the young kids from the church to play some music we liked and explain what the music meant to us. They felt completely disconnected from our music and thought we could help clarify things for them by explaining our music.

There were about five or six of us from our group that volunteered. Don McLean's *American Pie* was the first album that us kids saved up our money to buy. A lot of it is about Vietnam, but I didn't realize that at the time. I was just drawn to these really melancholy songs. There is a song on it called "The Grave," a lovely song about flowers and the graves of people who have died in Vietnam. After I played this song, I stood up in front of the ministers, the parents and the other kids. I explained how this song meant a lot to me; it made me realize that I wasn't a Christian. My father's jaw dropped. If there were a God in the world, a God wouldn't allow this to happen. I just got turned off. I didn't really want to hear about anybody's religion any more; I wasn't really interested in any of them. Christianity was hypocritical; I couldn't stand it.

Dad came out to Canada in the late summer of 1973 and decided he loved Canada and he wanted to move there. He came back in the fall, after the harvest, and my family went to Canada in 1974. I came to Canada for the summer of 1974, but I didn't want to emigrate then so I went back to Ireland and boarded at the Quaker school while I was finishing up high school.

In 1976, I started at the University of Manchester in England. I wasn't happy in England. I really felt like a second-class citizen. The English had stereotypical views of who and what I was. And while I was freer there than in Ireland, I felt confined. It was harder for me to live there than in Canada. I worked on my off-hours at a little hotel that had a little club at lunchtime for businessmen in Manchester. A lot of them were involved with the newspaper business. I remember some really horrible racist remarks being made about the waitresses, who were all Irish. They really treated us as though we were their servants.

I remember one of them commenting on my hips and saying that I had good Irish hips — good for bearing children. We were just Irish and it didn't matter whether we were Catholic or Protestant. That was the thing: As Protestants, we grew up in the North of Ireland believing that we were special and that we were really important to Britain. And yet when we were in Britain they don't see you as special; they just see you as Irish and a troublemaker. That's the real contradiction you find in colonial states.

I officially emigrated to Canada in June of 1977. I landed in Edmonton, Alberta. I'll never forget the sky, that flat prairie expanse of the open sky that was blue and warm and so open. It gave me a spiritual and emotional openness that just didn't exist in my life before. I took the bus from Edmonton up to Dawson Creek, about 380 miles. You don't travel that kind of journey in Ireland. There was room to move and room to expand and room to do what you wanted. And the blue sky just made it all seem possible.

Along with many people, I was really moved by the Bobby Sands hunger strike, when Bobby Sands died in May of 1981.[5] We always call it "Bobby Sands," but there were others who died. The Irish Prisoner of War Committee was founded at that time in Ontario and Vancouver to heighten awareness and understanding about what the hunger strike was about, what the prison conditions were like and what the British regime was like for people living in the North of Ireland.

When I came to Vancouver in 1983 I noticed a flyer and went to one of these Irish events and met some people. I was struck by their commitment, by the issues themselves, and by the integrity of these people. So I became involved. What that meant was organizing pub nights. Talk about reinforcing stereotypes about the Irish and pubs! The pub nights would be a mixture of social interaction, where people would just sit and yak to one another, and maybe someone would talk about a current important event.

It would occasionally feature a guest speaker who would come from Ireland or another part of the world.

The Irish Prisoner of War Committee in Vancouver was part of the CNLM, the Canadian National Liberation Movement, made up of groups from Chile, the Philippines, El Salvador, Palestine and other national liberation struggles. These other groups would have their own events and we would have a presence there by making an address or bringing educational material. I began to make little cards out of photographs of wall murals, taken when we were in the North of Ireland in '83. There are some beautiful murals painted on the walls, and I took photographs of them and put them on cards and envelopes and sold those and the money went to the committee.

At that time a lot seemed to have happened at once. It felt like I had an understanding of politics and an understanding of my own political perspective. I had worked at the University of Waterloo, where I got my degree, and through the student movement I felt I'd had a good exposure to political issues. So the Irish politics came easily. As a Protestant going into the Irish Prisoner of War Committee, I felt very strange — at the beginning I felt like I needed to apologize, or I needed to explain why I was there. I didn't want people to assume I was a Catholic because I was there: I wanted them to know I was a Protestant and that therefore I might offend someone. I wanted to be careful.

When we moved out from Ontario, I had it in mind that I wanted to work with a women's organization. It was primarily motivated by social needs. I had mostly men friends in the work that I had been doing prior to that and wanted to develop more women friends. So when I first came to Vancouver, not only did I meet up with the Irish Prisoner of War Committee, I also went to the Vancouver Women's Health Collective and began to do some volunteering there. I used to volunteer once a week in the evening, after doing a training program, and I grew more and more interested in that health-related work.

I didn't deliberately set out to discover feminism or to become a feminist, but I wanted more exposure to women and women's issues. A lot of my desire to discover women's issues came out of my own experience. I had married and I got pregnant when we were living in Ontario. The only gynecologist in town was a man vehemently opposed to abortion. I had tried to get a diaphragm fit with him because I had been wearing an IUD. I didn't want to wear an IUD any more because I felt they were dangerous. He refused to fit me with a diaphragm, claiming they were messy. Then when I insisted he said, "Okay. You make an appointment." By the time I got back I was pregnant. That wasn't his fault by any means, but he wouldn't help me.

I found that experience very isolating. My husband didn't deal with it very well at all and I felt really discriminated against as a woman. There weren't enough services and I didn't understand enough. That's why I came to the Women's Health Collective. I knew the Collective to be a pro-choice, self-help organization. It wasn't a deliberate attempt to become a feminist or become a pro-choice activist — it wasn't anything; it was just my way of understanding myself better and learning more.

I was working at the time, for money, with a family services organization as a family counsellor, volunteering at the Women's Health Collective and also beginning to do some of the Irish solidarity work. My husband was a student at university. Our lives were full and relatively free because we didn't have many responsibilities.

In 1984, an opportunity came up to work for money on a grant at the Health Collective so I began to do that. Over the five years that I was involved with the Health Collective I wanted to increase the profile of the organization, make it more an advocacy group and to some extent increase its respectability, I suppose. The Health Collective is, I think, the oldest Canadian women's health organization. It was founded as a self-help organization for women who had medical issues or problems to solve. It has over and over proven to be a leader on many questions, such as PMS, IUDs, birth control pills and the Dalkon Shield.

My job was an administrative job, but it helped me understand a lot about the different kinds of medical practice. And quite early on, in 1985, I began to do a lot of work with women who were injured by the Dalkon Shield IUD. We got a lot of calls because during the late seventies the Health Collective had been very involved in trying to set up a Canadian class-action suit against A. H. Robins, the company that made the Dalkon Shield. The aim was to win compensation for injuries from using the Dalkon Shield IUD. I helped found a national network, Dalkon Shield Action Canada, as a result of the numerous inquiries we had. Over the course of three years, groups were established across the country, including Halifax, Montreal, Quebec, Toronto and London, for women who were injured.

We did a lot of advocacy, a lot of media work and a lot of information-sharing. Establishing this organization was a dream I had from the beginning, and it became a very important part of the work I did at the Health Collective. At the same time, I also became involved in pro-choice work. I was representative from the Health Collective to the B.C. Coalition for Abortion Clinics, established in 1986. The goal of the coalition was to establish an abortion clinic in Vancouver. We had an extremely anti-choice provincial premier and health minister who were considering taking abortion off the medical services plan, thereby forcing women to pay for their abortions. Their political party, the Social Credit Party, is a very evangelical type of party that I would parallel very closely with the Irish Protestant Loyalists in the way that they view the world.

From the beginning I became one of two spokespersons for the B.C. Coalition for Abortion Clinics and over the course of the next few years I worked long and hard to turn around public opinion on the issue. When we first campaigned for choice in abortion, a poll of 1,200 people showed only 51 percent of British Columbians polled were in favour of free-standing abortion clinics. But over the next two years, public opinion swung around completely so that about 78 percent of British Columbians thought that abortions should be available in clinics as well as hospitals. This campaign was the beginning of building a strong organization that could withstand the barrage of criticism and abuse that we were going to get when the free-standing abortion clinic was eventually established in Vancouver.

My daughter was born on February 15, 1985, at home with midwives. Caila was certainly one of the reasons I wanted to make things better for people. There was an incredible set of contradictions that had manifested themselves in the work I was doing. Many of the women that I worked with on the Dalkon Shield issue were never able to have children because they had been injured so seriously by the Dalkon Shield. And then other women who were pregnant, but didn't want to have children, couldn't have abortions.

All of this work, particularly the abortion coalition work, became very, very demanding. The Canadian Supreme Court ruling in January 1988 struck down the abortion law but set up a separate system of medical care for abortion. The bottom fell out of the box the government had tried to contain this abortion issue in. The Vander Zalm government actually did take abortion off the medical services plan. Immediately the horror stories began: Women were being denied service because they didn't have money. I was under a lot of pressure working for choice.

Around that time my marriage began falling apart. I had been married for six years and had been together with Larry for eight. My work was very demanding — as was his — and on top of that we had our daughter Caila to care for. If he had a meeting or work to do in the evening, I would be with Caila and vice versa. We began spending less and less time together. In the end I learned that Larry just wasn't able to give me the kind of support and care I needed during that hectic time. I was beginning to see that my childhood in war-torn Ireland and my contact with the church gave way to republicanism and feminism, which are all interconnected, like a big patchwork quilt. I had made my commitments. Our lives were going in different directions. I had clearly chosen to challenge traditions in a very direct service-oriented way.

I have questioned and challenged the church, imperialism, patriarchy, and now the institution of the family in a very direct, personal way. Now I see the interconnectedness of these themes and know that as I continue to grow I will have to face new challenges. I remind myself of that huge blue Alberta sky that tells me anything's possible.

Notes

1. Hugh O'Neill, the Earl of Tyrone, still fighting in the early 1600s, was the last to resist the English. After his defeat at Kinsale, he fled the country. The English Crown seized lands in the North, turning them into the counties of Armagh, Cavan, Coleraine, Donegal, Fermanagh and Tyrone. To make sure that colonial planters outnumbered the Irish, the Crown invited Scottish and English settlers to colonize the seized lands.
2. Set up in 1971 from several smaller Protestant paramilitary groups, the Ulster Defence Association (UDA) is the largest such group.
3. A derogatory name for Catholics.
4. Rev. Ian Paisley founded his virulently anti-Catholic Free Presbyterian Church in 1951 and still runs it. He set up Ulster Protestant Action "to keep Protestant and Loyal[ist] workers in employment in times of depression, in preference to their Catholic fellow workers." In 1971, he set up the Democratic Unionist Party. Paisley appeals to Protestants who fear Catholics will get their jobs and their homes. See John O'Beirne Ranelagh, *A Short History of Ireland* (Cambridge: Cambridge University Press, 1983), pp. 255–68.
5. Following the end of Special Category, or political status, for both Republican and Loyalist prisoners, some Republican prisoners went "on the blanket," refusing to wear prison-issue clothing. Women Republican prisoners jailed at Armagh went on the blanket after male guards beat them following a search for "uniform skirts."

In 1980, Republican prisoners at the "H" Block in Long Kesh (The Maze to the British) waged two hunger strikes. The first ended 52 days later, after the British government promised concessions. They reneged. Hunger striker Bobby Sands, a working-class man from Belfast, was elected as British MP for Fermanagh/Tyrone and won more votes than then–Prime Minister Margaret Thatcher did in the General Election. Women Republican prisoners held at Armagh waged a hunger strike. Sands and nine other hunger strikers died.

Corn Fields and Heather

Nancy Mulligan-McCaldin

*Nancy Mulligan-McCaldin emigrated to Montreal, Quebec,
in 1958 at 26 years of age, and still lives there.*

Growing up in County Down, my brothers and sisters all used to
say this poem:

> *County Down where I live, corn fields and heather,*
> *Blue hills and high hills all sitting down together,*
> *Rainbows and dewdrops and moss is everywhere.*
> *Oh, County Down is beautiful and I live there.*

I remember everything so clearly. From every hill we looked
onto the Mourne mountains: I can still smell the heather; I hear
the reapers in the fields; I hear the corncrakes and the cuckoos and
the magpies. Every day was an adventure: We'd find badgers,
hedgehogs and porcupines; we'd find frogs and tadpoles,
snowdrops and beautiful spring flowers. I see all the beautiful
sheep running free over the mountains. I can still smell the ocean.
I see the harbours and all the fishing boats, the fishermen and the
happy faces in that beautiful County Down.

Culture

My Mother Said: Always Hold Your Head Up High

Dorothy Taylor

Dorothy Taylor lives in Toronto, Ontario.

I was born in Ireland — Dublin — in 1925. My mother was from Westmeath. My father was from Meath. I spent a lot of my early childhood visiting my grandparents in Loughpark, Castle Pollard, Co. Westmeath — very near a lake there called Lough Lein. I had one sister, my sister June, and one brother, Leo, who thankfully are both here in Canada. My father was a very strict disciplinarian, but my mother was a very good-humoured, very full-of-life sort of person. Unfortunately, while they were two wonderful people, they were completely incompatible.

I suppose most of the influence that I had in my life came from my mother. Early on in my childhood I realized there was a slight difference between my mother and father — everybody seemed to be knocking at our door looking for Mrs. Walsh. Mrs. Walsh to deliver some baby down the road. Or Mrs. Walsh to get somebody out of trouble. This was my mother. She was a very good neighbour. Whenever anybody had a problem they would call for my mother, which led to my father being very aggravated if his dinner wasn't on the table when he came home in the evening time. She always felt that her first duty was if somebody needed a handout, that's where she would go first; my father was a capable man and could wait for his dinner. At one stage I had to give up my bed for some unfortunate person she brought in out of the cold one night and had nowhere to go.

My father had his very sensible way of doing things and my mother had her very lackadaisical way of doing things. She hated housework, but she cleaned up the house when it was absolutely necessary. My father liked everything to be perfect, very prim, very proper, a throwback — his father before him was very Victorian. My father was a salesman. He worked for a tea company. He was a very good salesman, great talker. Although he was a very stern man, he had a very good sense of humour underneath all that, but it was always hidden by "the right thing" to do — you had to learn how to sit at the table properly, how to eat properly, how to speak properly, and how to carry yourself through life.

Where my mother also went for those things, but she figured that it wasn't wrong to see the funny side. She loved music, she loved dancing, she loved singing. She loved to travel, but she never travelled anywhere further than Belfast. She was full of life.

After several years, when I was around about fifteen, they went their separate ways. That would have been around about 1940–41. The war was on and tea was becoming scarcer and scarcer — he used to have a van, then a car. From the car he went to a bicycle. Then he could almost walk around and hand the tea to shops out of his pocket because we had rationing in Ireland at that time. The tea companies closed down for the remainder of the war — they only needed a skeleton staff and he went to England.

When my father went to England, he went to work in a factory. He didn't like that because he had been very prim and proper and factory life to him was a step down. Over the years we heard less and less from him — letters became very spaced out, maybe once a week, once every two months, once every four months — and we didn't see him again for eleven years.

In the meantime, my mother was left with three children. It was very hard for her because we were in a time when women didn't go out to work. And it was looked on peculiarly, a woman on her own. She went to the thing that she could do best and that was cooking. She got a job in a restaurant and worked as a cook and put us through school. We had a wonderful time. My mother was a story-teller — we're talking about the days before television. We would spend hours sitting around the fire, and she would regale us with stories of her youth, and times in the country, and sing songs. She loved to sing. We never really missed my father because we had a very close relationship between the four of us.

Unfortunately, my mother was an extremely heavy smoker. My mother would light maybe one cigarette a day, but smoke about two or three packs, just lighting one cigarette from the other. In recent years, my sister and myself used to say: How come we can never make stuffing the way Mammy used to make it? So we figured it was because she always had a cigarette in her mouth and she used to probably blow the ash off and it went into the stuffing. That was the flavour that was missing!

In 1952, my mother died at a very early age of fifty-four from lung cancer. We had heard from my father again, and although he didn't come back, at least he was in contact. At that point, I was about twenty-six. My brother was sixteen and my sister was nineteen. I was going steady at the time, with my husband. The day that we were to be married, the 25th of September, was the day my mother died. So we had to postpone our wedding and were married the following April, in 1953. We'll be thirty-nine years married this year. I always look on my mother's death as the closing of a door on a particular part of my life that opens in memory only.

Ireland had its own form of a recession in 1956. My husband lost his job. We lost our house, and we moved to — I had two children at this stage, my two girls — Manchester in England where we lived for six years, where my two youngest children were born. When we came back to Ireland in 1962, we couldn't find a house or an apartment to rent. This was in Dublin. I decided to apply for a Corporation house, the equivalent to Ontario Housing. We got a house in Finglas. I wasn't very keen on Finglas, it's a bit on the rough side. However, they were building a particularly wonderful new conception in building in Dublin in a place called Ballymun, or Baile Muna in Gaelic — the town of the shrubs.

It was built on land as you go out towards the airport. They were going to turn this into a new town, and all the architect's drawings and the models were fabulous, so we applied to move there. Originally these houses were to be sold to existing tenants of Corporation houses, but they decided they would charge us a higher rent. We moved there. These were beautiful houses — we hadn't seen them before in Ireland. They were centrally heated; they were spacious; they were anything that you would want in a lovely house. We were very happy.

We moved in 1966. And in 1967, they decided to build the Ballymun Flats. At this stage, I had become involved in forming a tenants' association with some other people. I became the public relations officer for Ballymun Tenants' Association. When the Ballymun flats were first built, they were lovely. But they built elevators with very inadequate material; they were always breaking down. People were living from one to fifteen storeys which they had never done before in Dublin. They never built any launderettes so people had nowhere to hang their clothes or wash their clothes. They used to hang them out on the balconies. The Ballymun flats had seven beautiful tall skyscrapers — named after the signatories of the Republican Proclamation. So, because of a lack of laundry facilities, here we had Pearse, Connolly, Ceannt, Plunkett, Clarke, MacDonagh and MacDiarmada festooned with laundry from top to bottom, flapping in the wind!

I had been involved in Finglas in Ladies' Clubs so we had formed in Ballymun a Ladies' Club, St. Pappin's Ladies' Club. The idea behind this was to get women to meet every second week. The club was made up of working-class women from the estates. This was 1967. We would bring people in to talk about childcare, maybe bring them in to talk about cooking. We would have all sorts of talks from doctors on health and how to bring up children properly and we'd always be looking for new ideas. We were a member of the Federation of Ladies' Clubs of Dublin, an amalgamation of all the different ladies' clubs.

The kids were buying bottles of Coca Cola and if they managed to take a packet of Aspro — sort of an aspirin in Ireland — or a few of these Aspro and a bottle of Coke, you could get as high as a kite. This was a bit of a problem in a lot of the local schools. With all the other Ladies' Clubs in Dublin, we had the

Coke analyzed and they discovered there was an ingredient in the Coke — the name of it completely escapes me — but combined with the Aspro, this ingredient did make the kids go up the walls. From the pressure of the Ladies' Clubs, we were able to have this element removed from the Coke and so they could take these aspirin and it would make no difference. It was like taking water: It didn't do them any good.

That was our first idea. The strength of women's clubs was that women banded together and pushed something so they could make a change. Then Dublin suddenly realized that it had something that it had always wanted to shove under the carpet — deserted wives. When I say deserted wives, they were deserted children because these were girls sixteen years old, seventeen years old, twenty. A girl of twenty with four babies: The eldest was four, then there was a three-year-old, a two-year-old sitting on the pram, an infant in the pram. When the going got rough, the daddy off to England and would never be heard of again.

We, the Ladies' Club, discovered that we had all these young women who were coming to the club — to find out if we could run a benefit for them. They didn't have a pram, or they didn't have a cot, or they didn't have clothes for the children. We became very concerned about this. We did run benefits, but we figured out that's only a stop-gap. They were too young to work. They had babies and even though they had relatives to look after the kiddies, it didn't make any difference. A lot of these young women — when they would be left and they couldn't afford to pay rent on their homes — they would be stuck into these flats in Ballymun and they were basically left there to rot. It was a case of not just one, so we decided to do a survey, and we went around knocking on doors.

It started in the surrounding area, but it branched out to other areas, working-class areas. At that stage, we were St. Pappin's Ladies' Club, after the local church — a very old church which unfortunately has been let fall into disrepair; it was built in the time of the Famine — very old, but it was the only church we had at that time. So we called ourselves after St. Pappin's, and we got the use of the hall. We went around. I would knock at a door and I would say to the young girl answering, "Could I speak with your mother, please?" and would discover that I was speaking to the mother — she would be that young. We discovered that we had not just one or two or three families, but we had hundreds of young women, all between the ages of sixteen and twenty-five, who were deserted wives.

At this stage there was a column in the Monday edition of the *Evening Herald* that used to report what was going on in Ladies' Clubs. They reported that we were trying to help deserted wives and this triggered off other people in other areas being interested in what was happening. We were approached by Nuala Fennell — a TD[1] with the Fianna Fáil[2] government. Fennell and her friends were trying to push through the government a deserted wives' allowance which would mean they could pay rent and they could bring up their children in some form or other of decency. These wives weren't getting anything from the government — they were just making do on their children's allowance. Or the odd pound or two that they would get from a deserting husband, in-laws, their own family, charity, St. Vincent de Paul, was all they were getting.

This society, which they called AIM — Act, Inform, Motivate — through their work and the work of the Ladies' Clubs, they managed to get through this bill. Because of the pressure of women, the government decided to make payments to deserted wives and payments for each child. This would have been about 1970–71. We just felt that women, if there was something really serious that needed to be looked after and done, then women as a whole could push it through by banding together. They used to have a laugh and joke and say that if the men would only band themselves together, God knows what we could all do. We could all push together instead of men just sitting on the sidelines and letting these things happen.

We did have the usual run-in with the local clergy. You always have that. They felt we were interfering — the Vincent de Paul were doing a great job and we should leave things be. I suppose it all goes back again to when we opened up the new church. We did have a new church, the Holy Spirit Church, and we also did voluntary work. We would help the priests out, and we used to go in every weekend and clean up the church for them because we figured we would make ourselves useful in the area. That was around 1970–71, where things were changing in the church and men were allowed to get up and give the first and second readings.

We as ladies in the Ladies' Club decided we should be allowed to do the same. Our priest at that time was pretty well scandalized. Women do not go behind the altar rails — those were the days we had altar rails. It's unheard of for a woman to go behind except to put flowers on the altar or to clean it, but not in any other way to be involved. We said, "Fine, we accept that, but from now on, if we're not good enough to go behind the altar rails, then we're not good enough to clean the church." So I was the first one to read the lesson, behind the altar rails! You can push a little and shove a little.

We would create a fuss when there was an increase in bus fares. We would call up the paper and have a meeting and invite them to our Ladies' Club. We actually did in one case have the fares reduced. This was all in Dublin. Being very involved in all of this, and in the Tenants' Association being the public relations officer, my name would appear from time to time. And my kids hated it. The younger two didn't mind, but my two older girls figured that their friends knew everybody in Dublin — not just their friends, but everybody from the President down knew who I was and knew that *they* were my children. Of course, that was a lot of rubbish. Nobody cared who you were. But as far as they were concerned, everybody knew.

The Ladies' Federation was a mixture of classes. You had different types: You would have a Ladies' Club in Foxrock who wouldn't have working-class women in it. Or you would have a Ladies' Club maybe in Killiney, who wouldn't have working-class women. St. Pappin's was, of course, working-class women. But basically there were a mixture. You would have different types of classes. I hate class distinction.

Dublin, I think, has to be the capital city of class distinction. I don't know about the rest of Ireland, but I know about Dublin and it has always bothered me. My mother used to always have a quotation: You should always be able to walk with the cabbages and the kings. It doesn't make any difference where you come from, what you are, where you're going: You should always hold your head up high. You're as good as anybody else. All through my life, that's how I behaved. I would meet Mr. Haughey[3] and I would feel the same with Mr. Haughey as I would feel with the guy down the road who's looking for a handout — which was another thing we got involved with, the itinerants. I hate class distinction.

Before I was married, when I was working, I was middle working-class. I was working in an office — it was a sewing company in Dublin — and I had graduated to being assistant manageress. My boss was a Galway man and he was the manager. He lived out in Clontarf. I lived in Drumcondra. It was my job when somebody would apply for a position in the company to go through the letters to get out the best selection of letters that I thought were suitable for him to interview. He would always say to me, "When you're selecting those letters I don't want any ones with Corporation addresses or National School education." That to me was the typical example of class distinction. I know people who live in Corporation estates in Dublin whose kids have all gone to universities and I know people who these people couldn't even hold a candle to who live in working-class areas. Some of these Corporation address letters were brilliant and some of them that would be really good letters I'd put them in. Then he'd just discover that they went to a National School and he'd say, "Oh, Miss Walsh, why did you put that there?" It made no difference how good the letter was, he was branded.

In later years children in Ballymun, or Finglas, or Whitehall, or Coolock — these are all working-class Corporation areas — would apply for jobs and never even get their letters replied to. How we worked that out was one particular family that I know had relatives living in Sandymount, a very upper-class area. We sent off two letters to the same company, one from the working-class address and one from Sandymount. And got called on the Sandymount address. Both were identical, but the one from the Sandymount area got a reply and the one from the working-class area didn't even get acknowledged. Maybe it's changed a little — I've been nineteen years away from Dublin now, and Dublin is my soul; I love every hole and corner of it and nothing will ever change that — but I see it with its warts.

The six years I spent in Ballymun were six of the happiest years that I can remember. There was a great sense of community. There was a fantastic sense of friendship. We didn't know each other when we moved in there, and through the clubs and the community councils there was a fantastic sense of belonging. It has changed. The Ballymun of today is not the one that I left, but at that particular stage, we formed youth councils, we formed drama clubs. We were a good bit away from entertainment and everybody couldn't afford TVs, so we showed movies for the kids on a Sunday afternoon. There were just a fantastic sense of being in really close-knit community that I have never experienced since.

What happened afterwards was when the rot started to set in, and the rot started to set in a year before I left. People started to leave Ballymun. It's very hard to understand what makes the working-class Dublin person tick, but you cannot put them onto the fifteenth floor — not in Dublin. You can't put them on the fifteenth floor of an apartment building, with a rickety old elevator going up and down, with no laundry facilities, no gardens for the kids to play in. That's not the way they are. They can't live like that, so they move out. What started was the Corporation could not give people on a housing waiting list — no matter how desperate they were — a flat in Ballymun because the people wouldn't take it. They would rather go and stay on the waiting list for ten years than take a flat in Ballymun.

What you started to get was squatters. When an apartment would become empty they would break the lock, they would go in, and they would claim squatter's rights. They would go in there and you couldn't get them out. They had no feeling for the place, so the place started to deteriorate rapidly. All the people that I had known and all the people that I had worked with all started to move out. I also looked around and discovered that you could go around to these people, as we had done as a community, and knock on their doors and they would tell you to f-off. That was their attitude. The Corporation couldn't get them out. They advised us to leave them be, not to interfere with them, and gradually, they started to take over. Young people then started to come up and take over squats. They had the communes in these apartments — most of them seemed to be very high on drugs.

This was now 1972. Most of the people who had been involved in the Ladies' Clubs and the community had bought houses, moved out to other areas. They just wanted out; they were fed up. The situation was their husbands were having better jobs, their kids were growing up and starting to work, so money was more available and houses were cheaper. Those who couldn't afford to buy a house transferred to other Corporation areas that were less rowdy.

My sister by this time was living here in Canada. And as always happens, when one member of a family goes to another country others will follow. My other two were still in school and my friends were all scattered all over the place. We had tried to put in for "purchase houses" — they were building a big slew of purchase houses in a place called Baldoyle where the racetrack used to be. We put our deposit down, but the government had a system where it was a lottery. There were 250 houses and a couple of thousand people put in for them. We decided that if we drew that house we would stay. If we didn't draw the house, we would leave. We figured out that it was only going to be a matter of time before the oldest children, Barbara and Gina, would be living in Canada. The other two would be leaving school and they would shortly follow. My parents were dead. My husband's parents were dead. We really had nobody, only just a few cousins, that were in Ireland.

We said we want to be where our kids are. We really are a

close-knit family. When I grew up, my family was close-knit. My community was close-knit. My husband was very understanding and very supportive of everything I ever did and had no compunction about babysitting whenever I was rampaging off somewhere else. As we lost the lottery, we decided to emigrate. We had lived in England before, but living in England doesn't seem to be all that much different from living in Ireland.

As a person coming from a Republican family, I always thought that everybody in England had to be devils, had to have a forked tail and horns and cloven feet. That was the way I was brought up by my uncles. I discovered that they were just the same as me. They were very helpful, very warm-hearted people. I loved England. I didn't want to live all my life in it, but I had no complaints about it and I have no complaints about the English people that I met there.

Going to Canada was different altogether. We arrived on a cold Friday, December 6, 1973. In Montreal first and then transferred down to Toronto. My sister June jumped over backwards to make us happy and feel welcome. But coming to Canada from Ireland and going to England are entirely different. To me it was devastating. Two days after we arrived, it snowed. Never in my life had I ever seen so much snow. It was up to my knees! I can never remember feeling as cold as I did. My God, I would have been forty-seven — too old for emigration. I left behind wonderful friends, all the activities.

I was in a strange country. I discovered that the people, even though they looked the same as I do, they were entirely different. While my sister assimilated into Canada — I think from the day she arrived she became Canadian — I somehow have great difficulty becoming a Canadian. I just felt lost. I didn't know what to do with myself. I didn't know the country. I didn't know the customs. I was having difficulty with the snow. I was having difficulty with my children and their homesickness.

I had to do something, so I took up the telephone directory and I joined the Irish Choral Society — I was about six months here at the time — and discovered there was only about two people in it that were Irish. There were every nationality under the sun except just one or two Irish people. I just wasn't on the same wavelength. Another few months passed and I picked up the telephone directory again and I saw "Irish Immigrant Aid Society." "Well now," I said, "I'm an immigrant, dreadfully in need of aid." I phoned up the Irish Immigrant Aid Society.

The late Gerry Kenny and I got chatting and I told him that I was feeling very left out of things and I didn't know enough about Canada. He said, "What hobbies have you got?" I said I was very interested in drama — at home in Dublin, St. Pappin's Ladies' Club had its own St. Pappin's Drama Society; we won a lot of awards. "Oh," he said, "for years I've been trying to get people interested in drama, but nobody ever does anything about it. I'm a great fan of theatre myself."

"Yes," I said, "I went a couple of weeks ago to see *Juno and the Paycock*" — down at St. Michael's College they were putting on *Juno and the Paycock* by Sean O'Casey — "and with all due respect to St. Michael's College, it wasn't O'Casey as I know it." He said, "Oh indeed, that's the story all around. Would you be interested in drama if you could get a few people together?" And I said yes. "Well," he said, "we have a little newsletter we put out and I'll put a note in it. If anybody's interested in forming a dramatic society, they'll meet here next Monday."

This was 1975. I'd been in Canada about a year and a half. I came along — it was February or thereabouts — and I was amazed. There was maybe about twenty or thirty people turned up at the Irish Immigrant Aid Society. All interested in drama. All Irish. He said, "We have a little thing here called Caravan[4] that we do every year in the summer. That would be a good place to start now, if you want to do something about it." And I said, "There's a one-act play called *Cathleen ní Houlihan*, why don't we do that? It doesn't take up much time." He said he knew somebody who would be delighted to direct. His name was Pat Hunt.

Cathleen ní Houlihan is by Yeats. It's the story of Ireland. Cathleen Ní Houlihan refers to Ireland because during the Penal Times you could be arrested for talking about Ireland in a rebel fashion. They had this habit as always referring to Ireland as a female. People got together and they used to refer to Ireland as "My Dark Rosaleen" or "Cathleen Ní Houlihan" or "The Old Lady" so if the British heard them, they did not know who they were talking about. They would not realize that they were talking about Ireland if they said, "Maybe it's time the 'Old Woman' said no." Or "maybe it's time that 'Dark Rosaleen' stood up for her rights. They would not realize that they were talking about Ireland.

Cathleen ní Houlihan is a very lovely story about this old lady who comes looking for people to help her. She's come looking for her sons to come and fight for her. Yeats wrote it for Maude Gonne MacBride, the love of his life. She actually did play that part of Cathleen Ní Houlihan. We decided that would be a good starting point for us. It was very short, only about half an hour.

Gerry got Neil McNeil Public School — where they used to hold Caravan — to give us the main stage to put on *Cathleen ní Houlihan*. Pat Hunt, a theatre arts teacher at Michael Power High School, directed it. We had so many people that we were able to set up three different casts. Gerry Crowe was in it, and myself, and my sister June was in it. There was D. J. Kelleher was in it and Sylvia Bonny was in it. And Nora and Bill Pollock. There was lots of people. I played Cathleen Ní Houlihan. It was a wonderful production. That main hall — it must hold probably at least 700 or 800 people — and Pat Hunt got them to close the bar while we performed *Cathleen ní Houlihan*, which was a great success.

That was the formation of the Toronto Irish Players. That was our first performance. I was the first president. We decided we would do nothing but Irish plays. We figured everybody else can do other plays, but we've got the real feel for Irish plays. We know where it's coming from. We've got the heart for it. We wanted also to present the playwrights and the plays to the Toronto public to get them to know these plays.

We have done Synge. We've done Yeats. We've done O'Casey. We've done Friel. We've done Behan. We've done Bernard Farrel. We've done McGuinness. We've done all the new ones. We've done Heno Magee. We'll do any play. All of them. We could be going on forever and still not do the same play twice. We just keep on every year doing two or three performances per year at the Irish Canadian Centre. We were an itinerant group for a long time, going around trying to find places to put on our plays.

The most memorable play is for me is *Juno and the Paycock*. There's so much comedy in it, there's so much family problems in it, there's so much tragedy in it. Juno is the backbone — she's the typical feminist. Juno has a no-good husband who orders her about and demands his breakfast. But basically, he's afraid of Juno. He's a layabout. He wouldn't work a day in his life. He goes under the title of Captain Boyle. He's never even been on a steamer, or a boat on the Liffey, never mind on a ship, but he calls himself Captain Boyle. He has a sidekick called Joxer. These two wouldn't work a fit, while Juno goes out and works. Tries to keep the home together. She has a son who's had his arm blown off in an IRA incident and who is an informer.

It's a Republican play, but Juno is the mother of sorrows. An Englishman comes into their life. He's a teacher and he tells them they'll come into money. Of course, they go out and they buy all this stuff and he gets the daughter pregnant. There's never any money in the first place. The IRA come and take away the informer son and kill him. Juno is left with her pregnant daughter, her useless husband, her dead son and the bare stage because the bailiffs come and take everything. She goes off into the night with her arm around her daughter, saying, "The baby will have not one mother but two mothers." The ending of that play is Captain Boyle comes in saying, "Where's the chairs, Joxer? Where's the chairs?" and he just dead drunk falls down on the stage. His last words — most wonderful line in the play — is, "Ah Joxer, the world is in a terrible state of chassis." He means "chaos," of course, but can't pronounce it properly.

Juno and the Paycock is successful in Moscow. It's been done all over the world. It's universal: You've got the layabout husband; you've got a woman who's trying to keep all ends of the picture together. Always brushing and cleaning and trying to get her husband to smarten up and go after that job. And he goes off and somebody comes in and says, "Oh, I saw Captain Boyle down in the local pub." That's as far as he gets going and looking for the job. Thinking then that they'd come into money and she goes out and buys a tea-set and a gramophone, something that she's always wanted. The only little touch of luxury, to have it whipped back from her again. Her daughter coming and telling her that she's pregnant and the man is gone.

In those days there was nothing for a pregnant young woman. She makes the choice that she'll go and take her daughter. She'll look after her daughter and the baby. She'll mourn her dead son. Even though divorce wasn't recognized, she decides that's it and she leaves her husband. She doesn't want him anymore. And she walks off into the night. This is Juno. I think that's universal. A lot of women when they see *Juno and the Paycock* can relate, no matter what language it's in. They can say: That's a mother of sorrows; she's lost everything. But she still manages to pull her shawl around her and lift her chin up and walk off into the night with her daughter. No matter how hard it is.

When I played Juno, I became Juno. I felt it all. I had an uncle who was in the IRA before I was born and I remembered my grandmother telling me how she felt — he was sentenced to hang, in the Civil War, 1920–21. I remembered how she told me she — at six o'clock the morning he was to be executed — was at the altar, and somebody ran into the church and whispered in her ear that he had escaped the night before from jail in Mullingar. She collapsed on the altar. Most of the neighbours thought that he'd been hanged and that was why she collapsed. But the reason was relief that he had escaped. That helped me to relate to that part of Juno.

Having daughters of my own, I related to how Juno felt about her daughter being pregnant and how the daughter had been deserted. He'd had his good time and he left her. So many people I knew had Captain Boyles for husbands. I know quite a lot of them who always seem to have enough money to go down to the pub but never seem to have enough money to help buy the loaf of bread.

Captain Boyle — he's never seen the stars from the bow of a ship in his life. And he says, "What is the moon?" He's contemplating all these wonderful things. He hasn't got a clue and most drunken Irish men don't have a clue. They're wonderful, they can talk, they can charm — I'm not talking about the aggressive ones; there are those too, of course. The only instance of violence in the play is when Captain Boyle goes for his son. He gets into a violent rage and goes for his son, and Juno steps between them. He falls short of hitting her.

The male violence against women is not an Irish thing, it's a world thing. I don't think that we're holding on to the handle there. Male violence against women I deplore. I absolutely deplore. In Ballymun, I did see an instance once where I saw a woman who had been beaten up pretty badly by her husband. The thing that never ceases to amaze me is why do women always feel she is the guilty person? I can't understand that. Who is putting it into the woman's mind that she is to blame? I have read books and seen the movies about violence against women by their husbands, but I am always amazed that it's still the same: They always seem to feel there is something that they have done, that they deserve this. If a man ever raised his hand against me, it would be the last time he would get the opportunity to do it. I would be gone. If I had children, they would come with me.

There's a selfish aspect to Juno. Early on in the play — while they're all having a wonderful time at a tea party — there's another woman living in the tenement house whose son has been killed, by the British. They're going to the chapel and she comes in and says her piece: "I bore the pain in bringing him into the world, now I must bear the pain in seeing him go out of the world." When she is gone, Juno turns around and says that she was always giving the IRA reason to be seen going into her room and so the British murdered her son. It serves her right. It comes back to Juno in the end because she repeats the things that the woman had said. I felt it was very insensitive. Juno thinks she's fallen on good times. It makes her act a little bit I'm-all-right-Jack. Why did O'Casey paint her that way? She was such a stalwart person in every other way. Why did he give her that mean streak? I think he just wanted to show that there's a flaw in all of us.

I'm not really involved that much with the Irish community, other than the Toronto Irish Players and with music too. Sometimes I sing and sometimes I read passages from plays, like with Kevin Kennedy and Jonathan Lynn. While I was at home in Ireland, apart from all the other stuff, I used to write a lot. I would write short stories. I wrote articles in the paper. I wrote for radio. I read them on the radio, Radio Éireann. I was very active in the social side of my goings-on. When I came to Canada, I lost it. I felt I was in a completely foreign environment that I couldn't reach, that I couldn't feel. With the Toronto Irish Players and the drama I can be quite at home. I'm fine. I'm in an element that I know, an element that I love.

The Irish community here, it's very fractured. You've got three levels of Irish community. You've got your class distinction. We brought it with us. You have the top-level people in the Irish community who have no knowledge of what the lower level of the Irish community is all about, the working class. They don't integrate. They don't mix. They are the big companies being run by Irish directors. There's the middle-class Irish — they almost give me the impression that they're ashamed of their roots. They've done very well here, gone up in the world. They came from poverty both in city and in country in Ireland. And now that they've gone up a few rungs in the ladder they don't want to remember where they came from. They keep out of things.

Then you have what I call the intellectual Irish — they're not all upper, because you've got some of the middle-class who are intellectual as well. They figure that they're really too high up in the scale intellectually to get down to the nitty-gritty of the ordinary guy who's not afraid to turn around and say, "Listen, I was a street-sweeper when I was in Dublin, and I've gained myself an education, and I've bought my big house. So recognize me." But they don't want to do that. They don't want to recognize that. There's a lot of them here. A lot of them.

I know people who lived in Ballymun. They were way down working-class who have come here. These people have pulled themselves up by the bootstrings. They got themselves an education and they got themselves good jobs. They remember their roots. But you get the guy from up here who's got a bigger job, a bigger house, and he doesn't want to know that person. You should be very proud of your roots. I have no compunction about saying that I lived in Ballymun. When I say that I lived in Ballymun, people say, "Oh, you mean Ballymun Avenue." I say, "No, I don't mean Ballymun Avenue. I mean Ballymun Estate, up the road." Still irritates me that people again set you off because you've got a good job.

In Toronto, you'll find at different functions you will see some people. At other functions you will see the working-class people. At the other functions you will see maybe a smattering of the middle-class people. You won't ever find the highly upgraded Irish down where the lower-graded Irish are. You never see the big knobs at the Irish Centre. Very rarely. They'll have their functions that they will attend at $150 a ticket. You'll find them in the King Edward Hotel when Phil Coulter is on for $125. You'll find them in all the big noise events. But you will not find them at a get-together or a benefit for somebody who's died here and needs to be transported back to Ireland. They won't come along and be there. The Irish are always divided. We're divided in our own country and we're divided here.

Right now you have the St. Patrick's Day parade, you have the Celtic Arts Society down at St. Michael's, you have Conradh na Gaeilge which is trying to instil some pride in language, you have the Toronto Irish Players trying to put on the plays, you have the Ireland Fund trying to get big-monied people to help the Irish in Ireland, and you have the big shots up in their ivory towers who really don't want to know what's happening to anybody. That's the way it'll be fifty years from now. You'll always have this fragmentation. So is the country divided, so is the Irish community in this city.

I suppose you can't blame them. They don't need the aggravation. You come out and you say the wrong thing and you rub them up the wrong way. Case in point, yesterday at the St. Patrick's Day parade — a couple of girls going down with leaflets from the Irish Freedom Society. There were mostly Irish people along where I was, and those poor unfortunate girls got a terrible tongue-lashing. That was a case of don't rock the boat. We're all okay, now leave us alone. Don't talk about the British occupation of Ireland. That's over there. There are so many people here who are afraid of anything becoming political. They shy away from the six-county question. They don't want to know. That's dangerous. They're forgetting their roots.

The other night my sister said, "Did ya see that program on the Queen?" I said, "The Lord save us! I have seven uncles and the grandfather who must be really and truly rolling around in their graves!" I said, "No way, my Republican blood wouldn't allow me to look at it." Same reason that I haven't become a Canadian citizen. When they say you pay allegiance to Canada, I'll become a Canadian citizen. I can't pledge allegiance to the Queen. I was raised on my Republican uncle's stories, and my grandmother's stories.

My mother was very political, a very, very staunch Republican. Very staunch. My mother was in the Cumann na mBan in 1916 during the Revolution, and she was all for 1916. She was all for getting rid of the British. Ireland for the Irish. And she was a great admirer of the Countess Markiewicz who was chief of the Cumann na mBan. So my mother joined the Cumann na mBan, which was the female equivalent of the Irish Citizen Army. Cumann na mBan did the gun-running for the Irish Citizen Army. My mother was a dispatch rider and she delivered messages from one post to another, Boland's Mills and Mount Street and so on, during the Revolution. There was no radio in those days, so someone had to go around and tell what was happening at the

General Post Office. She would pass the messages on to someone who would pass them on to de Valera who was holed up in Boland's Mills. The British came up the Liffey and bombarded the GPO and blew half of Sackville Street into kingdom come. There was one Cumann na mBan friend of my mother who dressed herself up as a wife and she had a pram and she was wheeling it across O'Connell Bridge to go to Mount Street. And in the pram was ammunition for the beleaguered soldiers in Mount Street.

My father, during the Civil War of 1920–21, was in the Army with Collins when he met my mother. And my mother was on the other side. There was the split which happened when the Treaty was signed in 1921 and we lost the six counties to the British to avoid further bloodshed. Arthur Griffith and Michael Collins went to London to sign the Treaty. But de Valera disagreed completely; he felt we should have fought to the bitter end to get rid of them altogether and have 32 counties. My mother was on the de Valera side. When Michael Collins came back he formed an army, because the British Army left the 26 counties, and it became the Irish Army under Michael Collins. My father joined Collins's army. My uncles did not like my mother associating with my father. They advised her to advise him to buy his commission out of the army, which he did.

I find it very hard to communicate with Canadians, the people who are maybe six generations here. I have worked with very nice Canadian girls and I've talked to them about this: I come into this city, I don't have to worry about English. I can read directions. I can find where to go. I only get lost sometimes in the dark. I can find out where I have to go. I can get myself a job, answer all the questions, fill in all the forms without having trouble. But some people come in and they don't even have English as a second language. They look different. Their culture is different. Their background is different, and they must have a heck of a hard time assimilating into the community.

As Irish people we don't experience any racism. It's not that long ago that we did experience racism, which should make us very sympathetic to people who do suffer from that today. About thirty years ago it didn't do well to be Irish. There were some jobs in this city that you couldn't get if you were Irish. My generation here and now maybe have not felt in any way intimidated by the fact of being Irish. But the people who came before us thirty or thirty-five years ago did. Even their religion came into it. If you were Catholic, some places here, it was very difficult to get a job.

Irish women don't experience the difficulties today that Third World women experience in Canada. The only difficulty that Irish women would come up against would be one which is universal, one of adjusting to a different lifestyle. Even though we're speaking the same language, we do have little differences. There are subtle differences like as to when we eat, the things we say.

But you can't get Irish bacon. It breaks my heart. I love Irish bacon. And black and white pudding, Irish style. Bread is sweeter here. What they call bacon, we would refer to as flank bacon or rinds because it all shrivelled up. When you go back home you take the bacon and it tastes very salty for a couple of days because your taste buds are all gone. It's just like jet lag. You have to adjust back.

When I came to this country, I was forty-seven. From the time I was married until I came to this country, I would only work when the mood took me, for pin money, for extra little things. When I came to this country, I discovered I had to work. I could not live without two wages coming in. It was a bit of a culture shock. I was very lucky. When I was here for a couple of months I got a job with a travel agency. I've been everywhere that I ever wanted to be. I was very lucky and Canada was very good to me in that respect. I would never in a million years have gotten a job in a travel agency living in Dublin. They would never have hired a forty-seven year old woman, for a start. Here they took the trouble to train me, even though in my background I had never worked in a travel agency. I loved my work. I retired a year ago.

The reason for my voluntarily retiring was I found out last year I had cancer. It took me five or six months to have this problem solved. It wouldn't have been fair on my boss to take that amount of time off sick because he was a small office. So I voluntarily retired, even though he didn't want me to. If I had stayed on, I would probably be fine. But once having left your work, to get a job again at sixty-seven is an almost impossible task. You could get a job in a donut shop, if you get a job anywhere.

We're here twenty years. I don't like aging in Canada. There was no possibility for us to save for retirement. We never were able to afford to buy a house because we just managed to earn enough money. We'd go home nearly every year. We just took it that it would be fine, that we would get pensions and figured that it was the same as at home. When we retired, the number one shock was to discover we weren't here twenty years, so neither one of us get full pensions. We get full old age pensions, but only partial Canada Pension. Both of these pensions are taxed to the hilt. I don't know of any other country in the world that taxes its pensioners and people on unemployment — you pay into unemployment and when you get it back they tax it.

Other than your OHIP card, which everybody has now, there's nothing for pensioners. You go around and you join seniors' clubs, but there basically is nothing. There are senior citizens' homes, but if you want to put your name down and wait for a thousand years, you'll probably get a senior citizen's apartment. A lot of these associations that cater for a retired person assume that every person who has retired is affluent. They send you out these luxury cruises that are going out to the Mediterranean for two months and it's only going to cost you five and a half thousand dollars. And time-share in Florida.

There must be hundreds of people who couldn't make provisions. I find that the people who have not made provisions are not being looked after. If anything, God forbid, happened to my husband, I don't know where I would go because my income is below the poverty line. As long as my health would keep up, I could probably get a job, but then who wants to hire a woman going towards her seventieth year, irrespective of how clever she is, or what she could do, or what she could give to people? There are thousands of openings for volunteers. You can go and volunteer until the cows come home, but that won't put bread on your table.

My one joy right now is my senior citizen's Metropass. I do not drive so that enables me to visit libraries, go down to see concerts downtown, go down to the art galleries, go down to Harbourfront, chase all over the place. And what do they do? They turn around and they put the Metropass up another seven dollars. Seven dollars may not seem like much to Mr. Leach of the TTC,[5] but that seven dollars is a crucial figure. If I was to go home to Dublin tomorrow, I would be almost 75 percent better off than I am here. I would have free transportation, all over the country, not just in Dublin. I would have one pound of butter a week free. I would have a free telephone. I would also have a certain amount of units of electricity free. In the winter, if I had a fire, I am entitled to a bag of turf a week, or its equivalent if I have central heating.

It's not in me to be bored. I am extremely busy. I help my daughter looking after my grandkids. She goes out to work early. Because my grandson is still fairly young, I make sure he gets up and goes out to school. I'm there then when they come home in the winter with a hot drink and stuff for them. I help out at the local school. I'm on the committee of the Toronto Irish Players.

And I scribble. Because I have four children living in this country and they are probably never going to go back to Ireland — I'm going to have grandchildren and great-grandchildren and great-great-grandchildren — I decided to start a family journal so they will have all the information of their background, going back as far as I can remember — to my great-grandfather. I can't remember too much about my great-grandmother. My great-grandfather was 104 when he died; I was five. My great-great-grandchildren when they come along will remember where they came from and how I felt and what Ireland means to me.

I have great admiration for the Native People. I follow their footsteps, what they are doing all the time. I admire these people and their ancestors for the way that they struggled. The Irish were so much pulverized in our past by the Danes, the Normans, the

Saxons, the British and everybody that wants to try to have a poke at us. To me there's a similarity there. Others have tried to put us down. They did deprive us of our language — they made a good job of that. They tried to change us and they have to a certain extent changed some people into little models of British. I am not involved with the Native Peoples, except I wore a red ribbon on my arm for them during the time of Oka to support them because I felt they were right. People with money came in and tried to take their land away to lay a golf course — now I get annoyed about those kinds of things. I wouldn't presume to enter into their arguments of what's right and what's wrong for them. But I support them and so I wore a red ribbon.

In a conversation the other evening, we were talking about the Constitution. My son was getting very hot around the collar about Canada and the Constitution. He said he wants Canada whole. He doesn't want them messing it up into all different sections. He was voicing his views on Canada as *his* country. "I'll always have Ireland in my heart," he said, "but I'd fight to die for Canada." And I was very proud of him. But I haven't got that feeling. I have tried. I have gone all around Toronto. I've gone to all the lovely places and I'd say to myself: Why have I no feeling? I love Canada as a country. It's been very good to me. I've also crossed Canada and seen it from East to West. It is an absolutely beautiful country and has a lot to offer.

But I get off a plane and I'm in Dublin and my feet go. And no matter where they go, I'm home. I'm back with the ghosts of the past. Maybe it's the ghosts that keep me coming back to Ireland. The ghosts are the people who walked the streets before me. My ancestors, my past, the whole psyche of the city. I can't get rid of it. I've nobody at home to stay with. We have to rent a flat. And I live like I was back home. I go out and I do my shopping and I chat with all the neighbours, and I feel as if I'm part of it again. I have friends back home who look at me when I come back home as if I've never been away.

Notes

1. A Teachta Dála or Deputy in the Dáil.
2. Named for the legend on the insignia of the 1913 Irish Volunteers, Soldiers of Destiny, and founded in 1926 to secure "the political independence of a united Ireland as a Republic," restore the Irish language and promote land reform and economic self-sufficiency.
3. The Taoiseach or head of government.
4. An annual multicultural festival in Toronto.
5. Head of the Toronto Transit Commission.

To Ann,

Well to-night Ann
you should be here.
It's just wonderful,
I love you so much
You are so much a
part of my childhood —
that we carry always
with us.

Trust in yourself.

Norita.

Keep the Life in Ourselves First

Norita Fleming
(Norída Ní Dhonnachú)

Norita Fleming lives in Toronto, Ontario.

My earliest years go back to Freemount, in the north of County Cork. That's where I spent the first ten years of my childhood. Freemount is a little village near the river Allow, a mile from Gortnaskregga, where my grandmother lived, and two miles from Coolbane, my grandmother's childhood home. When I was a child my sister Kathleen and I used to go to Coolbane to collect the eggs. Along the way we kicked the stones to shorten the journey, and in the summer we picked primroses and cowslips growing along the side of the road. We made daisy chains also.

The farmhouse in Coolbane was settled on high ground, with a very long avenue which we used to call a "passage" leading up to it. Turning the corner into the old kitchen, we would be anticipating the bread that Aunt Nell used to make. She made it from flour and buttermilk. Then she'd put it into the warm bastable, with the lid on top. In Cork and Limerick we called it a bastable, which was a pot about six inches deep and eighteen inches across. She'd lower the bastable which was on a pothook over the turf fire in the hearth, and then she'd put coals over the lid. We'd sit beside the fire watching and listening. And every once in a while Nell would shout for us to turn the bellace to encourage the fire.

We'd be tired from the journey, so we'd sit and dream, and Nell would tell us: *Lig do scí* (rest). There was lots of time for dreaming in that slow time back then. It took what seemed an eternity for that bread to come out of the oven. And then the pot would be hauled over to the side of the hearth. The smell of the bread was gorgeous. As she lifted it out of the pot and wrapped it in the damp towel, 'twas nearly too much to bear to see it going away from one. Then she'd set it on the old dresser in the kitchen to cool. I'd always look at Aunt Nell and ask her for a slice before it would go cold, so I could put the butter on and let it soak into it. Now Aunt Nell was very practical and she didn't like spoiling children that way. But every now and again she'd give in.

The taste of that bread! And the glass of fresh milk from the bucket from the corner of the dresser that went with it! I'll never forget it. Aunt Nell used to marvel at the fuss I used to make about the bread. Even as a young child, that bread was at the heart of everything.

In my mother's time the flour came from Shaughnessy's mill that was just across the road from the farm. It was a water mill which was on the River Allow. It was going into ruin when I remember it, but it was very much used during my mother's time.

There were all kinds of characters around there. There was these two sisters who lived on this little farm near Coolbane. T'would be very small. They kept a couple of cows and a goat, and the cows grazed along the sides of the road. The goat was an ould *peatach* — pet — with them. Now in Switzerland the cows had bells, but this goat in County Cork had bells all around its neck. Every time we'd pass the gate, Peg would be out to us to ask us how we were and to tell us the latest news on the goat. Everything the goat did was told to us. They had a beautiful front garden with dahlias and daisies and things. They were very independent women.

My mother was a teacher. There were seven children, and my mother would get up at six every morning to bake the bread for the family for the day. There's an old Gaelic saying: *Nua gach bíd agus sean gach dighe.* (Food should be eaten as fresh as possible, and drink should be well matured.) We'd have the fresh bread for breakfast, and we'd have it for lunch with butter and homemade jam on it, and a bottle of milk. Later on in the evening again we'd have the bread for tea as well. I remember as a child when visitors would come, as soon as a car would pull up at the gate my father would go out to see who it was because anyone who came to the gate would be coming in, and my mother would have a batch of scones in the oven baking by the time they hit the back door. The kettle was always on the simmer and she'd pull it over to bring it over to the centre of the range, and by the time the coats and hats were off and all the hello's said, the tea would be made. This woman had it all down to an art. We had a lot of visitors.

Daddy was very involved in Muintir na Tíre (People of the Country), and he went everywhere with Canon Hayes, its founder. It was to get the people together and to get them talking and to show how valuable the country people were. They had fireside chats in their homes and in the local schools. I don't know what they chatted about, but it seemed important. My mother's proudest memory is the time Canon Hayes came into the kitchen to her and he told her he wanted to meet Bill's garden — my father's name was Bill and he counted us as the garden. She was just delighted that he was so interested in us children. My father loved company and it was a great chance for him to get out of the house. So our house was a kind of centre. People were always coming.

In my own life today people are always coming and I'm still baking the bread. It feels good to make the bread. When I make the bread I think back. I think of all the times I took the bread to the fields during the haymaking. I think of the dances in Lynches' kitchen when I was thirteen years old coming from the pattern[1] in Dromcarra where my Auntie Bridie lived and where I went on my holidays.

When I was a child I never thought Aunt Nell was that important to me, but when I make the bread I think of her. I think of how capable she was. She fed her family very well, you know. She had different recipes from the rest of the parish because she had spent two years in America when she was a young girl. She used to make potato salad — German potato salad — beetroot and cold boiled mutton for Sundays. I never ate anything like that anywhere else when I was a child. She was a great worker. The bread just brings up things. The bread is always company because there was always company in our house.

Today I have a catering business. I see it as a part-time job. The food I prepare is nourishment for people. I use basic country food whenever I can. It was after my sister's death five years ago; my health suffered badly. Then I got interested in the holistic foods I grew up with in my childhood. The more I looked at them, the more I realized the food we grew up with as children was what is now called holistic food. I love making a sauce that has been made for two hundred years in my family. It's a grand feeling to stuff the goose with potatoes like my grandmother did long ago in the old farmhouse.

When I prepare the sauce or the goose or when I make the brown bread I *feel* their history. I want those foods to stand. I do the cooking for the Cork Association events here in Toronto. I wanted to reintroduce Irish recipes like the cabbage with an onion gravy, good potatoes, and ham done the old way with breadcrumbs and brown sugar. It's a great feed for them. They say they couldn't get it anywhere else. Leave it to a Cork woman! I also make elegant foods for weddings and funerals and office functions. They're fancy but they're simple. I try to educate Irish people to their heritage. They must know they have a food heritage that mustn't get wiped out by plastic and foam and package and biscuit mixes and things.

I love having a box of potatoes in the kitchen, so I can look at them. I see them with butter melting on them. I can make them into potato pancakes, mashed potatoes, or any food that can stand on its own. Potatoes can satisfy a hunger in a way that nothing else can for me. I don't hold it against the potato that it failed during the Famine. The potato isn't responsible for all that died on the roadsides. It got worn out from feeding all the poor. I feel a responsibility to all the Irish who died from injustice and lack of food during the Famine, because of a people who did not want us on our land. When I think of the Famine I feel an anger against the invaders at the abuse of the food in our land, and the way they denied it to our starving people. When I look at the potatoes today I see a plenty, a full table. But I get angry at the abuse of that plenty, a coddled people, pampering their whims while people lie starving on the streets of Toronto. We see it under our noses, the starvation, the hopelessness. We repeat history when we turn away.

Maybe the bread and the potatoes are important to us as Irish people because we remember the starvation. The Famine destroyed our food habits as a people and we must reclaim them and rediscover who we are. As I get older, those foods are a comfort for me. The simple foods. A simple life.

When I prepare the food I call down blessings on the food. The Gaelic language is full of blessings. Prayer is part of everything. I call for blessings to travel out to everyone who eats my food. I feel that food has a story to it. It's also a spirit. The Celts are soaked in the spirit. We can't separate from it. Neither can we separate our bread from it. When we share our bread together we share ourselves. We share love and that love is a bond. Sharing has always been part of us as an Irish people — going outside of ourselves sharing what little we had. We didn't have much of the world's goods, but we shared joys and sorrows many a time over a cup of tea and a slice of brown bread and butter. In Ireland, we had little of the material things, but any house you walked into, you got the tea and bread and maybe scones or a bit of apple pie.

Baking and cooking remind me of my grandmother too. A lot of the basics I have go back to my grandmother. When she'd be preparing the food she used to say, "Keep the life in ourselves first." To do a good day's work you had to have a good feed. You couldn't work on an empty stomach. And with thirteen children and three hired hands and themselves, sickness had to be kept away from the door.

I have an intuition about what goes together. I can look at a table and know what's right for that table. My mother did say that her mother was a very good cook. My mother was also good. Maybe I've inherited it. My food is wholesome. I make everything from the basics. I do all this catering, but sometimes I feel conflict. Some people have too much food. They've never known hunger. That comes from our materialistic society. Everything is fast food.

There's no feeling in it, no nourishment. It's hard to get a group of people around the table to eat. I like to sit for a long time around the table.

Food is a very important medium. It's like language, singing or talking. It's one of the basic ingredients of life. Think of all the communication that takes place over food. These cups, they hold a lot of secrets. When people put the cups to their lips, they hold many thoughts. If the cup is listening, it'll hear a lot. When the stomach is full you feel mellow. It's hard to be idealistic on an empty stomach. When you feed a person, they feel content. You have happy conversation. Many friendships are nurtured over food, and bad feelings are mended over food. When I do my catering, I pray over the food that every person who eats it will be touched by the spiritual feelings I send to it. I pray for healing for the people who eat my food. Food is spiritually nourishing also. But you have to feed people first before they can grow and develop spiritually.

I also put all the leftovers in a compost. By composting leftovers I'm helping nature in a small way. Composting is a way of returning to the earth and nourishing the earth which will in turn produce more food. That's the cycle. We must align ourselves with the earth. We are slowly damaging the earth with our pollution. We don't need to use all these chemicals which harm our water. We don't need all this packaging. I see food as part of the natural cycle of life and earth. We must use what we need and not abuse the earth. That way we'll be kinder to ourselves and to the earth. I like that old philosophy of looking back seven generations and looking forward seven generations before we make decisions. It eliminates selfishness.

Note

1. A pattern is an open-air dance that dates back to Celtic times. Local musicians played. In Celtic times, the *Patrún* was a day of merrymaking with food, dancing and singing. It was also a day where

differences were settled, physically if necessary. Later, in Christian times, it became known as the well day, when people gathered around a holy well to pray; the dancing and merriment were revived later.

And Their Spirit Will Come Through in the Music

Ena McClearn-O'Brien

Ena McClearn-O'Brien lives in Toronto, Ontario.

In East Galway, where Ena and I come from, location is very important in conversation. Ena's description of the crossroads where the bonfire took place is typically East Galway. Also typical is her use of the maiden name of the married woman who danced the half-set. In Ireland, a woman is often called by her maiden name, followed by the name of her husband and the place he is from.

When Ena plays "The Bag of Spuds," it carries memories of my father as he held a bag of them in his clay-covered hands and told us in terse sentences the story of the Famine, as the sun would be setting in the distance over Limehill bog.

My family name was McClearn. Back in the early 1900s the name was spelled McClearnon and it is still pronounced that way around home. I was born in the late forties. I grew up in a rural farming community outside Killimor, about fifteen miles from Ballinasloe and about five miles from Portumna, Co. Galway. We were a split family: I'm the youngest of eight and the next one in line to me was about a year older, then there was an eight-year gap and there were six kids all together, steps of stairs, close together in age. My sister Dympna and I did everything together.

I can remember, even as a little kid, the house being full of people on a Friday night. Friday was our night for the hooleys, or the céilís. Certain houses were open to these kinds of get-togethers. Some houses were open to card games, but our house was definitely the music house. It was the neighbours who came, and some people from maybe six or eight miles away — from outside of Killimor, or down towards Eyrecourt, or down towards Ballinasloe or in near Loughrea. It was maybe a couple of Fridays a month that we'd have a hooley.

My brother was the only musician in the area back then. And I was the up-and-coming one. All our neighbours were farmers and the work went on until about seven or eight o'clock in the evening. It took them till that time to get finished milking cows and feeding the calves and getting the evening chores done, so you didn't see anyone until after supper. We were allowed to stay up because we didn't have to go to school next day.

We would start off with the gramophone, the old wind-up gramophone, in the kitchen. We'd do a certain amount of dancing until my brother Joe would arrive — he might have been at the pub, or nipped out to do something, and he'd get back around nine or nine-thirty. He would arrive back with a couple of friends who were also musicians: Padraig Boland, from outside of Killimor, and a neighbour of ours, Paddy FitzGerald. They both played the accordion. Furniture was scarce. You certainly didn't have to spend much time moving furniture — just the table and the chairs — and then we'd start into the dancing. My sister Dympna and I sat and watched for a bit and eventually somebody would invite us out to dance. As kids, you were usually left till last. I was about six years old now; my sister was maybe seven and a half. My brother Joe would be in his early twenties. And there was my Mom and Dad. The rest of the family were all grown up and gone away.

My brother and Padraig Boland were good musicians. The hours they sat playing! They would sit until maybe two or three in the morning. The only thing that would be served would be tea and maybe some cake, if you were lucky. If you were really lucky, maybe one bottle of beer. And the brown bread, of course. If it was after Christmas, there might be some cake. But mainly there was brown bread and homemade butter and jam, and all the good things that we don't have any more. They'd be playing jigs and reels and hornpipes and old-time waltzes. They'd dance what we called a half-set. Then we'd do the Barndance, a horn-pipe dance.

We'd then take a little break, have the tea and get back into it again.

At this point I didn't play, but I really was interested in music. The influence was my father. He was a tin-whistle player back in his very early days. I will admit I never heard him play, but in terms of lilting a tune or telling you when you were playing it wrong or right, he was able to do it. All our music came from the McClearn side of the family. My mother's name was Hardiman. She was about five feet tall, very Irish-looking, short and stocky. A lot of these Irish mothers, after having eight children, were inclined to be a little bit heavy, but it didn't bother them. My mother had jet-black hair, and when she died at seventy-two she still had jet-black hair. There didn't seem to be much music on her side, but she was a lovely dancer and she certainly enjoyed these hooleys.

When they were growing up they used tilly lamps hooked on to the ceiling or left sitting on the mantelpiece. You had to buy the paraffin oil and sometimes the lamp didn't work. By the time my sister and I came along we had electricity. We had a big wide hearth, with a huge fire. No heat. It was all going up the chimney! There were two hobs and a cement floor, a good big kitchen. There was quite a large home-made table. My brother made the table out of mahogany. It would seat about eight people, ten if you wanted. It was unpainted, unfinished, which to us back then didn't look fancy. I suppose the reason I didn't like it is that every Saturday we had to scrub the table and chairs with a scrubbing brush and Vim to get the marks off.

We looked on paint and wallpaper as being fancy. We had a dresser with the plates all sitting on there, the Willow pattern, of course. Some of them were used every day and some of them weren't moved for months, maybe even years. And there was the big serving dish. To remove that you had to move about twenty glasses to get at it at the back. We didn't have a TV back then.

Us being the second family, my Mom and Dad had gone through the poorer times. They were no richer now, but they had built a new house. So we weren't living in what my older sisters and brothers lived in, a thatched house. The new house had a slate roof and three bedrooms. It was not modern at all — just your average cement walls, cement floors, bit of linoleum on the bedroom floors — but nevertheless a little bit of a step up. A bit easier for my mother to cook and to serve out meals. It had a little bit more room too. We had just got the radio.

My older brothers and sisters went to school in Gortanumera, outside of Portumna, on the way to Abbey. My sister and I also went to school there. That was a five-mile walk, there and back every day across the fields and the bog. In the springtime, when everybody got out of rubber boots and wore shoes, we still had to wear our rubber boots and bring our shoes in our bag because we had to go through so many fields every morning.

I don't remember the day I started school. Low infants and high infants — kindergarten and junior kindergarten here — would get out about two o'clock in the afternoon. Then the regular classes would get out at three-thirty. My sister Dympna was allowed out at two o'clock with me because I wouldn't have known my way home and it was nearly five miles. I remember falling asleep on the way home. My sister Dympna used to carry me on her back for a certain distance, and then she would put me down on the side of the road and we'd both have a rest, and then we'd walk or she'd carry me the rest of the way.

When we got a little older, we used to cross the front yard of a particular family on our way to school. We got a little cheekier and we used to steal their apples on the way home. They had a great orchard! We had our own little hole made in through the ditch, or the hedge, to the orchard. One or two kids would go in — the bravest ones! My sister was brave — she would be one of the ones who would go in to steal the apples. And make sure you could fit enough in your pocket for the other kids when you came out, because if you didn't you wouldn't be very popular. The family who owned the orchard ended up going to the school to complain.

I can remember the landscape on the way to school. The stone walls. We had to go by road and the route was to cross in over someone's land, climbing over a wall. Sometimes the rocks would fall on your feet. In the spring, all the flowers and the hedges were budding. We used to delay on the way home picking flowers by times. Primroses and cowslips were very early spring flowers and they grew wild everywhere — I've never come across them over here. We used to pick those on the way home and we used to string them together and make necklaces. Then coming into the summer, on the way to school you'd hear the cuckoo in the morning, and further into the summer the corncrake.

The hazelnuts came out in the autumn. There was a place we passed by on the way home from school and we always stopped to pick hazelnuts. We were expected home at a certain time. We didn't wear watches — nobody owned a watch. Keeping the time limit in mind we would run to this place, and as quickly as we could we would pick as much of the nuts as we could. They grew very, very plentiful on the way down from Gortanumera School, right by the side of the road up on Curragh Hill. The trees were quite high on either side.

My sister liked housework, I didn't. I liked working outdoors. Picking the spuds. Our day to do that was on a Saturday in the autumn, around September going into October. It was tiring. You had to do it a certain way and go between the drills with the horses and plough. My brother was careful enough. We had two horses. One was a lovely white mare, very gentle. On the other hand, we had a red horse that would bite anyone except my brother. So we were always cautioned not to walk under the horse's mouth. I do recall seeing him bite my father — took a good chunk out of his shoulder. Unlike today, nobody went to the doctor for a tetanus shot. It just healed on its own. I was afraid of that horse. The last thing I remember about him was him having to be put to sleep. The way we did it was to shoot the horse, on Christmas morning. The horse got lockjaw and there was no cure. So we borrowed a revolver from the butcher. My brother was assigned to that chore. That was kind of sad.

My brother did the ploughing of the spuds, and my father did the major picking of the good ones. My sister and I followed him and picked the small ones — the stray ones, as we used to call them. The potatoes were put in a pit — a dug-out — and they were covered with straw and clay. That protected them from the frost. We picked the potatoes in the aluminum buckets, made by the tinkers.

Tinkers used to live on the side of the road in caravans. When they came to the door, my mother used to give them bread or whatever she had. The husbands — the fellas — made different things out of pieces of tin and aluminum. Buckets and all sorts of pots. One day a really talented tinker musician, Syke Ward, came to the door when my brother was playing. It was a wet day and you couldn't do anything outside. So my brother spent the morning playing music. When the tinker came to the door and heard the music, he commented on it and we brought him in. He played the harmonica and he sang. These people are floating around, but nobody knows much about them.

Every evening after he got finished his work, my brother would play the accordion for two or three hours. Eventually, he started to teach me to play when I was about seven. I didn't learn by note, I just learned by ear. Teaching someone without the notes is quite difficult. I could lilt all these tunes. The accordion came up over my nose because I was so small. But I really and truly loved to play music. It didn't take me that long to learn.

Around the same time I got involved in traditional Irish dancing. I took dancing lessons in Portumna. Not having a car, my mother made arrangements with our teacher who lived in Portumna that every Thursday I would bring a second lunch to school and a half crown — two shillings and sixpence — for the dancing lessons. I would stay back after school, get a ride to Portumna with the teacher. I took lessons in the convent and then I got a ride home with my first cousin who had a betting office in Portumna. I loved the dancing lessons.

Listen and learn, I was told by my brother Joe. Do your practising at home and do your playing when you are skilled at doing so. I was seven or eight years old, just learning, and the people who would be playing were skilled musicians. Not professionals, but they were skilled at what they did because they had put hours and years at it. So they'd hold back and let me do my thing. But that was holding up a session as far as my brother Joe was concerned. When you've gotten to their stage, you can sit in and do the same as them, so do your practising at home.

It was a good lesson to be learned. And I did that. I do that with my children today. Do your learning at home, I tell them. Don't go out and try to do in one year what has taken somebody else twenty years to do. I think that applies to a lot of life. People just don't get told these things, or if they do, it hasn't been explained the way it was explained to me. I've dealt with musicians who've only started playing six or eight months ago and they get quite upset if they're not included in everything that's happening.

The schools in Ireland, they were quite interested in dancing and singing. Stuff that the kids pay for today we had for free back then. The teacher used to encourage me to bring the accordion to school, but my brother wouldn't allow me to take it because it was a valuable instrument. Paying a couple of hundred pounds back then for an accordion was like paying a couple of thousand dollars today. I wasn't allowed to move it out of the house. But my mother would sneak the accordion out of the room and hide it down in the bushes, just outside of the farm gate. We'd get ready for school and I'd sneak it out of the bushes at the gate. Then I'd carry this accordion that weighed about forty pounds about five miles to school, dragging it between my sister and I.

I got to play at quite a few concerts and I got to meet some very prominent musicians. I was influenced by a fellow who has made a great name for himself. He's known as the King of Accordions, Joe Burke, from Killnadema, near Loughrea. I remember seeing him at concerts and thinking how long his fingers were — the longest fingers I have ever seen on any man. They definitely could be women's fingers! I watched him and listened to him time and time again at concerts in Killimor, Portumna, Kiltormer and

Loughrea. We weren't allowed to go to too many places over and above the local places. I would have been around eleven or twelve that time.

My one wish was to go to an All-Ireland Fleadh Ceol — that's a Gaelic term meaning Festival of Music. I finally got permission to go to one in Swinford, Co. Mayo, around 1961 when I was in my early teens. My brother took me and my older sister Nancy who was home from Dublin at the time. We had such a great time. People go to compete. I didn't at that one. These festivals are an annual event on Whit[1] weekend towards the end of August. It would start on a Friday night, and though the competitions would go on all through the day on Saturday and Sunday, music took place all over the streets at random corners and in the pubs. Day and all-night music sessions. Musicians came from all over Ireland. Flute players, fiddle players, banjo players, singers, accordion players, set-dancers in the streets. Old and young. Storytellers.

You'd meet great characters at those places. It was the one and only one I went to before I came to Canada. I went to various local country Fleadh Ceols — one in Portumna where I competed. I loved to play, but I was never interested in competitions.

During my teenage years, most of my friends went to dances with show bands or rock and roll. My choice was just to hear the traditional Irish music. I remember my mother and my sister going for a walk on a Sunday evening. We used to stand up on the top of a hill where we could hear music coming from the local hall. A band would be playing. You could hear it loud and clear. When you live in the country there is no traffic. The most you'll hear is a dog barking.

It was beautiful. We used to sit down at the side of the road and we'd listen for hours to the music. We could even hear it coming from Tynagh, about eight miles. It might be the Tulla Céilí Band, the Kilfinora Céilí Band, or the Killimor Céilí Band. It got so hot inside they would open all the doors of the hall. In the marquee they would lift the canvas flaps at the sides. You'd get maybe three hundred people in these places dancing till one o'clock in the morning. The music would carry over the fields on a summer's evening. That was our Sunday night's entertainment until we were old enough to go to the dances.

I remember bonfire night — June 23rd, St. John's Night.[2] We used to wait till about ten o'clock to light the bonfire. It's pitch dark out in the country, but the moon seems to be that much brighter than in the city. It seemed like gold. The bonfire is traditional but I'm not sure of the history of it. It had something to do with Pagan times. They were great traditionalists around our place; any excuse at all was used to dance a few sets or have a hooley. On bonfire night these large fires would burn and people sat around them. In some areas they sat and they told stories.

Our chore of the evening was to go and collect the makings of this fire: sticks and lots of wood. We'd set the fire up at our road gate. At our gate, up a little boreen from the house, there were three roads, one leading to Portumna, one to Killimor and one to Tynagh. It made for a little crossroads at our main gate. So we had the fire up there. About nine o'clock the music would start and people sat around and chatted. When I eventually learned how to play properly, I remember sitting there playing and shouting. I don't know what the significance of this shouting and yahooing and making lots of noise was. People would dance a set — and a half-set, which was the East Galway dance — right at the crossroads. Our neighbours would come and our cousins who lived a couple of houses over would be there. The Quirkes, and FitzGeralds, other McClearns from down the road, and the Traceys would be there.

In the summertime in Ireland nights are so still in the country. There was a tranquility and darkness. The only light is the light from this fire, blazing and crackling with the old wood. The smell of that wood burning. The light of the moon. The smell of the hay — that was the time of the year when we cut the hay, and many an hour we spent at it. That particular evening you had to get the hay finished early — on a summer's evening, the evenings were longer so you made hay up to nine o'clock at night. But on bonfire night we made sure to get it finished a little bit quicker, get in and have the supper, and say the Rosary. Then we'd get out and start the bonfire, and the music and dancing and yahooing would break the stillness of the night.

Other times for hooleys would be around Christmas, on St. Stephen's Day[3] — Boxing Day in Canada. We called it the Mummers or the Wren Boys, depending where you came from in Ireland. Where I came from we called it the Mummers. We painted our faces or wore masks and we had a group of dancers. They used shoe polish for paint — usually black shoe polish or brown. We might have head scarves, old sunglasses and masks. We used to call the masks féasógs, the Gaelic for mask. Anything to disguise. It took very little — you were so involved in what they were doing and the music, or trying to decipher who they were by the instrument they held, you forgot about how they looked.

You had to make sure you had enough people for a half-set, four people. We had two or three musicians and a driver — someone who was willing to drive from house to house all day and have little or nothing to drink. At the end of the evening he was compensated by way of a couple of pounds. The Mummers started early on St. Stephen's Day, about twelve noon.

When I was about seven or eight years old I used to watch for them. I recall very, very clearly being scared of the Mummers — when they came in all dressed up in raggy clothes and masks and painted faces, I didn't recognize them. They came in briskly, shouting and dancing through the door. They would grab the first person that they came upon inside the door to join them in a dance. I remember one of them grabbing me and I ran and cried. Not only did he scare me, I didn't like the idea that he took my mom out to dance. I had this fear of him knocking her down or hurting her in some way. I wanted to listen to them play from behind a closed bedroom door. So when I'd see them coming I always liked to go in the bedroom and lock the door or push a chair to the door, and I'd listen to them from there. They were just neighbours in disguise.

My own brother used to go out in the Mummers. We always had a piece of cake for them and a few shillings. My father never hesitated to pay them some money, even though money wasn't plentiful with us. The instrument was the first thing I would look at. It might be an accordion, or a flute, or a fiddle. It was hard to distinguish between one flute and another, but it was easy to distinguish between one accordion and another. I had such a great interest in music that I knew the colour and size of the accordions played by the local musicians. I'd recognize them anywhere. But I got fooled by that. I remember a group of Mummers coming in — great dancers — who I thought were also great musicians. I encouraged my Dad to give them a pound, a lot of money back then in the sixties, and he did. One of them was my brother Joe. I didn't recognize him because he wasn't playing his own accordion.

Other times we played music would be at thrashing time and the evening of a station, a Mass said in the house. The station wasn't customary all over Ireland, but it was common in East Galway. Mass would be held in the house and a breakfast served, and it lingered on through the day, and then ended up to be a bit of a hooley that night.

I learned to play the spoons, kind of drumming to the music, playing these spoons. It's like when people play the bodhrán, the goat-skin drum. In my teens I played the odd concert with my brother in local places: Killimor, Portumna, and Ahaskragh, outside Ballinasloe. I didn't play too many places while I was going to school.

Eventually I finished high school, but there weren't very many jobs available in Ireland. My going to Canada came up around the early sixties, when I was in my teens. Letters came from my older sister in Canada — there's more than a ten-year difference between us. She was encouraging me to come to Canada and my mother and father were in agreement. My father, as a rule, didn't want you to agree to anything you didn't want to do. He would never deprive you of an opportunity. My mother was passive, which wasn't unusual in Ireland back then. The women tended to go along with what men suggested.

It came to pass that I finished school, and all of a sudden I was making arrangements to come to Canada. I always wanted to travel. My mother took me up to Dublin to the Canadian Embassy. Because I was under age, we were experiencing a lot of difficulty with clearing Immigration. It started the early part of the year of '63 and went on into '64 — I would get clearance to go and then something would happen that I couldn't go. Little I understood about it, of course. I learned afterwards that because I was so young, we had to get clearance from the local Garda[4] to make sure that I wasn't running away from home. I was really looking forward to coming to Canada. I didn't know what I was coming out to.

It came to pass on December 15, 1964, when I was still a teenager, that I was coming to Canada. I remember getting presents of envelopes with a pound note or a five-pound note from neighbours and relatives. I was so excited but this was naiveté on my part. My one wish was to be able to buy a watch. I had never owned a watch, and I always wanted one. So I bought a watch in Killimor, in the chemist shop, of all places. It cost me seventeen shillings and I was so proud of this watch. It was a plain old watch with a brown strap, but to me it was the ultimate. I longed for one with a bracelet but I couldn't afford it.

Then I had to buy clothes. I had an idea in my mind about what they would wear in Canada: Everything would be very fancy and frilly and beautiful. So I ended up leaving a lot of practical and useful stuff behind that I had to send for later on. I had never worn slacks before and I bought a pair of slacks at the airport the day I was leaving. My mom bought me a beautiful suit. I had a suit before, but nothing as expensive as this. I bought dresses in Portumna and Killimor and a new winter coat, new shoes, and the necessities. I was very pleased and happy with myself with all this stuff.

On the day I was leaving we went to Shannon Airport. It was quite an ordeal back then, a whole-day affair. I don't remember too many details about leaving. I remember having my suitcase packed. I was so excited. Not excited in a super-happy way, but excited because this was a new adventure. The furthest I had been away from home was England. I had never been on an airplane, and having to travel on my own was quite an adventure. On the morning I was leaving I remember everybody rushing around trying to get all the farming jobs done. My father summoned my cousin to come over to the house that morning to take care of all the milking and feeding the calves and keeping the fire down until they came back.

We left the house around nine o'clock in the morning and my cousin drove us to the airport. My father and mother came. My sister Dympna was already in England. My mother's sister came. My brother Joe was there. We got to Shannon Airport and checked in and then we had time to sit around a bit and we went and had tea and cake. I remember my father and mother being extremely sad. Now, I was very sad. My father hadn't spoken for most of the morning. He had spent most of the time crying. My mother didn't cry until just before I boarded the plane. Now I cried too. I am a very emotional person. I really didn't know what I was doing. I didn't know how far away I was really going; the miles didn't mean a thing, or the difference in culture.

The sadness that overcame them was a different sadness. They cried because they knew that I was going to a foreign country I knew nothing about. I was just a child. So it was the fear that made them cry; they didn't want to part with me. I didn't realize that until I was here and I learned what it is like to have to part with children of your own. I certainly wasn't longing to get away. I had no reason to. I had a lovely childhood and I always enjoyed being around my father and mother. They gave us anything they could and lots of their time. I don't ever remember any unhappiness. But there were no jobs in Ireland. I do remember looking at my father and thinking: This man is crying really hard. So was my mom. It made me sad and I cried when I was on the plane. But it didn't sink in until I got here.

I arrived in Toronto, dressed in a nice tweed suit and a purse to match, and high-heel shoes, feeling that I looked like everyone else. At that time you had to walk down the steps from the plane and across the tarmac into the terminal. The walkway wasn't covered then, so I stepped into a foot and a half of snow in my high-heel shoes! I knew nothing about Immigration or how it worked, so I just followed the crowd. I was only about three minutes off the plane when I was tapped on the shoulder and my name was called. Through sheer innocence and naiveté again, I thought, here I am three thousand miles away from home and somebody knows my name!

I was brought into this office and the man explained to me that my sister who was meeting me would have some forms to sign because she was "sponsoring" me. I didn't know the meaning of "sponsor." He explained to me that if we didn't make contact with my sister, I would be sent back on the next plane. That bothered me because it was all too confusing. When he was saying this to me I thought: What if I don't recognize her? She was much older than me and because she had been living in Canada, she hadn't been home that many times. I was very scared at that point. He said we should first go and get my luggage, and we did. And as we were going down the escalator, I saw my sister.

We headed for Toronto, where she lived, and I was fascinated by the lights on the Gardiner Expressway. It was a whole sea of lights. I was overwhelmed by the lights and the lanes of traffic and the speed of the cars. It was at night and I couldn't see much of the city except for the lights. All the houses were decorated for Christmas. You were lucky in Ireland to see the odd house here and there with a Christmas tree that had "fairy lights." It seemed that every house in Toronto had umpteen lights and beautiful decorations. It was like a storybook. And there were all these street lights that I wasn't accustomed to after coming from rural Ireland.

We got to my sister's house about nine o'clock at night. I remember thinking that her house was beautiful. My brother Pat was living in Toronto then. He was close in age to my sister. I had met him on a couple of occasions before. Something clicked with this brother of mine, some bond that to this day has never been broken. Now he lives back in England and is miles away from me again, but this bond between us has never been broken.

I got up the next day and decided to go out. I was terrified of the traffic and scared to go too far away from my sister's house in case I wouldn't know my way back. So I kept looking for landmarks, what was on the corner of the street — a drugstore, Woolworth's, whatever. I was only going about a half a block away from the house, but I was so afraid. My sister encouraged me to go downtown in order to find my way around. There was no subway on Danforth Avenue then, just streetcars.

One day before Christmas I took the streetcar to Yonge and Bloor and then the subway down to Queen Street. She told me I would see a sign for Eaton's and I could do some shopping. It was about one o'clock in the afternoon. I found my way to Eaton's and I went in and looked around. I was just overcome by the size of the store, trying to shop for Christmas presents. I had learned very quickly that Christmas presents are quite the thing in Canada. That wasn't so in Ireland: When you got finished with Santa Claus in Ireland, there wasn't much in the way of presents for adults. I was trying to cope with this different money, and I had no idea how it came about — these dollars and cents in comparison to pounds, shillings and pence.

I remember looking at this gorgeous window at Simpson's and all these toys, fascinated by the fact that they moved. They had these little beavers set up, cutting wood. Even though I was in my teens, it still took my interest very much. When I was a kid I longed to go and see Santa Claus in person in Ireland. We were always too busy, or my mom just wasn't free to take us to Portumna. Santa Claus used to come to O'Shea's drapery store in Portumna which was always set up with toys for Christmas. Not every store would have toys back then. I was comparing that with this beautiful window which displayed countless moving toys. And inside the store sat Santa Claus! I recalled how I longed to get a sleeping doll for Christmas, and I never did get one. To this day I still go into the stores and I look at the dolls.

I spent a couple of hours shopping and then it was time to go back to my sister's house. I had written directions to get to Eaton's and I had planned to double back in order to get home. When I set out for my sister's place I found myself up on the street. It was now pitch dark and I did not know which was north, south, east or west. I had made my way from the store, bypassed the subway, and I was now up on the street. I hadn't a clue where I was. Then I saw these streetcars and thought: maybe that's Bloor Street. I thought the streetcars only ran on Bloor Street. I was desperate and scared, so I phoned my sister. She gave me directions to get home and I found my way back on the subway and the streetcar. That was my first and last time ever to get lost in Toronto.

It was moving closer to Christmas and then reality set in. I had this idea when I was coming to Canada that everybody would be a musician. I thought I would arrive in this Irish community where everybody played traditional Irish music. I never thought of anybody being a different religion. The first thing that hit home was the realization that I certainly didn't hit on an Irish community. There are a lot of Irish people in Canada, but not everybody played traditional Irish music or was ever interested. All of a sudden I was missing all this music that I lived with on a daily basis in Ireland, here in Canada without an accordion. I was lost. Completely lost. I remember borrowing an accordion from someone, and playing it day and night. All of a sudden I realized I was in a strange country. Was I going to be able to cope with this?

Christmas Day, we went out for dinner and we were invited back to my brother's house afterwards. I spent the better part of Christmas Day and during Christmas dinner crying. Having no experience, having been in England once, Dublin maybe twice, but other than that having never left home. Out of school to Canada, this great, vast country.

We went to my brother's house for tea and dessert. I remember walking up the steps and hearing the Tulla Céilí Band playing. Tulla is in Co. Clare. I just went in and I sat on the couch and I cried and I cried and I cried. Eventually, we got out to dance a half-set. Living beside my brother was a lady from Killimor, Kathleen Dealy, who is married to Kearns from Sligo. My brother and myself and Kathleen Dealy and my sister all danced a half-set. That kind of appeased me a bit. And the night went on and I ended up staying at my brother's and went back the next day to my sister's house.

Then a nice surprise came my way. One evening in January, just after that Christmas, my brother came to my sister's house and asked me to go for a drive with him. Somewhere on Bloor Street, way out in the west end, he went into a store. I saw him handing a document over the counter and he got a large box. We came out and got into the car. "Here," he said. "Happy Christmas! It's late, but this is your Christmas present." I opened it up. It was an accordion! That's the accordion I have today. He had sent to Italy for it, before I came to Canada. I have never, never been so excited in my life. I played this accordion all the way home in the car! It was a road between Canada and Killimor. All of a sudden, that gap was closed between Canada and Ireland. Just being able to play brought me back home again. And I felt very much at peace.

Having the accordion, I made myself available to play at dances and competitions to earn some money, but also because I loved it. I used to play at intermissions at Irish dances for no reason but just to play. I played at the Maple Leaf Ballroom in Toronto, and the Locarno and places like that. I didn't do it for money; I just loved playing so much. I used to bring the accordion to a dancing school I joined and when I wasn't dancing myself I used to play for the dancers.

Out of all that came a couple of odd jobs playing in clubs. One was the Windsor House, here in Toronto. I remember playing there for about $25, just at intermissions and in between the main groups. Someone had seen me play there and asked me to play at the El Mocambo down on Spadina Avenue. There used to be an Irish night there every Thursday night for about thirteen years. That was around 1968 or 1969, but it was going from the fifties — long before I came to Canada. I took over the Thursday nights along with another fellow from the North of Ireland. From there I met up with another musician, Norman Payne from Athenry, Co. Galway.

At the end of the sixties and the beginning of the seventies was the start of the music in pubs here in Canada. We got together — Norman and myself, and another fellow, Davie O'Donohoe from Limerick, and a woman from Liverpool, Jean — and we formed a band, the Travelling People. We got a three-week engagement at a club in Toronto's west end. Before our three weeks were up the manager renewed our contract, and we ended up there for three and a half months.

In that time we quit our day jobs and made music our profession. While we were there, we met a talent agent from Calgary, Alberta, who was booking mainly for the west coast. We drew up a contract with her and we ended up playing most of the Canadian Pacific hotels, all across Canada. We played Winnipeg, Sudbury, Sault Ste. Marie, Calgary, Lethbridge, Edmonton, Red Deer, Vancouver, and as far north as the Northwest Territories. We played about 40 percent traditional music and the rest folk. It was mostly a Canadian audience, so we played what the audience could recognize — a lot of ballads and country-type music — and then we did the jigs and reels in between.

That was 1970 to 1973. Then I checked out for a year and decided I'd work through the day, but in that year I ended up caught up in another group here in Toronto, playing at night and working through the day. One day in the early part of the seventies I was playing at a dancing competition. A day-long affair. You sit and play from nine until six. Quite tiring, quite aggravating at times because if the children don't win, the musician gets the blame. I noticed this little red-haired six- or seven-year-old boy in a kilt; he was taking in what I was doing. Now he was a dancer.

He was cute, very Irish-looking. Towards the end of the day his parents asked me if I would teach him to play. He wanted, above all other things, to be able to play the button accordion. The button accordion is more difficult than the piano accordion. So I promised them that I would take their number and I would teach him but I couldn't say when. I contacted them about a year later.

I taught this child to play. He would come to my place on a Saturday for a lesson, about an hour and a half long. He was a delightful child and he turned out to be a terrific musician. Anything he forgot after he left my house, he used to phone me. He would play the part of the tune over the phone for me and I'd have to leave the phone down and get the accordion and play it back for him.

I grew very close to this young fellow who was growing up into a lovely teenager, tall and good-looking and a pleasure to be around. His two sisters were equally beautiful. They got involved in traditional Irish dancing. I became very close with the family. His mother used to knit sweaters and socks and make things for my children. All through high school he continued to play. I got him some jobs playing and he became quite well known in Toronto. He bloomed into a very fine young man who still loved traditional music and he played in Massey Hall.

On March 16, 1989, he died very suddenly at the age of 21. That left a big void in my life. The saddest thing I've ever done was play at that man's funeral. I played "Boolavogue," his favourite tune.

I left music in 1977. I was in a fairly steady relationship in Toronto, and thinking about marriage. I would still get the odd phone call from the Irish American Club in Detroit and go down maybe and play for a weekend. I continued playing for dancing competitions.

I got married in 1979 to a fellow from Co. Kilkenny. Chose in the middle of the relationship to check out of the music, out of respect for the other person. My husband wasn't very keen on traditional Irish music. A year or two before I got married, I got myself a day job, one that I liked, dealing with people. I didn't involve myself very much in music while I was married except in house get-togethers. I would go to someone's house and I'd play a few tunes. I also played at dancing competitions. I didn't accept a lot of bookings in the evening or out of town because I had young children. I used to play at home too for the kids. It was quite okay because I devoted the time to the children. I never lost the ability to play because of the marriage or anything else.

As time went on both my children got involved in traditional

Irish dancing. They like music and they're very involved in the cultural aspect of Ireland. They've won many awards in Irish dancing. They both play the piano and now the violin and the banjo. One of them plays the bodhrán and is quite good at it.

The music eventually picked itself up again, in the last four years. I got involved in Comhaltas Ceoltóirí Éireann, the traditional musicians of Ireland. It's a body of people who get together to promote traditional Irish music in Canada, Australia, New Zealand, the U.S., and all over the world. It's quite a big organization and it promotes the playing of the music — not for money, just to promote the culture. We had the Comhaltas Congress here in Toronto, in 1984 or 1985. Delegates came from all over the world. Gradually, I kept on playing and picking up whatever jobs were available. I didn't find it a problem with the children. I just took them along with me. At that point they were about five and seven. I'm still involved in Comhaltas, but only indirectly. If there is a function and I'm asked to play, I go along and I play.

I never did find it a problem being a woman in the music field, among predominantly men. I was able to help a lot of them who were just starting out and learning, so they never did look at me as a woman playing music. In Ireland, it's a bit of a problem — not many women are out playing music. Years ago it didn't seem to be the accepted thing. Maybe today it's a bit different.

Any time I go back home to Ireland on holidays, even though I've been gone a good number of years, time stands still. I walk into a pub, and I feel like I've never left. I sit down and play the tunes that will always be played. That's the nice thing about music: It's so universal there's no gap between musicians. I go back sometimes after a three-year span, and could walk into any pub in Killimor or Portumna, and it's like it was just the day before.

I didn't have many hopes and dreams when I left Ireland — I didn't know enough of what I should expect. Canada is a super country, definitely in terms of work. My deep-down wish, though, would have been to stay in Ireland. I miss the simplicity of what I knew around my home. But the work wasn't there so I had to leave and earn a living. If I could bring the landscape and the simplicity of the people and the friendliness of Killimor over to Toronto, coupled with the music, and have it here, I'd be very happy. I do miss the sensitivity of my people, the small community atmosphere, being able to stop and say hello to everybody, being able to stop and help someone.

I really haven't thought about the future. At this point I'm raising two children by myself. I work a nine-to-five job, and I play music for fun and for money. I look at the children and I'm glad they're well and I'm well. I plan that the children will have a good education, and I will direct them a bit more in their career than I was directed as a child. When I went to school a teacher or counsellor never came to you and said: This is what you would be best at. It's too bad that we didn't have people to direct us. I worked at jobs, mainly secretarial, but I didn't always enjoy them. I didn't know any better because nobody counselled me in any different direction.

If I had my choice, I would play music. "The Bag of Spuds" was my father's favourite tune — he always asked for that tune; it's a good tune too, good and lively. When I play "The Bag of Spuds," I see my father sitting, listening very attentively, hoping that I didn't make a mistake, clapping his hands, stomping his feet, keeping time with the music. Enjoying the music while it lasted. It didn't matter what hour of the night the hooley went on to. As long as there was music being played it could spill into the small hours of the morning, and it didn't bother my father.

My father has passed and gone and any time I play that tune now I think of the night of their fiftieth wedding anniversary in 1977. It took the place of the wedding they never had. We had a Céilí at the Westpark Hotel in Portumna for them. The party spilled over from there back to our house and we sat around the hearth and continued on playing and drinking, and making sandwiches. That party ended about six-thirty or seven o'clock in the morning, with everybody going to Mass.

My mother loved "The Battering Ram," a very well-known jig. When I play that tune I remember her rushing around getting tea ready, the tea and the raisin bread, the brown bread and jam for these hooleys in the house. If someone was at home on holidays or it was a special occasion, then we had hot roast-chicken sandwiches.

We would be playing in the kitchen, so she did her preparing — the one and only time the parlour was used. All the china cups were taken out and she set up the table and cut up whatever cake she made and prepared the tea in there. Then when we took our break from the music and dancing we went in to have our tea and sandwiches in the parlour.

Each time I sit down to play, my father and mother come to mind. Sometimes I start to cry. Nobody seems to notice if the tears are running down my face. It often happens for an entire concert. It's the feeling and the memories of this huge Irish kitchen, the floor full of people dancing, people sitting on the wooden chairs, and the fire in the big hearth that had to be tended all night. It all comes back to me when I play. This fire and the people and my father sitting there enjoying the music and my mother running and rushing around. Sometimes when I play I get goose bumps when I think of it: It's a feeling of warmth, a feeling that they're still there. So long as I can play music, my mother and father will still be alive, and their spirit will come through in the music.

Notes

1. Whitsunday is the seventh Sunday after Easter.
2. The summer solstice.
3. The winter solstice.
4. Police.

Something of My Heritage

Margaret O'Connor-Lefas

*Margaret O'Connor-Lefas lives and works
in Winnipeg, Manitoba.*

I'm from Arklow, Co. Wicklow, and I came to Canada in 1977. I was just twenty-one when I came to Winnipeg. I met my husband here, who's Greek. We have three children, Katherina aged eight, Georgia who's six, and Demetri who's a year and a half. I got involved in Irish culture here in Manitoba mostly because of my children. It's very important to me that they have something of my heritage.

I did Irish dancing at home myself for a while, but I didn't keep on with it. My oldest daughter Katherina has a flair for Irish dancing. She does very well at the competitions. It's very important to her that she has something to show her Nana and Granddad that's Irish. She's always talking about her Irish dancing costume, and if anyone ever comes to visit, right away she wants to dance for them and show them the costume.

I'm very involved with the Irish Association in Manitoba; I'm a director there and one of my functions on the board is to look after the Women's Auxiliary. This year it was my job to pull it back out of the woodwork. St. Patrick's week is a very busy week for us. We have a banquet, usually the Saturday night before St. Patrick's Day. It's a very big function which we help organize. I'm in charge of the decorating for all these functions. On St. Patrick's Day we have a luncheon down at the club. This year we decided that the women would cater it — a big responsibility because we get a thousand or more people at lunchtime. We have bacon and cabbage and potatoes and Irish Stew. Soda bread, of course. A few of the women get together and they make the soda bread and freeze it.

The first Tuesday of every month we have a traditional Irish night at the club — it's all traditional Irish music and they all just meet there. You don't have to be a member of the club or anything, and it's not just Irish — visitors from all over can come. If you're just in town — say on your holidays — and you play a musical instrument you can just come down. If you want to sing, you can sing, or just sit around enjoying the music and talk.

The Irish club here is a place for us to go and it brings us that little bit closer to home: You can go there and you know you'll meet some Irish people and have a chat. Women are very involved in the traditional nights. There are a few really nice singers and a few ladies that play different instruments. A lot of ladies are involved in the Tara Players. The Tara Players have been invited to go to Minneapolis later on this year to put on the play *Crystal and Fox*.

There are a lot of the Irish people here that are married to different nationalities, so it's good for them to all entwine, just like myself. Quite a lot of my friends are Irish, but I also have Jamaican friends, a few Greek friends. Usually we spend an awful lot of time at the Irish club. My husband really likes it down there. He finds the people very friendly and he's even got involved himself this year in the Tara Players Theatre Group and he does some of the set construction for them.

I like to be involved in the Irish culture. It makes it a bit easier for me because sometimes I get very homesick. If I'm involved with the Irish club it's a home away from home. That's important to me because I feel so drawn back to Ireland.

It's My Step and I'll Dance It

Violet Moore

Vi Moore lives in Vancouver, British Columbia.

My mother was born on Patrick Street, in the heart of the Liberties in Dublin between Christ Church Cathedral and St. Patrick's Cathedral. It was an overcrowded and poverty-stricken area, but the wit of the people in the Liberties was not to be matched anywhere in Dublin. They were poor people but colourful people. George Bernard Shaw hung out around that area.

My mother had fifteen or sixteen pregnancies and miscarriages, and God only knows how many self-induced abortions. I grew up in the early forties on a street where the average-size family was twelve. Large families had twenty-two children. There were twelve children in my family. In my formative years I often heard women aiding and abetting each other inducing abortions. Now there's such a furor about it, but it was very much a part of our upbringing. Women considered themselves lucky when they had their period.

I remember many times going down the street with my mother, and meeting a neighbour, my mother saying, "How are ya, Mary?" and Mary answering, "Oh, I came on, May." And my mother saying, "Thanks be ta Jasus! I hope I do." My mother was lucky enough not to get pregnant while she breast-fed — for the first eight children that were breast-fed there is nearly two years between each of us. But after my father returned from the war, the last four were not breast-fed and there's barely nine or eleven months between them.

My father was not present for the first few years. He would come back and forth from England. I know that he was involved in the First World War. There was some rift between my father and his brother Dan, who was in the IRA. Uncle Dan was entrenched and invested in the movement, as were many of my relatives, and he had to flee to England for protection because of his activities in Dublin.

After we moved to Crumlin, Dad got a job with the White Swan Laundry on Donore Avenue off the South Circle Road as a van driver and I think he was earning about £25 a week. There was never, ever, ever, ever enough money, and oftentimes not enough food. But there was always potatoes — always spuds. I think spuds saved our lives. Still we were a healthy bunch. I never, ever went to the doctor until I was coming to Canada and had to have a medical.

Poverty was not something that I grew up resenting. I only ever had a glimpse of something different during my tenth year, when I discovered one of the girls at school was an only child. People used to point at her and say, "She's an only child!" And all of my friends and I would wonder what that felt like, to have the whole house with no brothers or sisters, and just your mother and dad, and have a whole bedroom to yourself instead of sleeping five to a bed. At least the girls in our family did well. There were five of us, and as much as it was uncomfortable sharing a bed with four other sisters, the boys were worse off. They were seven to a bed. We lived in a two-bedroom house and my mother and father were in the other room along with the current baby.

Shortly after we moved to Crumlin, I discovered Irish dancing. Some of the neighbourhood children went around to the next street to a woman who taught the dancing. It cost sixpence — a fortune — and there was no way we could release sixpence a week for dancing lessons for me. I was fascinated by the kids on the street doing bits and pieces of their dances. My mother'd say, "Oh, I know the reels and the jigs," and she'd do them for me. There was such a yearning and a longing in her voice when she talked. I see her dancing in the kitchen. And at that point I see why I made a decision: I would become an Irish dancer. But how to do this with no money?

What I found myself doing was lying in wait in the house watching out the window for the girls coming back from Irish dancing. When I'd see them coming I would say to Mammy, "I'm just going out to see Ann or Rosaleen and I'll be back." I'd go over and ask them to teach me the steps they had learned. This went on for a couple of years. It would be eight or nine o'clock at night when I'd return and ordinarily she would argue, but she knew why I was going out. So I was waiting a couple of years before I eventually got to go to Irish dancing. The dancing teacher would say, "Okay, won't you show the good teacher the one-two-threes." Then I'd do the one-two-threes and continue for the whole reel. Then she would begin to teach me the jig, but I already knew that too. So she would say, "Well now, what don'tcha know?" I figured I'd wasted so much time not being there that I just sponged it up. It wasn't very long at all before I was out in somebody's second-hand costume at the Feis.[1]

My life was never the same. My mother by this time was hooked: She realized I was talented and she was determined to make available to me whatever it was that I needed to go to dancing. Dancing became my life. My dancing teacher also realized that I had a talent to teach, and having so much experience at home with so many younger children to look after I was successful teaching the children. Very soon after I began taking classes I became assistant teacher on Mondays and Fridays and then we went to a place on Parnell Square[2] on Saturdays to do céilí dancing. My own classes were on Tuesdays and Thursdays. Wednesday, I stayed home and washed my hair. Every single Sunday there were competitions in the FOS, a union hall on Parnell Square. It had a dingy old basement with a broken-up old floor that we danced on. The rest of the kids would go to the pictures and I'd be off to the Feis with Ma.

I have a vivid recollection of walking down Rutland Avenue one Sunday. Here I was being taken off to dancing and I should be grateful. We were walking together on the way down to the bus stop and the rain was beating down, hopping off the ground. There was a squishing sound coming out of me Ma's shoes because they were letting in rain. I felt in a blackened mood and I did not want to be going to this Feis. And the rest of the journey till we stood at the bus stop and waited and got on the 22 Bus to go to Parnell Square, I prayed, "Please God, let me win for her." That way I could justify these sacrifices she was making. I don't know that I won anything that day, but I did go on to win enough awards to satisfy her.

It caused a lot of friction in the family. There were times when the competitions would run over and we'd miss the last bus home. And often I was in a daze of tiredness with the hanging around for these competitions and then coming home late. One time my father had his bicycle cuffs on and he was just getting on the bicycle to go out looking for us. It was two o'clock in the morning before we arrived home and a bunch of women had got together and shared a taxi, which was an enormous luxury. It was my first time ever in a motor car.

My father was just on his way out the door with the bicycle and his face was white with anger at the hour of the night it was. My mother had to do some explaining. The Feis was held in Dun Laoghaire and I had won my very first championship. Everybody was thrilled. I think people realized how much it meant to my mother so there was a bigger than normal reaction to the result of my championship.

My mother held up this cup and nothing could faze her now. It wouldn't make any difference what had happened now that she had this trophy; it was proof positive that she wasn't wasting her time on me. But if I hadn't won anything, there was murder in the house after we returned. I'd be doubly jeopardized because I had caused this trouble and friction.

The crux came when I was fifteen years of age and I started to lose interest. I just got very, very bored and very tired. I was doing more teaching than dancing and I wasn't growing as a dancer. I really was fed up with my life. At the time I was working in Jacob's Biscuit Factory in Dublin, so I was up at the crack of dawn to go to work and the work was dull and repetitive. The office staff and the supervisors had to be referred to as Miss and Mister and there was a definite level of hierarchy. I was on the very bottom level. We were working for a pittance doing piecework and there was very little time to even chat with your neighbour on the factory line.

My body just gave up the dancing. I wanted to continue for my mother but my body just stopped. This threw her into a bit of a tizzy. It was her ambition for somebody in the family to somehow transcend this abject poverty. Having won medals and cups, I was earmarked.

It was announced one day that I was going to Canada. I got this notification from my sister in Winnipeg: She had organized a loan with the Bank of Canada to pay my fare out and I was initially going to look after her first child. After her second child was born, I would be expected to get a job to help pay back the loan. I came to Canada in 1956 when I was sixteen. I was quite numbed. I don't ever recall breaking down or crying, even when I was leaving my mother, but when I got to Canada, I went to pieces because I didn't belong here. I had no means of identifying with anybody my own age. My closest friend after I'd been in Canada for three months was 32 years of age, a woman from Belfast who was just insanely homesick. Her and I got together regularly whenever there was an opportunity. Just talked about Ireland.

I got a job at the Winnipeg Clinic in the records department and earned $100 a month. Out of that I paid $40 to the Bank of Canada and $40 board and room to my sister and sometimes managed to send $10 or $15 to my mother. Whatever was left over paid for my bus tickets.

I decided I would not put foot to floor again. I was so delighted to be out from under the Irish dancing that I didn't care if I never danced again because it was all connected with this obligation to my mother. It felt wonderful being away from it. I did actually get roped into a couple of St. Patrick's Day concerts. There was somebody in Winnipeg teaching dancing and the kids wore tap shoes — it was a combination of tap dancing and bits and pieces of Irish dancing. Some of the Irish people that had their children going to this person said they would like me to teach Irish dancing. Being too polite to say no, I would go to their houses and teach their children dancing but it wasn't something I enjoyed at all.

The dancing went by the board until after I was married and moved to Vancouver in 1962, saddled with a baby getting ready to be born and an unemployed husband. I managed to hook up with a woman through the Irish Society, who was teaching dancing here and had loads of Irish dancing pupils. So I was teaching for four hours on Saturday and getting $12 for my four hours. It gave me an opportunity to be earning the $12 which I needed at the time. I was invigorated when I started dancing again and then began thinking about what I was missing, how my life was diminished without the dancing. Then I began to think about how I could organize it in a fashion where I could do it my own way and pass it on to the children of Irish immigrants. I felt it was very worthwhile to be passing on.

Irish dancing is like no other ethnic dancing. I have been involved with the Canadian Folk Society for twenty-odd years now and I'm familiar, for the most part, with the dances from all over the world. They are invigorating and inspiring and energizing, but none of them have the intricacy that Irish step-dancing has. Irish dancing strengthens all the muscles in your legs from your feet all the way up to the tops of your thighs. Then there's deportment: Irish dancing is stately and regal. You have to be straight of stature to carry out this intricate foot movement. There are other benefits too.

I have often wondered why I didn't give up the dancing. I wasn't earning enough money to live on just dancing alone. It never paid worthwhile money, so I was forced into sitting down and thinking what it was about dancing that I was hanging onto so tenaciously. And I discovered that dancing is an exercise in meditation. I would go into that studio sometimes, that shed in the back garden. Canadians call it a studio — it's a ramble-down old shack! I would go in there bedraggled and tired and fed up and just pissed off with the world and within minutes I would be transformed. Dancing empowered me. It is a tradition that was passed on to me through bigger and better people than I, and I discovered I could be a medium to pass it on to somebody else.

A whole floodgate has opened with respect to Irish women in

history. Aside from the suffragettes — who I still don't know enough about but I fully intend finding out about — there are the women of Irish mythology. There's Queen Maeve of Connaught from Celtic times who, when asked whether or not her husband gets jealous when she goes off with her team of warriors, replies, "Well, it wouldn't do for him to get jealous because one gets lonely out on the plains. And one must keep oneself amused with one's warriors." Compare that with the victimized woman of today and you begin to understand where the anger is coming from. There is this strength in Irish woman's tradition but she has been disempowered, reduced to — forgive me — a snivelling, victimized individual who has no faith in her own judgment, as a result of patriarchy. She knows the world is a miserable place, that she could do a better job, but she has lost her connection to make a contribution that would be far more valuable than what's happening in the world today. Women of the entire world have been sublimated to what they thought to be a better power. And it's turning out that it isn't a better power.

I formed a shell of a dance drama around the mythological story "The Children of Lir," from a feminist perspective. The story goes back to Celtic Ireland and is about this "wicked woman" Aoife, who came into the Kingdom of Lir and turned her poor, unfortunate step-children into swans because she was insanely jealous of the love their father and her husband, King Lir, had for them. She was the wife, the youngest sister of his widow, which made her the evil step-mother.

Now let's look at this story from the point of view of a woman. This very handsome warrior King Lir went into the Kingdom of De Danaan because his first wife died on the birth of their second set of twins. He is shown the youngest and prettiest daughter of the high king, De Danaan, who becomes his second wife. It so happened she had been in love with him all the years that her sister was married to him. After marriage she went with him to the Kingdom of Lir, imagining that she was going as his lover, expecting to find happiness when all he was interested in was a caretaker for his children. He would go off warrioring with his warrior friends and he'd be gone for long periods and when he came back it was the children he came back to. He even moved them into his bedchamber sooner than be away from them. Even the small amount of time that she would have with him, private time in the bedchamber, was taken away from her.

Finally, Aoife fell ill and was close to death and they were giving her potions. When she came out of this illness she was caught in the grips of dementia and determined she would destroy these children, so she could get his love. She had come on the premise that he was taking her as his wife. She was expecting love and caring and a relationship and found instead isolation and loneliness. There are parts of the story where she really extended herself to these children. When she wasn't successful in having the children killed she cast a spell on them and turned them into swans. They had to swim the lakes of Ireland for nine hundred years. In turn, her father, King De Danaan, who could do nothing to undo her spell, turned her into a demon of the air, a Morrígan[3] who everybody was terrified of because if they looked upon a Morrígan they became afflicted with some terrible disease or they died. Nobody would look at Aoife. For the rest of her life she was left to roam the skies isolated and tormented.

How to interpret this into dance? The way that I did it was to play up her sense of isolation, to show that she was victimized by the treatment that she received from Lir and not the other way around. My interpretation is to offer a different perspective for people. First, how the whole notion of evil step-mother came into effect. And swans are sacred in Ireland; it is believed that swans are human beings. The swans in Lir did become human beings after nine hundred years, but they were old and decrepit, and with the coming of Christianity they were baptized before they died.

It's significant that this should all have taken place with the coming of Christianity. Queen Maeve and Gráinne[4] and all these magnificent female figures in Irish mythology were rendered powerless with the coming of Christianity. It then became necessary to completely defame, to turn woman into the evil step-mother. Woman is now demon of the air: You have to be very careful lest you be engulfed by her. She's a woman who operated independently, not a woman who came in under the fold. In Christianity you either came in under the banner of patriarchal religion or you were not a woman; you were some kind of evil witch and deserving of punishment.

I'd always been a devout Catholic and whenever I had these conflicting thoughts I would offer them up to God. I could not see my strength. I was tied up in a Church where women have spent much energy repressing their strengths because of the Church's conditioning. In Ireland, a working-class man would have a difficult time supporting a huge family on very meagre wages; nevertheless, he was the king of his castle. Being a woman in Ireland meant being conditioned that you have to serve this man. We were taught to believe that this is the will of God and it is the will of the land. This is woman's place.

Then I reached a point when I really felt I was losing my sanity. My own kernel of truth was trying to break through this wall of conditioning. I had an incredibly interesting, strong maternal grandmother who, having lost her husband at an early age, brought her family up alone and was quite a figurehead in the Liberties. That strength inspired me. My mother was a mass of spirit and full of energy right up until she died at 84 in 1988. She died very shortly on the heels of my brother who was killed in a car accident at 42 years of age. His death didn't make any sense to her at all. I remember one incident after his funeral. One of the women came in off the street, a very Catholic religious woman, and said, "Oh well, God wanted him, Mrs. Duff. Don't fret yourself. It's because God wanted him." My mother's answer was, "Well, fuck Him anyway. He could have had me any day and four fatherless children wouldn't be left behind!"

My mother fed me things I think that even she was not aware of: There is a better life than this, trust your own intuition, you know what's right for you. I made a decision that I would get out of my marriage. Then what came into question was the whole religious thing. For the next five years I struggled mightily. I was bombarded with bits and pieces of ideas and feelings that were conflicting and had no choice but to sit down and try to decipher them. At the end of the five-year struggle I came out of it no longer a Catholic and no longer married. That's over twenty years ago.

With Irish dancing you go into a knowledge outside of you that you have access to by somebody out there teaching you. You bring this information inside of you, assimilate it, and then allow it to manifest itself through you. The way you manifest that information is through your own interpretation of it. Your own creativity comes into play and you can become empowered by somebody encouraging you to project in a more assertive way. For the girls in my class Irish dancing is an instrument. They can learn that they can dance as good as anybody. Then in later life when they're being taught — as they will be in the schools and the universities — that their point of view or decision or impression of life is not as valuable as a boy's or a man's, they know they have had this empowering experience of the dancing. They can believe in themselves. What it all comes down to is this: There are times in your life when you have to stand up and say: This step I'm dancing may be different to yours, but it's my step and I'll dance it.

In 1990, Vi Moore set up a program to teach Irish dancing to working-class, inner-city children in Vancouver. Her students include children of many different races.

Notes

1. Dancing and singing competition.
2. Named after the nineteenth-century Irish nationalist leader, Charles Stewart Parnell.
3. In Celtic mythology, Morrígan was one of a triad of fierce and sinister war goddesses.
4. In Celtic mythology, an aggressively erotic woman.

Bibliography

Adams, Nancy, Linda Briskin, and Margaret McPhail. *Feminist Organizing for Change: The Contemporary Women's Movement in Canada*. Toronto: Oxford University Press, 1988.

Agnes, Sr. Mary. *The Congregation of the Sisters of St. Joseph*. Toronto: University of Toronto Press, 1951.

Agonito, Rosemary. *History of Ideas on Women*. New York: Perigee Books, 1977.

Akenson, Donald Harman. *The Irish in Ontario: A Study in Rural History*. Kingston and Montreal: McGill-Queen's University Press, 1984.

Akenson, Donald Harman. *The Orangeman: The Life and Times of Ogle Gowan, the Irish Scoundrel Who Made Canada Orange*. Toronto: James Lorimer, 1986.

Anderson, Bonnie S., and Judith P. Zinsser, eds. *A History of Their Own*. New York: Harper & Row, 1988.

Anderson, Kathryn, and Dana C. Jack. "Learning to Listen: Interview Techniques and Analyses." In *Women's Words: The Feminist Practice of Oral History*, edited by Sherna Berger Gluck and Daphne Patai. New York: Routledge, 1991.

Anderson, Margaret, ed. *Mother Was Not a Person*. Montreal: Black Rose, 1972.

Armstrong, Frederick. "Ethnicity and the Formation of the Ontario Establishment." In *Ethnic Canada: Identities and Inequalities*, edited by Leo Driedger. Toronto: Copp Clark Pitman, 1987.

Armstrong, Karen. *The Gospel According to Woman: Christianity's Creation of the Sex War in the West*. London: Pan, 1986.

Backhouse, Constance. *Petticoats and Prejudice: Women and Law in Nineteenth-Century Canada*. Toronto: The Osgoode Society/ Women's Press, 1991.

Bagchi, Amiya Kumar. *The Political Economy of Underdevelopment*. London: Cambridge University Press, 1982.

327

Baker, William. *Timothy Warren Anglin—Irish Catholic Canadian.* Toronto: University of Toronto Press, 1977.

Bannerji, Himani. "Introducing Racism: Notes Towards an Anti-Racist Feminism." *Resources for Feminist Research* 16, no. 1.

Bannerji, Himani, Linda Carty, Kari Dehli, Susan Heald and Kate McKenna. *Unsettling Relations: The University as a Site of Feminist Struggles.* Toronto: Women's Press, 1991.

Barber, Marilyn. "The Women Ontario Welcomed: Immigrant Domestics for Ontario Homes, 1870–1930." *Ontario History* 72, no. 3 (1980).

Barry, Ursula. *Lifting the Lid: Handbook of Facts and Information on Ireland.* Dublin: Attic Press, 1986.

Baxter, Sheila. *No Way to Live: Poor Women Speak Out.* Vancouver: New Star, 1988.

Berger Gluck, Sherna, and Daphne Patai, eds. *Women's Words: The Feminist Practice of Oral History.* New York: Routledge, 1991.

Bird, Pat. *Of Dust and Time and Dreams and Agonies: A Short History of the Canadian People.* Toronto: Women's Press, 1975.

Brand, Dionne. "Black Women and Work: The Impact of Racially Constructed Gender Roles on the Sexual Division of Labour." *Fireweed*, no. 26 (Winter–Spring 1988).

Brand, Dionne. *No Burden to Carry: Narratives of Black Working Women in Ontario 1920s to 1950s.* Toronto: Women's Press, 1991.

Brickman, Julie, and John Briere. "Incidents of Rape and Sexual Assault in an Urban Canadian Population." *International Journal of Women's Studies* 7, no. 3.

Brodie, Janine, Shelley A.M. Gavigan and Jane Jenson. *The Politics of Abortion.* Toronto: Oxford University Press, 1992.

Calliste, Agnes. "Canada's Immigration Policy and Domestics from the Caribbean: The Second Domestic Scheme." In *Race, Class, Gender: Bonds and Barriers*, edited by Jesse Vorst *et al.* Toronto: Between the Lines, 1989.

Cameron, Anne. "Classism, Racism, and Academic Elitism Run Head-Long into Low-Rent Criticism." In *Feminism: From Pressure to Politics*, edited by Angela Miles and Geraldine Finn. Montreal: Black Rose, 1989.

Campbell, Bruce. *Canada Under Siege*. Ottawa: Canadian Centre for Policy Alternatives, 1992.

Canadian Advisory Council on the Status of Women. "Women, Paid/Unpaid Work, and Stress." Ottawa: Canadian Advisory Council on the Status of Women, 1989.

Carty, Linda, and Dionne Brand. "'Visible Minority' Women—A Creation of the Canadian State." *Resources for Feminist Research* 17, no. 3 (1988).

Cohen, Marjorie. *Free Trade and the Future of Women's Work: Manufacturing and Service Industries*. Toronto: Garamond, 1987.

Colleary, John. *Ireland's Case*. Grimsby, Ontario: Innisfree, 1985.

Condren, Mary. *The Serpent and the Goddess: Women, Religion, and Power in Celtic Ireland*. New York: Harper & Row, 1989.

Conway, Sheelagh. "Campus Critique Leaves Women on the Margins." *The Globe and Mail*, October 24, 1991.

Conway, Sheelagh. "History Weaves a Blood-Red Tapestry." *The Globe and Mail*, November 1, 1991.

Conway, Sheelagh. "The Montreal Massacre—Madness or Misogyny?" In *Women's Experience, Women's Education—An Anthology*, edited by Anne Innis Dagg, Sheelagh Conway and Margaret Simpson. Waterloo: Otter Press, 1991.

Conway, Sheelagh. *A Woman and Catholism: My Break with the Roman Catholic Church*. Toronto: PaperJacks, 1987.

Conway, Sheelagh, Anne Innis Dagg and Margaret Simpson. "Sexism in Universities: The Myth of Academic Excellence." Paper presented to the Commission of Inquiry on Canadian University Education, Toronto, 1990.

Cooper, Barbara. "The Convent: An Option for Quebecoises 1930–1950." *Canadian Women's Studies* 7, no. 4 (Winter 1986).

Cross, D. Suzanne. "The Neglected Majority: The Changing Role of Women in 19th Century Montreal." In *The Neglected Majority: Essays in Canadian Women's History*, edited by Susan Mann Trofimenkoff and Alison Prentice. Toronto: McClelland & Stewart, 1977.

Curtis, Edmund. *A History of Ireland*. New York: Methuen, 1936.

Dagg, Anne Innis, and Patricia Thompson. *MisEducation: Women & Canadian Universities*. Toronto: Ontario Institute for Studies in Education Press, 1988.

Daly, Mary. *Beyond God the Father: Toward a Philosophy of Women's Liberation*. Boston: Beacon, 1973.

Daly, Miriam. "Women in Ulster." In *Irish Women: Image and Achievement*, edited by Eiléan Ní Chuilleanáin. Dublin: Arlen House, 1985.

Das Gupta, Tania. "Introduction." In *Race, Class, Gender: Bonds and Barriers*, edited by Jesse Vorst *et al*. Toronto: Between the Lines, 1989.

Davis, Angela. *Women, Race & Class*. New York: Vintage, 1983.

Degnan, Sr. Bernard. *Mercy Unto Thousands: Life of Mother Mary Catherine McAuley*. Westminster, Maryland: Newman Press, 1957.

Devlin-McAliskey, Bernadette. "Building a United Women's Movement." *Spare Rib*, December 1991–January 1992.

Dickason, Olive Patricia. *Canada's First Nations: A History of Founding Peoples from Earliest Times*. Toronto: McClelland & Stewart, 1992.

Diva 3, no. 2 (March 1992).

Eichler, Margrit. *Families in Canada Today*. Toronto: Gage, 1988.

Elliott, Bruce. *Irish Migrants in the Canadas: A New Approach*. Kingston and Montreal: McGill-Queen's University Press, 1988.

Evans, Phil, and Eileen Pollock. *Ireland for Beginners*. London: Writers and Readers Publishing Cooperative, 1983.

Fairweather, Eileen, Roisin McDonagh and Melanie McFayden. *Only the Rivers Run Free: Northern Ireland: The Women's War*. London: Pluto, 1984.

Fireweed, no. 25 (Fall 1987). "Class Is the Issue." Special issue on class.

Fireweed, no. 26 (Winter–Spring 1988). "This Is Class Too." Special issue on class.

Fox, Bonnie, ed. *Hidden in the Household: Women's Domestic Labour Under Capitalism*. Toronto: Women's Press, 1980.

Friedan, Betty. *The Feminine Mystique*. New York: Dell, 1963.

Galarneau, Diane. "Alimony and Child Support." *Perspectives on Labour and Income*. Statistics Canada Catalogue 75-001 (Spring 1992).

Gallagher, Thomas. *Paddy's Lament: Ireland 1846–1847, Prelude to Hatred*. New York: Harcourt Brace Jovanovich, 1982.

Gannagé, Charlene. *Double Day, Double Bind: Women Garment Workers*. Toronto: Women's Press, 1986.

Globe and Mail. "One Million Children in Poverty." December 19, 1991.

Gorman, Thomas, Cathal Stanley, Marian Lyons-Hynes, Desmond Roche and Seamus McEneany, eds. *Clanricarde Country and the Land Campaign*. Galway: Woodford Heritage Group, 1987.

Grace, Beverley. Ph.D. thesis in progress on listening in storytelling, Ontario Institute for Studies in Education.

Greene, David H. *An Anthology of Irish Literature*. New York: Modern Library, 1954.

Gunderson, Morley, Leon Muszynski and Jennifer Keck. *Women and Labour Market Poverty*. Ottawa: Canadian Advisory Council on the Status of Women, 1990.

Haig-Brown, Celia. *Resistance and Renewal: Surviving the Indian Residential School*. Vancouver: Arsenal Pulp Press, 1988.

Harding, Sandra. *The Science Question in Feminism*. Ithaca, New York: Cornell University Press, 1986.

Hibbert, Joyce, ed. *The War Brides*. Toronto: PMA Books, 1978.

Hogan, Sr. M. Williamina. *Pathways of Mercy: History of the Foundations of the Sisters of Mercy in Newfoundland 1842–1984*. St. John's: Harry Cuff, 1986.

hooks, bell. *Ain't I a Woman? Black Women and Feminism*. Boston: South End Press, 1981.

hooks, bell. *Feminist Theory: From Margin to Centre*. Boston: South End Press, 1984.

Houston, Cecil, and William Smyth. *Irish Immigration and Canadian Settlement: Patterns, Links and Letters*. Toronto: University of Toronto Press, 1990.

Houston, Cecil, and William Smyth. *The Sash Canada Wore: A*

Historical Geography of the Orange Order in Canada. Toronto: University of Toronto Press, 1980.

Huberman, Leo. *Man's Worldly Goods: The Story of the Wealth of Nations*. New York: Monthly Review Press, 1968.

Jones, Charles, Lorna Marsden and Lorne Tepperman. *Lives of Their Own: The Individualization of Women's Lives*. Toronto: Oxford University Press, 1990.

Kealey, Linda, ed. *A Not Unreasonable Claim: Women and Reform in Canada, 1880s–1920s*. Toronto: Women's Press, 1979.

Lennon, Mary, Marie McAdam, and Joanne O'Brien. *Across the Water: Irish Women's Lives in Britain*. London: Virago Press, 1988.

Lerner, Gerda. *The Creation of Patriarchy*. New York: Oxford University Press, 1986.

Levitt, Cyril H., and William Shaffir. *The Riot at Christie Pits*. Toronto: Lester & Orpen Dennys, 1987.

Logan, Patrick. *The Holy Wells of Ireland*. Gerrards Cross, England: Colin Smythe, 1980.

Lorde, Audre. *Sister Outsider*. New York: Crossing Press, 1984.

MacCurtain, Margaret. "Women, the Vote and Revolution." *Women in Irish Society: The Historical Dimension*, edited by Margaret MacCurtain and Donncha Ó Corráin. Dublin: Arlen House, 1978.

MacCurtain, Margaret, and Donncha Ó Corráin, eds. *Women in Irish Society: The Historical Dimension*. Dublin: Arlen House, 1978.

MacKay, Donald. *Flight from Famine: The Coming of the Irish to Canada*. Toronto: McClelland & Stewart, 1990.

McGovern, Sr. Kathleen. *Something More Than Ordinary*. Toronto: Alger Press, 1989.

McKeown, J. C. *The Life and Labours of Most Rev. John Joseph Lynch, D.D., C.M., First Archbishop of Toronto*. Toronto: Sadlier, 1886.

Magnusson, Magnus. *Landlord or Tenant: A View of Irish History*. London: Bodley Head, 1978.

Malthus, Thomas R. *Essay on the Principle of Populations, as It Affects the Future Improvement of Society.* London: Macmillan & Co., 1926.

Mann Trofimenkoff, Susan, and Alison Prentice, eds. *The Neglected Majority: Essays in Canadian Women's History.* Toronto: McClelland & Stewart, 1977.

Mannion, John J. *Irish Settlements in Eastern Canada: A Study of Cultural Transfer and Adaptation.* Toronto: University of Toronto Press, 1974.

Mannion, John J. *The Peopling of Newfoundland.* St. John's: ISER Books, 1977.

Maracle, Lee. *I am Woman.* Vancouver: Write-On Press, 1988.

Mies, Maria. *Patriarchy and Accumulation on a World Scale: Women in the International Division of Labour.* London: Zed, 1986.

Miles, Rosalind. *The Women's History of the World.* London: Paladin, 1989.

Miller, Kirby. *Emigrants and Exiles: Ireland and the Irish Exodus to North America.* New York: Oxford University Press, 1985.

Millet, Kate. *Sexual Politics.* New York: Doubleday, 1970.

Mitchell, Alanna. "Divorce a Ticket to Poverty for Women, Figures Show." *The Globe and Mail,* June 4, 1992, p. A10.

Mitter, Swasti. *Common Fate, Common Bond: Women in the Global Economy.* London: Pluto, 1986.

Monture, Patricia. "Ka-Nin-Geh-Heh-Gah-E-Sa-Nonh-Yah-Gah." *Canadian Journal of Women and the Law* 2, no. 1 (1986).

Murray, Margaret. *The God of the Witches.* London: Oxford University Press, 1931.

Murray, Margaret. *The Witch Cult in Western Europe.* London: Oxford University Press, 1921.

Nelson, Joyce, Marlene Nourbese Philip and Ayanna Black. "Disturbing the Peace: Commentary on 54th International PEN World Congress." *Fuse* 13, no. 3 (Winter 1989–90).

Ng, Roxanna. "The Social Construction of Immigrant Women in Canada." In *The Politics of Diversity,* edited by Roberta Hamilton and Michele Barrett. Montreal: Book Centre, 1986.

Ní Chuilleanáin, Eiléan, ed. *Irish Women: Image and Achievement.* Dublin: Arlen House, 1985.

Nicolson, Murray. "Peasants in an Urban Society: The Irish Catholics in Victorian Toronto." In *Gathering Place: Peoples and Neighbourhoods of Toronto, 1834–1945*, edited by Robert F. Harney. Toronto: Multicultural History Society of Ontario, 1985.

O'Connor, Rev. M. Margarita. "The Institute of the Blessed Virgin Mary." In *The Canadian Catholic Historical Foundation*. Toronto: The Association, 1945.

Ó Corráin, Donncha. "Women in Early Irish Society." In *Women in Irish Society: The Historical Dimension*, edited by Margaret MacCurtain and Donncha ó Corráin. Dublin: Arlen House, 1978.

O'Driscoll, Robert, and Lorna Reynolds, eds. *The Untold Story: The Irish in Canada, Volumes 1 and 2*. Toronto: Celtic Arts Canada, 1988.

O'Gallagher, Marianna. *Grosse Île: Gateway to Canada 1832–1937*. Quebec: Carraig Books, 1984.

O'Gallagher, Marianna. *The Voyage of the Naparima: A Story of Canada's Island Graveyard*. Quebec: Carraig Books, 1982.

O'Gallagher, Marianna. *Saint Brigid's Quebec*. Quebec: Carraig Books, 1981.

O'Gallagher, Marianna. *Saint Patrick's Quebec. The Building of a Church and a Parish, 1827 to 1833*. Quebec: Carraig Books, 1981.

Ó Tuathaigh, Gearóid. "The Role of Women in Ireland under the New English Order." In *Women in Irish Society: The Historical Dimension*, edited by Margaret MacCurtain and Donncha ó Corráin. Dublin: Arlen House, 1978.

Ontario Native Women's Association. "Breaking Free: A Proposal for Change to Aboriginal Family Violence." 1989.

Pelrine, Eleanor Wright. *Abortion in Canada*. Toronto: New Press, 1971.

Philip, M. Nourbese. *Frontiers: Essays and Writings on Racism and Culture*. Stratford, Ontario: Mercury, 1992.

Prentice, Alison, Paula Bourne, Gail Cuthbert Brandt, Beth Light, Wendy Mitchinson and Naomi Black. *Canadian Women: A History*. Toronto: Harcourt Brace Jovanovich, 1988.

Punch, Terrence. *Irish Halifax: The Immigrant Generation, 1815–1959*.

Halifax: International Education Centre, St. Mary's University, 1981.

Punch, Terrence. *Some Sons of Erin in Nova Scotia*. Halifax: International Education Centre, St. Mary's University, 1980.

Radford Reuther, Rosemary. *Sexism and God-Talk: Towards a Feminist Theology*. Boston: Beacon, 1983.

Ranelagh, John O'Beirne. *A Short History of Ireland*. Cambridge: Cambridge University Press, 1983.

Ridington, Jillian. "Violence and Women with Disabilities." Toronto: The DisAbled Women's Network, n.d.

Roach Pierson, Ruth. *"They're Still Women After All": The Second World War and Canadian Womanhood*. Toronto: McClelland & Stewart, 1986.

Roberts, Barbara. "Ladies, Women and the State: Managing Female Immigration, 1880–1920." In *Community Organization and the Canadian State*, edited by Roxanna Ng, Gillian Walker and Jacob Miller. Toronto: Garamond, 1990.

Robinson, Mary. "Women and the New Irish State." In *Women in Irish Society: The Historical Dimension*, edited by Margaret Mac-Curtain and Donncha ó Corráin. Dublin: Arlen House, 1978.

Rossi, Alice, ed. *The Feminist Papers: From Adams to de Beauvoir*. New York: Bantam, 1973.

Scannell, Yvonne. "Changing Times for Women's Rights." In *Irish Women: Image and Achievement*, by Eiléan Ní Chuilleanáin. Dublin: Arlen House, 1985.

Schmitz, Nancy. *Irish for a Day: Saint Patrick's Day Celebrations in Quebec City 1765–1990*. Quebec: Carraig Books, 1991.

Sen, Gita, and Caren Grown. *Development, Crises, and Alternative Visions: Third World Women's Perspectives*. New York: Monthly Review Press, 1987.

Shaw, J. G. "Devotion to Our Lady at Cap de la Madeleine." In *The Canadian Catholic Historical Association*. Toronto: The Association, 1952.

Shiel, Michael, and Desmond Roche, eds. *A Forgotten Campaign*. Galway: Woodford Heritage Group, 1986.

Silman, Janet. *Enough Is Enough: Aboriginal Women Speak Out.* Toronto: Women's Press, 1991.

Silvera, Makeda. *Silenced.* Toronto: Williams-Wallace, 1983.

Smith, Barbara, ed. *Home Girls: A Black Feminist Anthology.* New York: Kitchen Table/Women of Colour Press, 1983.

Smith, Dorothy. *The Everyday World as Problematic: A Feminist Sociology.* Boston: Northeastern University Press, 1987.

Smythe, Elizabeth M. "The Lessons of Religion and Science: The Congregation of the Sisters of St. Joseph and St. Joseph's Academy, Toronto 1854–1911." Ph.D. dissertation, Ontario Institute for Studies in Education, University of Toronto, 1989.

Spretnak, Charlene, ed. *The Politics of Women's Spirituality: Essays on the Rise of Spiritual Power within the Feminist Movement.* New York: Anchor, 1982.

Stone, Merlin. *When God Was a Woman.* New York: Dial, 1976.

Strong-Boag, Veronica. "'50s Dream No Guide for '90s Women: It's Time to Stop Penalizing Women for Motherhood." *The Globe and Mail,* May 7, 1992.

Toner, Peter, ed. *Ireland Remembered: Historical Essays on the Irish in New Brunswick.* Fredericton: New Ireland Press, 1988.

Vorst, Jesse, *et al.,* eds. *Race, Class, Gender: Bonds and Barriers.* Toronto: Between the Lines, 1989.

Ward, Margaret. *Unmanageable Revolutionaries: Women and Irish Nationalism.* London: Pluto, 1983.

Weitzman, Lenore. *The Divorce Revolution: The Unexpected Social and Economic Consequences for Women and Children in America.* New York: Free Press, 1985.

White, J. *Women and Part-Time Work.* Ottawa: Canadian Advisory Council on the Status of Women, 1983.

Wood, Helen Lanigan. "Women in Myths and Early Depictions." In *Irish Women: Image and Achievement,* edited by Eiléan Ní Chuilleanáin. Dublin: Arlen House, 1985.

Woodham-Smith, Cecil. *The Great Hunger: Ireland 1845 to 1849.* New York: Harper & Row, 1962.

SHEELAGH CONWAY grew up on the land in the rural village of Limehill, between Loughrea and Portumna, County Galway. In 1970 she emigrated to England, where she lived in London and Southhampton. She taught in England and the Caribbean before coming to Canada in 1979.

Active in the women's movement since the early 1970s, Conway co-founded many women's groups in Canada, including the Windsor Women's Incentive Centre and the Canadian Caravan of University Feminists. She is a graduate of Southhampton University's La Sainte Union College of Education in England, the University of Windsor, Ontario, and York University, Ontario. She is in graduate studies at the University of Toronto.

Her first book, *A Woman and Catholicism: My Break with the Roman Catholic Church*, was published in 1987. Conway co-edited *Women's Experience, Women's Education: An Anthology*, published in 1991. She lives in Toronto with her two daughters, Siobhán and Ann, and the family collie, Toby.